The Fairness
of
Markets

Other Books by Richard McKenzie

Regulating Government: A Preface to Constitutional Economics
(1986, with Dwight Lee)

Economics (1986)

Competing Visions: The Political Conflict over America's Economic
Future (1985)

The New World of Economics (1975, 1978, 1981, and 1984, with
Gordon Tullock)

Plant Closings: Public or Private Choices? (1981 and 1984, edited)

Fugitive Industry: The Economics and Politics of
Deindustrialization (1984)

Constitutional Economics: Containing the Economic Powers of
Government (1984, edited)

National Industrial Policy: Commentaries in Dissent (1984)

The Limits of Economic Science: Essays in Methodology (1982)

Bound to Be Free (1982)

Economic Issues in Public Policies (1980)

Restrictions on Business Mobility: A Study in Political Rhetoric
and Economic Reality (1979)

The Political Economy of the Educational Process (1979)

Modern Political Economy (1978, with Gordon Tullock)

An Economic Theory of Learning (1974, with Robert Staaf)

The Fairness
of
Markets

A Search for Justice in a Free Society

Richard B. McKenzie
Clemson University

Lexington Books

D.C. Heath and Company/Lexington, Massachusetts/Toronto

Library of Congress Cataloging-in-Publication Data
McKenzie, Richard B.
The fairness of markets.

Includes index.
1. Economics—Moral and ethical aspects.
2. Capitalism—Moral and ethical aspects.   3. Wealth,
Ethics of.   4. Economic policy.   I. Title.
HB72.M35   1987   330   86-45958
ISBN 0-669-14801-6 (alk. paper)

Published simultaneously in Canada
Printed in the United States of America
Casebound International Standard Book Number: 0-669-14801-6
Library of Congress Catalog Card Number: 86-45958

The paper used in this publication meets
the minimum requirements of American National Standard
for Information Sciences—Permanence of Paper
for Printed Library Materials, ANSI Z39.48-1984.
∞ ™

ISBN 0-669-14801-6

87 88 89 90   8 7 6 5 4 3 2 1

To
Professor Gordon Tullock

Contents

Preface

My central purpose in writing this book is to reintroduce questions of fairness to economic discussions of public policy by economists and to demonstrate that economic reasoning can contribute much to our understanding of fairness of markets. Economics as a distinct discipline arose from moral philosophy more than two hundred years ago. Questions of the justice and fairness of markets were then central to the study of political economy; they underpinned the work of Adam Smith (who wrote *The Theory of Moral Sentiments* before *The Wealth of Nations*) and many of his followers.

In more modern times, however, economists have sought to skirt public policy debates involving justice and fairness issues. Instead, they have focused almost exclusively on the efficiency or inefficiency of markets and various forms of government intervention in markets. Many economists have maintained that their professional expertise does not offer any particularly useful guidance on normative matters. Public policy makers, who must deal more carefully and frequently with questions of fairness than with efficiency, have understandably ignored much economic advice for being insensitive to human needs or, worse, irrelevant.

In essence, my purpose in *The Fairness of Markets* is to break with this contemporary economic tradition and address directly the justice and fairness of markets and a variety of proposed public policies that would restrict market operations. Accordingly, I evaluate the fairness of proposals to give workers greater rights of participation in management decisions, to legislate wages, and to protect industries from foreign competition. I acknowledge that a strong case can be made on fairness as well as efficiency grounds for welfare; however, I also show

how an uncontained welfare state will ultimately work to the detriment of the poor.

In summary, as a promarket economist, I seek to join the public policy debate on terms largely prescribed by opponents of markets, who contend that markets are unfair and that greater fairness in the economic system can only be obtained through more expansive governmental controls on the economy. My central thesis is that markets are, admittedly, often unfair. However, many proposed governmental solutions to observed economic ills do not improve the fairness of the economic system; indeed, many governmental remedies are arguably unfair to the people the remedies are designed to help.

Acknowledgments

This book has, of course, benefited greatly from the comments and criticisms of many colleagues over the several years that it was written in the form of independent papers and articles. The most important contributors, who must be generously thanked but not held responsible for the final product, are James Buchanan, Dwight Lee, Gordon Tullock, Bruce Yandle, Hugh Macaulay, Clinton Whitehurst, James Childs, Jules Coleman, Walter Nord, Arthur Denzau, Murray Weidenbaum, and Kenneth Chilton. Ellen Frankel Paul, who read the entire next-to-the-last draft, was especially gracious and helpful with criticisms and suggestions for improvement and reorganization.

Richard Burr made major contributions to the manuscript through his editorial suggestions and substantive comments. Donna Cole and Donna Tingle were extaordinarily helpful in having the manuscript computerized.

The Center for the Study of American Business at Washington University in St. Louis, under the direction of Murray Weidenbaum, literally made the book possible by appointing me to their John M. Ohlin Visiting Professorship during the 1985–1986 academic year. That position gave me the time and resources to rework already published papers and to develop new chapters for completing the book. My debt to the center and its staff is considerable and heartfelt.

Several of the chapters have been published. Chapter 2 was originally published as an article in *Ethics*. Chapters 4, 5 and 6 were distributed by the Center for the Study of American Business. Chapter 7 is reprinted from the *Journal of Labor Research*, and chapter 9 was distributed by the Center for Policy Studies at Clemson University. Chapter 10 was published in the *Journal of Institutional and Theoretical*

Economics. All of these previously published works have been extensively revised for inclusion in this book.

This book is dedicated with considerable admiration to Gordon Tullock, my professor, friend, and coauthor. Those who know Professor Tullock understand that concern for matters of fairness and ethics have rarely been central to his substantial scholarly record. Nevertheless, they have been strategic to his dealings with his colleagues and friends. All of his colleagues who have had the opportunity to work closely with Professor Tullock are tremendously indebted to him for numerous insights that have inspired their own work for which he has not received credit. More than most, I am indebted to him, particularly for the opportunity to coauthor two books with him.

Part I
Ethics and the Making
of Public Policy

———

1
Fairness and Markets

Indeed there can be no question . . . that the valid criticisms of the existing economic order relate chiefly to its value standards, and relatively
much less to its efficiency in the creation of such values as it recognizes.
. . . [The existing market system's] only justification is that it is effective
in getting things done; but any candid answer to the question, "what
things," compels admission that they leave much to be desired.
                                                        —Frank Knight[1]

P rior to the election of Ronald Reagan to the presidency in 1980,
    the federal government was expanding in real dollar terms and as
a percentage of national production. In terms of total government
growth, not much changed during Reagan's first term. Contrary to
popular wisdom, the federal government continued to expand during
the first half of the 1980s. Indeed, total government spending expanded during the Reagan first term along the growth path set by the
Carter administration, which was not known for being tight with
taxpayers' dollars.* What appears to have changed most under the
Reagan administration is the perceived guiding social philosophy of
Washington politics, which has resulted in a restructuring of government expenditures and a redirection for government regulatory
powers. This book has been written partially in response to the social
controversy surrounding that change in governmental policy and
philosophy.

---

*In 1967, federal government outlays accounted for slightly more than 20 percent of gross
national product (GNP). In 1980, federal government outlays were slightly above 20 percent of
GNP and nearly 25 percent of GNP in 1985. For more details on the aggregate budgetary
consequences of the Reagan administration, see Richard B. McKenzie, "Taking Stock of the
Federal Budget," *Occasional Paper* (St. Louis: Center for the Study of American Business,
Washington University, 1986).

The Shift in the Social Agenda

Prior to 1980, contemporary government was largely directed by the fervently held belief that greater social justice and fairness should be or could be promoted most effectively through greater reliance on government. Through the expansion of government outlays, especially those involving the transfer of income among citizens, the nation gradually began to rely more heavily on political power rather than prices for signals on what should be done for and by people acting as investors, workers, and consumers.

If President Reagan has stood firmly on any guiding principle, it has been that the trend in past government policies should be reversed as much as possible. More reliance should be placed on markets to allocate the nation's resources and to determine people's incomes.

While his actual achievements remain questionable, President Reagan's obvious insistence on such a dramatic policy course reversal has not gone unnoticed or unchallenged. If he has accomplished nothing else in domestic policy—and he has had hosts of detractors, even among conservatives—the president has reignited the long-standing intellectual and public-policy debate over the fairness of markets.*

At virtually every policy turn, the Reagan administration's less-government, promarket policies have been characterized as unfair, if not inhumane. For example, his early efforts to curtail the growth in Social Security with the intent of encouraging people to rely more on their own resources for retirement income met with a hostile rebuff in Congress. After all, there are many poor elderly people. Accordingly, the Reagan administration has had to shelve any tentative dreams of privatizing or contracting out Social Security.

---

*Columnist Robert Samuelson concluded early in President Reagan's first term, "Reaganomics is dead—not because it failed, but because it never existed. Ronald Reagan never really had an economic program. . . . Hence, Reaganomics was born: neither an economic theory nor a social philosophy" [Robert J. Samuelson, "Economic Focus: Phantom Philosophy, Reaganomics is Dead," *Washington Post* (December 12, 1982), p. C1]. Libertarian Edward Crane drew the same conclusion only a few months earlier: "Reaganomics has not failed. Reaganomics is simply a fiction transmitted to us with unblinking innocence by the nation's media. . . . If Steven Spielberg can make adults teary-eyed at the sight of flying bicycles, then Ronald Reagan can make otherwise intelligent people believe he is going to reduce the size of government" [Edward Crane, "Reagan Never Meant What He Said," *Washington Post* (August 19, 1982), p. A19].

Reagan's emphasis on a defense build-up and efforts to reduce the growth in welfare benefits, including loans and grants to middle-class college students, caused his critics to wonder if he had any compassion at all for those in need. Such worries were dramatically reinforced when the U.S. Department of Agriculture, in an early major administrative blunder to reduce government expenditures, sought to define catsup as a vegetable in acceptable school lunch programs for the poor. Understandably, market economics quickly became equated in many quarters with blatant stupidity in public policy.

The Reagan administration's refusal to extend import protection to a variety of domestic industries (most notably, the shoe and textile industries), greater loans to farmers, and training and relocation aid to displaced workers—all of whom were perceived to be in various stages of economic crises—has caused many to wonder if the president's "high society" circle of friends and almost religious affection for free markets blinded him to the needs of ordinary American workers.

Repeated attempts by the Reagan administration to privatize government services and sell off government assets, buildings, and land have been met with scorn and fears that the president is willing to forsake the nation's treasures in his myopic quest to reduce the deficit, prevent tax increases, and pursue the Holy Grail of his right-wing ideology.

All of his efforts to cut and flatten tax rates and boost people's incentives to work, save, and invest have been met with the incessant charge of unfairness because only the well-off have benefited. "Supply-side economics" first became known as "voodoo economics" and then as "Reaganomics."

Clearly, the words of economist–social philosopher Frank Knight that head this chapter, although written for a political setting that predated the New Deal, describe the tenor of these political times. Even if efficiency of markets is conceded,* which many critics do

---

*Efficiency in markets in simple terms means that resources are used in the most effective ways to satisfy the most highly valued wants. In Knight's view, "[A] freely competitive organization of society tends to place every productive resource in that position in the productive system where it can make the greatest possible addition to the total societal dividend as measured in price terms, and tends to reward every participant in production by giving it the increase in the social dividend which its co-operation makes possible" [Knight, *The Ethics of Competition*, p. 48].

not concede, the overriding concern of policy opponents of the Reagan administration has been the fairness of the market system, or what Knight called value standards, that undergird the market system. Critics contend, in essence, that the domain of markets should not be extended for the simple reason that fairness will necessarily be sacrificed.

For too long, promarket economists have refused to debate the fairness of market-oriented policies, preferring to focus on markets' more "scientific" efficiency attributes and claiming that concepts like fairness and justice are "terms which have no content." In so doing, many market economists have conceded the policy debate. This is so partially because, at best, few policymakers appreciate the technical economic meaning of efficiency and, at worst, see efficiency as an apology for greed that presumably motivates the market system and for unwarranted profits that emerge from the system.

Joining the Fairness Debate

This book has one overriding purpose: to join the policy debate as an unabashed advocate for the market system. In doing this, I accept the terms for debate laid down largely by the detractors of the market system. Although the efficiency of markets will not be overlooked and will be considered with some care in various chapters, the fairness and ethical content of markets and market results will be the central value by which markets and proposed deviations will be judged.

In writing this book, I accept the reformist position that fairness is no less elusive a concept for judging social institutions than efficiency.* While efficiency is something markets produce, it is not everything they do or accomplish for social good and bad. Nevertheless, readers will, of course, find in the arguments presented a dedication to market principles properly understood. I make no apologies

---

*To economists, *efficiency* has a very definite meaning and graphical (and mathematical) representation. Conceptually, it is the condition in which resources cannot be reallocated without reducing the welfare of at least one person. Graphically, it is (for any given product) the point of intersection of the product's market demand curve and marginal revenue curve. However, efficiency is still dependent upon the elusive concept of people's values as expressed in what they are willing and able to purchase in the marketplace, which in turn is dependent upon the distribution of property.

for that. However, I acknowledge my role as a political economist and dedicated democrat, one who explicitly recognizes that all argument for or against any social or economic system is something of a hypothesis that must ultimately be tested for acceptance in open debate among the electorate.

Having said that, two caveats are worth emphasizing at the start. First, in the context of this book, markets are not seen as ideal social institutions but rather as systems that are tolerably effective in creating wealth and, at the same time, in promoting a reasonable degree of fairness and social justice in many areas of human endeavor. No system of social interaction can aspire to being ideal, which is tantamount to being hopeless, and simultaneously not subject to dispute, which the market system surely is.*

Second, markets are hardly seen here as applicable to all areas of people's social dealings. Casual observations of a wide variety of social settings indicate markets are not used pervasively in human affairs. Consider families and clubs within which cooperation emerges without explicit or implicit exchanges. Consider business organizations that are designed to reduce the number of explicit market transactions among different stages of production and the amount of bargaining in the assignment of daily work loads. Consider friendships that are founded more on altruism than self-interest.

The relevant issue this volume addresses is whether or not in specified areas of social life markets represent an improvement in fairness terms over alternative, frequently proposed governmental forms of social organization. That question is, of course, not addressed fully here. It is simply too big an issue for this author to handle in a small book. Rather than being comprehensive treatises on the fairness of markets, the following chapters consider the fairness issue through a series of case studies, that is, through an examination of several proposed reforms of the market system. Each of these reforms has been advocated on the grounds that greater fairness, as defined largely by the advocates of reform, will be achieved.

---

*This point was made by Frank Knight, who wrote, "Normal common sense does judge in terms of ideals, of some absolute ethics . . . , and not merely in terms of the best that can be done; else it would be linguistically equivalent to call a situation hopeless and to call it ideal, which is clearly not in accordance with usage" [Knight, *The Ethics of Competition*, p. 44].

Normative Economics Reconsidered

To a substantial degree, this book represents an exploration into normative economics, as distinct from positive economics. As such, the book
represents a significant departure from the conventional wisdom adopted
by many economists. Traditionally, economists have viewed their discipline as concerned almost exclusively with a positive economics that, as
Milton Friedman reminds us, is "in principle independent of any particular ethical position or normative judgment. . . . [I]t deals with 'what
is,' not with 'what ought to be.' "[2] Positive economics is concerned with
making predictions. In this regard, it is value free, and much has been
accomplished with the scientific approach.

Normative economics, on the other hand, which is concerned
with matters of value and what ought to be, is often spurned as
nonscientific. Analysis of matters involving personal judgment is
not likely to yield any particularly useful insights or settle any particularly interesting or challenging intellectual or policy debates, or so it
is argued. The main problem with economists assuming exclusively
the aloof status of the scientist is that they exempt themselves almost
totally from the mainstream of American political life, which necessarily deals extensively with matters of what people want in the type
of system that allocates resources, not with just how the system, once
entrenched, is likely to operate in practice.

The scientist qua economist who judges his or her analysis solely
by the correctness of its predictions—based, as they are, on abstract
models of competitive or monopoly markets and on empirical
methods of verification that impose severe restrictions on the kinds
of variables that can be considered—presumes that the issue of
"which economic system" has already been settled.[3] It is, accordingly, understandable why so much economic analysis is not taken
seriously by political operatives in Washington. Many economists
and much of the political world are, in large measure, talking at
cross-purposes to different audiences and not to each other.

The reluctance of economists to deal openly with the fairness, as
opposed to the measurable consequences, of government policies
may for several reasons appear strange. First, investigations of the
measurable consequences of public policies often mask the investi-
gators' dedication to market principles. Few would think that Milton
Friedman, Paul Craig Roberts, Herbert Stein, Martin Feldstein, Murray Weidenbaum, William Niskanen, James Buchanan, and James

Miller (all prominent economists, if not Reagan supporters or advisers) are indeed neutral on the issue of the intrinsic social value of markets. Although they often assume in their work the role of the detached observer-analyst, they certainly give every impression in their public comments that they consider the social value of markets to extend far beyond the efficiency of markets.

Second, there seems to be no particularly good reason why normative issues should remain outside the purview of economists as social analysts. Economics has always been as much art and philosophy as it has been social science. Clearly, economics as a distinct and modern discipline grew out of moral philosophy two hundred years ago. Even Adam Smith, the acknowledged founder of economics, was a professor of moral philosophy who wrote during a time when questions of morality, fairness, and justice could not be ignored.

The essential truths of economic order that Hobbes, Locke, Hutchinson, Hume, and Smith recognized, and which Smith so superbly systematized in his *Wealth of Nations,* were not grasped from models of human interaction that were devoid of normative considerations or that even attributed to social ethics a minor degree of importance. On the contrary, Smith's work on political economy emerged from his and others' more general concern with moral issues. It is important to understand that Smith's *Theory of Moral Sentiments,* a study in social ethics, predated *the Wealth of Nations,* a study of how market exchanges, constrained by the "impartial spectator" (in essence, the individual's conscience), could extend social cooperation beyond that which is achievable by relying on the important forces of love and friendship. It is equally important to realize that Smith and others have viewed markets as constrained, albeit imperfectly, by the "virtues of prudence, justice, and beneficence."*

---

*Smith is remembered for having written, "It is not from the benevolence of the butcher, the brewer or the baker that we expect our dinner, but from their regard of their own self interest" [Adam Smith, *An Inquiry into the Nature and Causes of the Wealth of Nations* (New York: Random House, Inc., 1937), p. 14]. However, he also wrote years before that "without the restraint which this principle [that is, the impartial spectator] imposes, every passion would upon occasion, rush headlong, if I may say so, to its own gratification. Anger would follow the suggestions of its own fury; fear those of its own violent agitation. Regard to no time or place would induce vanity to refrain from the loudest and most impertinent ostentation; or voluptuousness from the most open indecent, and scandalous indulgence. Respect for what are, or what ought to be, or for what, upon certain conditions, would be, the sentiments of other people is the sole principle which, upon occasions, overawes all those mutinous and turbulent passions into that tone and temper which the impartial spectator can enter into and sympathize with" [Adam Smith, *The Theory of Moral Sentiments,* included in *Adam Smith's Moral and Political Philosophy,* edited by Herbert W. Schneider (New York: Harper and Row, Publishers, 1970), p. 275].

What Smith was concerned about in *The Wealth of Nations* is how best to design a social system that would account for people's natural inclination to be less than prudent, just, and beneficent some (or maybe even most) of the time in their dealings with others. Granted markets might be less than perfect, subject to abuse and misuse by imperfect people, but Smith seemed reluctant to accept the facile conclusion that remedies should necessarily be sought through government because governments are also subject to the same human frailties.

To Smith and many of his followers, markets are "good" in an important social sense. They not only help build the "wealth of nations" through an efficient allocation of resources, but they also constrain social behavior, help disperse economic power, allow for individual freedom, provide for some reasonable means of sharing the fruits of productive activity, and offer relief of problems of the disadvantaged, especially over the long run.

Most conceptions of fairness of any social system contain elements such as the ones just listed. These elements of fairness are embedded in the modern tough-minded analyses of John Rawls, Robert Nozick, F. A. Hayek, Milton Friedman, Michael Novak, Israel Kirzner, and Geoffrey Brennan and James Buchanan.[4] If the supporters of market system from the time of Smith onward had not seen such benefits arising from markets, it is hard to understand how they could support the system for so long and with such intellectual vigor. While opponents and proponents of markets may disagree on many things, they do not necessarily have different fairness and other social objectives at heart in their commentaries, nor do they necessarily have disparate levels of compassion for people.

Third, it is also clear that the deficiencies of markets have been fully acknowledged, even by the market system's intellectual supporters. For example, Frank Knight has stressed in his critique of the "The Ethics of Competition" that:

> Markets fall far short of the abstract ideal of perfect efficiency of perfectly competitive markets;

> "There is some truth in the allegation that unregulated competition places a premium on deceit and corruption";

"The inheritance of wealth, culture, educational advantage, and economic opportunity tend toward the progressive increase of inequality";

"What is desired is more likely a matter of human relations than goods and services as such";

"The ownership of personal and productive capacity is based upon a complex mixture of inheritance, luck, and effort, probably in that order of relative importance";

"'Giving the public what they want' usually means corrupting popular tastes"; and

The system "distributes the produce of industry on the basis of power, which is ethical only in so far as right and might are one."[5]

Given such acknowledged criticisms, it seems clear that markets cannot be evaluated completely within an ethical vacuum, nor do they have to be discarded simply because they are imperfect either from an ethical or efficiency perspective. Governmental institutions are also defective to one degree or another. As Knight also warned, "It must be said that radical critics of competition as a general basis of the economic order generally underestimate egregiously the danger of doing vastly worse" than markets.[6] The critical problem faced by social philosophy is to acknowledge that all forms of social arrangements can be used in human society and "to find the right proportions between individualism and socialism and the various varieties of each and to use each in its proper place."[7]

An undergirding principle of this volume is that the search for "right proportions" can only be undertaken by an admixture of positive and normative analysis. Accordingly, the normative implications (involving matters of justice, fairness, and rightness) of conventional analytical findings (involving matters of predicted social consequences) are repeatedly sought and evaluated throughout the following chapters. This search has one overriding motivation, a desire to live in a society that is tolerably fair and free at the individual and collective levels.

The Meanings of Fairness

The concept of fairness can be criticized for meaning different things to different people and for being imprecise and unmeasurable. Nevertheless, fairness can be given some concreteness by simply acknowledging that to different people fairness tends to mean that:

Certain basic human rights are "inalienable" and should be equally available to all, and are not subject to violation without the consent of the people who hold the rights;[8]

Social institutions should be so arranged that people's behavior is consistent with commonly agreed-upon rules for behavior;[9]

Rules for social interaction are unbiased, that is, are not intended to favor those who make and enforce the rules; rules should be generally applicable and nondiscriminatory, to the extent possible;[10]

Cheating on agreed-upon rules is discouraged (and when cheating does occur, there are built-in mechanisms for correction);[11]

Special consideration and aid are given to the disadvantaged.[12]

This book reflects a certain degree of frustration, perhaps exasperation, in getting people who advocate constraints on markets to see that so many of the arguments made against this or that form of market control are, at their foundation, motivated by many of these fairness concerns. For example, consider the following several arguments offered by economists that may appear, on the surface, to be an affront to people's welfare because they represent arguments for greater reliance on impersonal markets.

Plant Closing Restrictions

For several years, I have been a staunch opponent of restrictions on plant closings.[13] In public debates, I have felt considerable resistance to my arguments against the legislation that would require prenotification of plant closings and severance pay for the affected workers. My arguments have tended to be equated with opposition to workers who, everyone agrees, are often hurt by the closing of their plants.

After all, plant closings can give rise to poverty, murders, and mental disorders.[14] While the details of my arguments can be sidestepped (to be considered in more detail in chapter 10), it is important to note that opposition to plant-closing laws is motivated by the fear that they will raise the cost of doing business in the United States and will restrict plant openings far more than they restrict plant closings, thus exacerbating the problems that distressed communities and their residents must face.

Water Rights

In another case, Terry Anderson and many other economists have argued for years that water should be allocated according to market principles.[15] His arguments have often faced the charge that water is too important to people to be subjected to the unemotional dictates of the markets. The high prices the water would command in many areas would push low-income people out of the market and make the resulting distribution of water inequitable and unfair. These conclusions are drawn in spite of the facts Anderson stresses: Water in arid El Paso and Albuquerque is one-third the price per thousand gallons that it is in Philadelphia, and water sold in 1980 to California farmers for $5 an acre-foot cost the federal government more than $300 to deliver. Not surprisingly, water is used far more heavily where it sells at low subsidized prices than where it is not.

Clearly, the way water is priced leads to market inefficiencies, but it also leads to questions of fairness, not the least of which is why poor people around the country ought to be required to subsidize through the tax system the water consumption of much higher income users. We may disagree on much about the pricing system, but we might agree here that fairness is not totally on the side of those who propose a continuation of the current system of allocation by politics.

Immigration Rights

Further, another flare-up over fairness occurred when University of Maryland business professor Julian Simon advocated in the *New York Times* an application of market principles that is radical by almost all standards.[16] He suggested that immigration rights into the

United States should be sold to the highest bidder. Several days later the *Times* editorialized against Simon's proposal, suggesting that the immigration question "has never been on how much gold but on how much door" we will have.

The *Times* also suggested other, more radical "kinds of currency" for allocating immigration slots: "like the number of days the bidder has spent in totalitarian prisons . . . or the number of years spent waiting to join relatives already in this country . . . or the length of time spent as an engineer." The *Times* concluded that "as it stands, the Simon proposal, while simple, would demolish the preference that the system now gives to refugees, relatives and highly skilled workers. These preferences are intended precisely to reward values that the United States has always regarded more highly than money."[17]

Clearly, prices and money are not everything, even to market economists. However, the *Times* editorial seems to miss the fundamental point Simon was seeking to expose: The current immigration system is, by nontrivial standards of human conduct, grossly unfair. It tends to discriminate against low-income people, especially from non-Western countries, such as Africa and Southeast Asia.* Under an auction system for immigration rights, many low-income people might be kept out, but it is an open question as to whether more or fewer will be kept out under the pricing system than under the current system, which permits broad administrative discretion.

Furthermore, the pricing system might result in the liberalization of immigration, because people would then be paying their own way. Under the current system, voters and politicians who determine how liberal the immigration system will be must worry that the people coming into the country will be a drain on the country and a competitive threat to the job security of Americans. Again, the case for the introduction of the market system in immigration on fairness grounds is not complete and cannot be developed at length here, but neither should it be dismissed out of hand simply because it appears on the surface to be unfair.

---

*Specifically, Simon argued at the start that "such a system would be fairer and economically more beneficial to the United States and the people in poorer countries than the present system. With each passing year, admission to this country depends more upon whom you're related to and less upon what you can contribute to American society" [Simon, *New York Times*, p. 27].

Capital Taxation

Many promarket economists often fret about taxes on capital, for example, the corporate income tax, stressing that capital taxation is shifted forward to consumers in the form of higher prices and backward to workers in the form of depressed wages and that it retards economic growth by deterring investment. Capital taxation tends to impose indirectly a tax on future generations through a reduction in the future income stream. Proponents of capital taxation sometimes insist that opposition is motivated by the private interests of capitalists who simply want to shift their rightful tax burden to others. The economists-opponents are, in effect, characterized as "hired guns" for the dominant economic classes, meaning that the whole debate all too often takes on the appearance of being between those who care about workers' interests and those who care about capitalists' interests.

While some opponents of capital taxation may harbor little concern for workers' welfare, it certainly is not always the case. This is especially true if it is recognized that workers' wages are critically dependent upon their productivity that, in turn, is dependent on the country's capital stock. University of Chicago economist Yale Brozen poses a question that should be of interest to those who are concerned about the fairness of capital taxation: What if the capital in the United States were doubled with no increase in the quantity of labor and no change in the technology available?[18] Brozen estimates that because the ratio of capital to labor would, as a consequence, rise dramatically (reducing the marginal productivity of capital and increasing the marginal productivity of labor), the national income would rise by about 26 percent. While the income of capitalists would rise by about 4 percentage points, the income of workers would rise by much more, 22 percentage points.*

---

*Brozen, "*The Economic Impact of Government Policy.*" Brozen adds, drawing on research done years ago,

> The effect of an increase in the stock of capital relative to the number of workers can be illustrated using Brazilian data from the 1950s. I worked out the relationship . . . in response to the accusation that the investment of American capital in Brazil exploited Brazilian workers. . . . I found that an increase in Brazil's capital stock by $1,000 per worker raised annual production in Brazil by $350 per worker. Of this *increase* in annual output per worker, $150 went to increase the annual wage per worker, which at the time was a little over $1,000 per year. Brazilian governments collected $100 per year in taxes levied directly on the investment and on dividends, leaving $100 as a return to those who invested their savings [Ibid, pp. 11–12].

The moral of these data is that we might legitimately disagree on the correctness of the calculations, but opposition to capital taxes does not necessarily spell support for making the income distribution less fair or more unfair. The same can be said for opposition to a progressive marginal tax rate system, such as the United States'. High marginal tax rates on high-income earners can also be seen as a tax on savings, mainly undertaken by high income earners, and a tax on capital. Hence, high marginal tax rates can be a means of indirectly taxing the wages of future workers.

Concluding Comments

In summary, the market system is a means of distributing power among people and for getting things done. It would appear that the distribution of power requires that people believe it is simply not arbitrary or capricious, meaning they generally accept the system by standards that go by the names of justice, equity, and fairness. This is especially true if the system is a matter of intentional human design, meaning that it has some social purpose. Clearly, getting things done through the efficient allocation of resources is one of the system's social purposes. However, efficiency presupposes sets of wants and distribution of resources, and the distribution of rights to resources cannot be justified solely by what is accomplished with the resources, given their distribution.

Furthermore, it seems difficult to understand how markets as a system could be judged solely by efficiency. Efficiency is necessarily that which results from unspecified prices that are dependent upon largely unknown wants and resources that are held by people, many of whom are not only unknown but unborn. Because they are designed to structure the future interactions of participants, social (including economic) systems (similar to parlor games) must be judged not so much on what does in fact happen during "play," but in terms of how "play" is devised and allowed to transpire.

This book attempts to come to grips with the fairness of the play in markets both fettered and unfettered by several specific governmental restraints. First, chapter 2 moves us into normative analysis by discussing the viability of ethical rules among various sizes of groups of people. A major point of that discussion is that ethics, as constraining forces on human behavior, have their limits, just as markets do. An important issue in institutional design is how to economize on the use of ethics in accomplishing social objectives.

Chapter 3 shifts the discussion to more specific complaints of opponents of free-market forces by addressing the question of whether free trade is tantamount to fair trade, a proposition proponents of protectionism often dismiss. The inevitability and fairness of economic failure in general is considered in chapter 4.

Chapters 5 and 6 initiate an extended discussion of the fairness of labor markets by evaluating the justice of proposals to give workers the right to participate in managerial decisions. In chapter 7, the case against legislated wage minimums is reconsidered. A major conclusion of that study is that all workers covered by such laws—not just those who retain their jobs—will generally be made worse off by them, a conclusion that raises serious questions about the fairness of legislated wages. Chapter 8 examines the case underlying the "equal-wages-for-comparable-worth" employment norm to determine if it matches its fairness billing.

Chapter 9 makes a strong fairness case for the development of a contained welfare state on the grounds that the poor, who are the professed concern, may not, on balance, benefit from an unregulated welfare state, whereas chapter 10 shifts the discussion once again to even more specific policy problems, namely the efficiency and fairness rationale for using states' powers of eminent domain to solve problems of plant closings and worker dislocation. Chapter 11 considers the fairness problems encountered in efforts to deregulate industries. The final chapter summarizes the major points developed throughout the book and assesses the long-run political viability of a market economy.

Notes

1. Frank Hyneman Knight, *The Ethics of Competition and Other Essays* (Chicago: University of Chicago Press, 1976), pp. 43 and 74.
2. Milton Friedman, "The Methodology of Positive Economics," *Essays in Positive Economics* (Chicago: University of Chicago Press, 1966), p. 4.
3. The limitations of the conventional positive approach to economic analysis have been extensively explored by Frank H. Knight, "The Limitations of Scientific Method in Economics," *The Ethics of Competition* (Chicago: University of

Chicago Press, 1976), pp. 105–147; and Richard B. McKenzie, *The Limits of Economic Science* (Boston: Kluwer-Nijhoff Publishing, 1983).

4. See John Rawls, *A Theory of Justice* (Cambridge, Mass.: Harvard University Press, 1971); Robert Nozick, *Anarchy, State, and Utopia* (New York: Basic Books, 1974); F. A. Hayek, *Law, Legislation, and Liberty*, three vols. (Chicago: University of Chicago Press, 1973, 1976, and 1979); Milton and Rose Friedman, *Free to Choose* (New York: Harcourt Brace Jovanovich, 1980); Michael Novak, *Freedom with Justice* (New York: Harper and Row, 1984); Israel M. Kirzner, *Discovery and the Capitalist Process* (Chicago: University of Chicago Press, 1985); and Geoffrey Brennan and James M. Buchanan, *The Reason of Rules: Constitutional Political Economy* (Cambridge, Mass.: Cambridge University Press, 1985).

5. Knight, *The Ethics of Competition*, pp. 45–61.

6. *Ibid.*, p. 58.

7. *Ibid.*

8. See Rawls, *A Theory of Justice* and Nozick, *Anarchy, State, and Utopia*.

9. See Brennan and Buchanan, *The Reason of Rules*, chapter 7.

10. See Rawls, *A Theory of Justice*, chapters 1–4.

11. See Hayek, *Law, Legislation, and Liberty*.

12. See Rawls, *A Theory of Justice* and David M. Byers, ed., *Justice in the Marketplace* (Washington: United States Catholic Conference, Inc., 1985).

13. See Richard B. McKenzie, ed., *Plant Closings: Public or Private Choices?* (Washington: Cato Institute, 1984); and Richard B. McKenzie, *Fugitive Industry: The Economics and Politics of Deindustrialization* (San Francisco: Pacific Institute, 1984).

14. These arguments have been forcefully made by Barry Bluestone and Bennett Harrison, *The Deindustrialization of America* (New York: Basic Books, 1982); and National Conference of Catholic Bishops, *Pastoral Letter on Catholic Social Teaching and the U.S. Economy*, 2nd draft (Washington, 1985).

15. See Terry L. Anderson, ed., *Water Rights* (San Francisco: Pacific Institute, 1984).

16. Julian L. Simon, "Auction the Right to Be an Immigrant," *New York Times* (January 28, 1985), p. 27.

17. "Immigration of the Fittest," *New York Times* (January 31, 1986), p. 26.

18. Yale Brozen, "The Economic Impact of Government Policy," a paper presented at the symposium, Economic Policy in the Market Process: Success or Failure? (Slot Seist, The Netherlands: January 29, 1986), p. 11.

2
Ethical Behavior and the Economy

The notion of morals implies some sentiment common to all mankind, which recommends the same object to general approbation, and makes every man, or most men, agree in the same opinion or decision concerning it. It also implies some sentiment, so universal and comprehensive as to extend to all mankind, and render the actions and conduct, even of the persons the most remote, an object of applause or censure, according as they agree or disagree with that rule of right which is established.

—David Hume[1]

E thics may appear to have no relevance to economics. After all, as noted in the first chapter, many economists have for a long time had a value-free approach to the study of social issues. They have, indeed, theorized about human behavior as if people were motivated almost exclusively by greed or self-interest and very little, if at all, by a sense of ethics, or what is proper or improper, right or wrong. Most of this book is a study of the fairness and ethics of markets and proposed social reforms. However, it must be firmly understood at the start that markets, as social institutions, are methods of constraining and containing human behavior, especially the excesses of human behavior. Ethics and other behavioral norms are also constraints on behavior; as such, they are viable alternatives to markets, but they, like markets, have their limitations in improving social welfare. In order to understand and appreciate the case for markets, one must understand and appreciate the limits of ethics and social norms as viable constraints on people's behavior.

This chapter seeks to initiate that search for fair and ethical institutions by raising the issue of why people would even be interested in or inclined to adopt constraints on their behavior, which the notions of fairness and ethics imply. The chapter starts with an examination of the purely economic reasons why people have to be ethical and fair and, quite apart from normative reasons, why they should. I start with basic points relating to ethics and group size that have been made by Mancur Olson and James Buchanan.[2] In extending their arguments, I focus on factors that tend to augment the deleterious effects that group size may have on the viability of ethical precepts. The importance of group structure and the dictates of religious institutions receive special attention.

Still, our discussion of the role of ethics and behavioral rules is useful for two reasons. First, it helps make the analytical transition from the way economists have at times thought about ethical issues to the normative matters considered in this book. Second, it helps explain why imperfect markets can extend the domain of human cooperation beyond what can be expected from reliance solely on ethical precepts. While much attention is given to the economic rationale for ethics and behavioral rules, the chapter concludes with an explanation of why people's pursuit of a fair, just, and ethical society cannot be completely economic (a conclusion that will not be very startling to noneconomists). The pursuit of improved social welfare requires, in other words, a rational passion for the irrational. It demands that people, to some extent, accept in what may only be called faith rules of behavior the value of which cannot be appreciated solely from their own experiences.

Group Size and the Limits of Ethical Behavior

The economic value of ethics is readily apparent. Ethical rules can make behavior among people within a group more predictable, and in this respect ethics is characteristically similar to the law. Knowing that others have agreed, implicitly or explicitly, to behave in certain ways, individuals can pursue their interests without having to determine how others will react to one's own behavior and to various circumstances. The more generally accepted the rules are, the more efficiently an individual can move among and interact with others. Further, if people agree to refrain from behavior such as lying, cheating, and stealing, the individual can save additional resources by not having to protect his or her property. The need for governmentally provided police protection, and the implied coercive power, is correspondingly reduced.

In this way, ethical and other behavioral rules contribute to the common welfare. They are, in the jargon of economists, "public goods," meaning that they benefit people generally regardless of whether or not payment is made. Since such rules are in the common interest, one may assume that they will be adopted and obeyed voluntarily even in large groups. Adherence to ethical precepts may be expected simply because of the common purpose they serve. However, Olson has argued rather convincingly that the common interest cannot serve as the basis on which large group behavior can be organized.* The explanation is simply that because the individual is such a small part of the total when taken in the context of a large group, his or her contribution to and influence on the group's attainment of whatever public good is at stake borders on insignificance. There will be, in other words, insufficient incentive for the individual to incur the private costs he or she must bear in order to contribute to the common interest.

For illustrative purposes, Olson relates his argument to the conventional competitive model. In that market, all competitors can benefit in the same way that a monopolist can: If an industry's output is restricted and the price is raised, total industry profits can be increased. In a sense, a public good, limited to the boundaries of the industry, can be generated. The individual competitor, however, because he makes a relatively insignificant amount of the industry's total output, has no incentive to cut back production. His behavior will have no detectable effect and, therefore, no realizable benefits. Additionally, if a surplus develops on the market, there is no private benefit to be gained by not cutting one's price.

Clearly, the common interest can be served if *all* restrict their output and hold the line against market pressures, but that end is not served. The incentive structure is such that the individual is led to do what is contrary to the interest of the group. His intent is not malicious; on the contrary, the competitor, because of his relative size, does not perceive that he is not acting in the group's interests.

---

*The dividing line between large and small groups remains unspecified because of the conceptual nature of the argument.

Similarly, the common interest cannot serve as the basis for an organizational structure, superimposed on the market, that can bring about the kinds of behavior necessary to generate the public good. If a structure is achieved, it is because private benefits are provided by the organization. A good example of what is implied here is membership in the American Economics Association (AEA). Olson would argue that economists do not belong to the AEA because of the *public* benefits that may be present. Rather, they belong because of the private benefits they receive from the journals and from being able to tell others that they belong. The private incentives are important because of the relative insignificance of the individual in the context of large groups.

Nobel laureate James Buchanan has developed a similar line of analysis, but his attention is squarely on the choice the individual makes between two fundamental ethical positions.[3] The individual may choose to follow a "moral law," something akin to the Kantian categorical imperative, or else a "private maxim." With regard to the former choice, the individual's subsequent behavior will be constrained by his or her prior decision to adhere to the ethical precept. In the case of the categorical imperative, the individual will do only those things that he or she can generalize to the rest of the relevant population. Doing what may be expedient in the narrow context of each situation is restricted or made more costly from a psychic point of view. Having chosen to abide by a private maxim, one's subsequent choices are left unconstrained. Purely expedient behavior, meaning that only the costs and benefits of the situation are considered, can be expected. This does not mean that the individual will not, in a given situation, do what is "morally" right; the morally right course of action may very often be the expedient thing to do.

Buchanan is unconcerned with the morality of the choice made at this fundamental level. His concern is with deducing the effects of group size on the choice that is made. Because the argument is involved and lengthy, we can only note here that Buchanan demonstrates with simple numerical examples that, even though the individual may prefer that he and all others adopt the moral law in large groups, the individual probably will choose according to a private maxim. Again, as in Olson's discussion, the perfectly competitive market model yields essentially the same conclusion. The insignificance of the individual and the absence of private, internal benefits in large groups make the adoption of the moral law an irrational act in terms of the expected benefits.*

Additionally, an individual may not perceive that he or she is, in choosing the route of expediency, doing anything that he or she considers morally reprehensible. Their behavior may not detectably affect others, and such external effects may be the central concern of his or her moral behavior. They are intrinsic in Kant's categorical imperative.

In small groups, the probability of an individual having a significant impact on the rest of the group is increased, and the adoption of the moral law is more likely; but, Buchanan writes, "there is some increase in group size that will cause him to modify his ethical rule and become a private maximizer."[4] In small groups, we do tend to find individuals foregoing strictly expedient behavior and adopting ethical or other behavioral rules that serve the common good. Buchanan cites examples:

> Volunteer fire departments arise in villages, not in metropolitan centers. Crime rates increase consistently with city size. Africans behave differently in tribal culture than in urban-industrialized settings. There is honor among thieves. The Mafia has its own standards. Time-tested honor systems in universities and colleges collapse when enrollments exceed critical size limits. Litter is more likely to be found on main traveled routes than on residential streets. Even the old adage, "Never trust a stranger," reflects recognition of this elemental truth, along with, of course, additional ethical predictions. Successful politicians organize "grassroots" support at the precinct level.[5]

To this list, we may add that small communities have many churches, many more than can be justified on efficiency grounds or on the basis of need for differences in approach. Churches are also internally organized with smaller subdivisions, such as circles and fellowship groups. Indeed, Buchanan's point has an unsuspected generality about it; it may be a major reason for highly decentralized

---

*The expected benefits must, of course, be appropriately discounted, to use economists' conventional terminology.

organizational structures within business and government bureaucracies. Failure to decentralize or departmentalize large bureaucracies may lead to a failure of personnel to adopt anything approximating a moral law. This may mean that the public good available to a group from ethical behavior will be lost; as a result, the firm's cost of production may, on balance, rise.*

More rigorously, we can conceptually segment organizational costs to a firm into two categories, overhead cost and moral cost. The overhead costs to the firm include relatively fixed costs, that is, given the size of the firm, of defining the departments with a structure, including a department head and line of authority. As the size of the departments is increased and the number decreased, the overhead cost attributable to any *one* department can decrease. The moral cost is the failure of the department to generate the public good through its members adhering to an ethical code. As implied in the Buchanan argument, this cost rises as the department size increases.[6] The total average cost combines overhead and moral cost.[7] From a strict efficiency point of view, an optimum department size is implied by these cost relationships. The firm wanting to minimize its organizational cost can increase the organizational unit, reducing the overhead cost but increasing the moral cost. At some point (that is, the optimum size) any further increase in the size of the organizational unit will cause the moral cost to rise by more than the overhead cost falls.†

The firm can reduce the size of the department and reduce the moral cost, but the overhead cost will be increased to the point where total average cost will be raised. It is because of this that the firm may allow a degree of unethical behavior (for example, personal use of office supplies) to pervade the organization, and this can be done rationally in the same sense in which the firm seeks to minimize all other costs. At the same time, the firm seeks to limit the amount

---

*The diseconomies of scale may still emerge to the extent that, although people may adopt the moral law within their small departments, the same rules may not be applicable to interdepartmental behavior. With regard to relationships outside one's own department, the private maxim may be adopted. Relating the argument again to the competitive market, the "public good" is generated within the individual firm; it is in the context of interfirm behavior that the public good is not generated.

†Perhaps employing marginal-costs concepts would be more accurate; however, this unnecessarily complicates the presentation and would not alter the general conclusions to be developed.

of unethical behavior: An increase in the department size beyond the optimum would increase the moral cost more than the decrease in the overhead cost.

If the size of the firm increases, the organizational structure becomes more complex with vice presidents, division managers, subdivision managers, and department heads. Further, the number of departments increases, causing an increase in the moral cost, among other costs, at the interdepartmental level. This implies that the overhead cost increases along with total cost, but the optimum department size then becomes greater. The important point to note is that the efficiency-motivated firm will permit a greater degree of unethical behavior; they do this in order to reduce the overhead cost to where, on the margin, it is no greater than the moral cost.

Our discussion of small and large group behavior may not be as sterile and unrelated to social problems and solutions as may be imagined. So much of the unethical behavior that pervades society (including markets) today in the actions of private and governmental bureaucracies can be a reflection of their sheer growth in number of people and the sheer sizes of the organizations they create. Street crimes and Watergate-type offenses in government and overcharges in private firms can be a natural consequence of growth in public and private organizations. The challenge to those concerned with the ethical crisis is one of finding more efficient ways of organizing people in groups. Otherwise, a reduction in the size of, say, bureaucracies or a return to decision making in smaller groups may be in order. One of the appeals of markets is that they do offer decentralized decision making, which can take place in small groups.

Mitigating Factors

Although one can point to many instances in which ethical behavior acquires considerable potency in small group settings, many instances can also be cited that demonstrate that ethical behavior is prevalent, and, indeed, is relatively powerful, in what may be considered very large groups. People litter, but, by the same token, many refrain in cases in which to do so would be expedient. Although many people know that they may go uncaught or, if caught, go unpunished, they do not take available opportunities to steal. People vote, some with a reasonable degree of intelligence, although the rational thing from a strictly expedient position may be to disregard the political process altogether.* Cheating may be prevalent in universities, but many students refuse, having decided to ignore the costs and benefits of the immediate situation and go out of their way to avoid even the suggestion that they are behaving improperly.

People do not take all opportunities they have to lie or divulge information about others, even in circumstances in which no one else can possibly learn what they have done and when lying may be beneficial to themselves. Roland McKean has listed the following examples: "Behavioral codes in certain cultures or during emergencies have caused individuals to sacrifice their lives. Numerous persons in Japan (for instance, the 47 Ronin), not just a few emotionally unbalanced individuals, have committed hara-kiri when the rules called for such action. In 1973, seventy-six passengers on a vehicle caught in a flood in India drowned rather than escape by means of a rescue rope that had just been used by passengers belonging to a different caste."[8] We can reasonably assert that the incidence of such behavior is not trivial and that much of it is revealed in the context of large groups.

This is not to suggest that the Olson-Buchanan position is unsound. On the contrary, there is every reason to believe that group size has the perverse effect they argue it does. However, as Olson and Buchanan both recognize, the problem is a multidimensional one; factors other than number can have an influence as powerful as ethics within a given group size. A complete theory must account for these instances in which ethics is effective within large groups. No pretense is made that the theory will be completed here. However, the purpose of the following discussion is to extend the Olson-Buchanan argument, to postulate what several of these other factors may be, and what mitigating effect they may have. In the end, we will see that we have to admit that much moral behavior remains unexplained by rationalistic means.

---

*For a theory that tends to support the view that voters should not be expected to vote and, if they do, to vote intelligently, see Anthony Downs, *An Economic Theory of Democracy* (New York: Harper & Row, 1957); and Gordon Tullock, *Toward a Mathematics of Politics* (Ann Arbor: University of Michigan Press, 1967). Admittedly, this theory is quite productive in that it explains the behavior of a substantial portion of voters, but it also fails to explain very well the behavior of many.

There are several points of departure. First, we must recognize that there are purely economic considerations at play. As McKean points out, although the benefits an individual may receive from contributing to a public good may be quite small, bordering on insignificance but not zero, the costs to the individual may be equally small, or smaller, making the act rational. If a person does not lie, he may contribute to the public trust. The benefits to him individually, from his *own* act, may be quite small; but because the lie may have been of trivial import to him to begin with, not telling the lie can still be quite rational. The cost-benefit ratio may be the same for a large number of people, so that the sum of the relevant individual actions can generate a certain degree of public trust as a public good.

Second, people may act out of a sense of duty, a sense of obligation to the community as a whole, that transcends the immediate circumstances of their own positions. This duty may have nothing to do with, and may be independent of, rational behavior as narrowly defined by economists.[9] Exploration of the Christian or Kantian motives for individual action, which makes the goodness of the act itself an end distinct from the gain to the actor, may yield useful predictions about behavior that can complement the economist's insights founded on economic rationality. One step removed from this level of discourse is the argument that even in very large groups people implicitly (by accepting membership in the group) or explicitly form a social contract that obligates them to certain forms of behavior. The force leading them to abide by such a contract may simply be an internal preference structure that makes keeping one's word an economic good in the same sense that a concert is a good.

Third, there is every reason to assume that ethical values and rules, like other goods, are the product of a rather elaborate development process that begins at birth with parental labor as the main resource input and continues through formal education with a substantial investment of resources. Values and rules are also developed and reinforced through the individual's everyday experiences and interactions with others. What constitutes acceptable or unacceptable behavior is learned or, using the terminology of the psychologist, imprinted. This does not mean that choice behavior is not present. The individuals producing the values must make decisions on how many resources should be employed in creating and maintaining the social values. The choice behavior of the subjects is an obstacle that must also be overcome in order that the value may be imprinted and in that way affect subsequent behavior.

The selection of ethical rules to be developed is not, of course, a random process. A group, be it small or large, has limited resources with which to accomplish what is wanted individually and collectively. There is a wide variety of rules that can be learned or adopted and obeyed, and it is reasonable to assume that the group does not have the option of developing all possible rules and ethical precepts. If the membership of a group constantly changes, individuals who make up the relevant group may rationally decide to concentrate their efforts on rules that can be generalized to the community at large. This means that information about what is acceptable conduct to others outside the group will be gathered by all groups in the fluid state. The fluidity of movement among groups, or the prospects of movement, makes it rational for individuals to develop and agree to something like a moral law that may make group members readily acceptable if and when they shift groups. Such behavior may make ethics more widely adopted than one might think from the limited-purpose argument of Olson-Buchanan.

Families, for example, are small groups that are continuously involved in establishing and reinforcing family values and rules. Parents, however, have a serious optimizing problem in dedicating their time to the development of values and rules whose benefits are limited to the family or to values and rules that reflect commonly held positions of the community at large. A motive for the latter application of resources is to make their children more acceptable and mobile in the larger community. Because the individual or family has little influence on the total community's values and rules, commonly accepted positions on ethics or other behavioral rules have a built-in inertia that can make them resistant to change. (It should be noted that the value of the norms and the rules that are accepted are not, cannot, always be fully appreciated by the group that adopts them. This is because they will never know what life would be like without them and may not understand why the values and rules were adopted or why they survived. More will be said about these points later.)

Fourth, embedded in Olson and Buchanan's argument is one of two assumptions: Either (1) the individual is assumed to be so insignificant that his or her behavior cannot materially affect anyone else even if the total impact is directed at one particular person, or (2) the effects of the individual's behavior are spread evenly over the entire group population with no noticeable effect on any one person. There are, in other words, no differential effects. In this way, an individual's unethical behavior in violating group rules does not have adverse effects, and the interpersonal costs and benefits discussed by McKean do not come into play as a means of restraining behavior.

Either of these two assumptions may describe with reasonable accuracy the relationships among competitors who must compete against the market and not each other, or among voters who may cast their votes for different candidates through secret ballots in a political contest. These are situations in which personal relationships are incidental to the forms of behavior; the people involved may just as well be isolated from one another. However, such assumptions may have little relevance to many problems of ethical behavior; that behavior is revealed characteristically in personal, one-to-one situations, where the impact is direct and differential effects are felt.

Most often a person lies directly, or befriends another directly, or steals from another, or snipes about another. The consequences of this behavior are not spread over the group evenly; there are differential effects, although there may also be external effects felt by group members not directly involved. This means that often, as opposed to treating the group members as a part of nature, the individual must operate strategically, reckoning with the consequences that his or her behavior may have on the behavior of others within the group.

In other words, a large group that may appear on the surface to resemble a competitive market may be better characterized as a web of interconnected and interdependent relationships (much like a set of oligopolistic market structures). To illustrate, I might behave quite ethically toward a friend because of the interpersonal costs-and-benefit structure that exists between us. These costs and benefits may constrain my behavior and force me to adopt, say, a moral law as a guiding principle. The same may be true of other friends. These friends may, having the same relationship with others I do not know, adopt similar rules for their relationships with them.*

---

*Clearly, an individual cannot handle an infinite variety of rules that govern his or her interpersonal relationships. He or she is, therefore, likely to try to economize on the resources employed in the development of governing rules by using many of the same rules with different people.

In this way, the size of the group within which a given set of behavioral rules applies can extend outward, possibly increasing the size of the group to where, in the Olson-Buchanan framework, it might be considered large. Here the group would be identified by common ethical precepts and rules; however, the group *structure* militates against the size having the deleterious effect suggested by Olson-Buchanan. This is because the group is, actually, a web of small groups. In this sense, the argument is consistent with Olson-Buchanan, but it focuses on group structure as opposed to group members.

The size of the web and the viability of the behavioral rules within the web will have their limitations. From a purely economic perspective, each rational party to the web can be expected to invest in personal relationships in a variety of dimensions (for example, time, space, and depth) until the expected additional benefits and costs are equal. The ability of the individual within the group to exact the costs and benefits necessary to maintain the behavioral rules (following McKean) will depend upon the strength and depth of these relationships. Persons who have strong and abiding friendships will incur considerable cost if those relationships are weakened by their own actions, such as by violating a commonly adopted ethical precept. On the other hand, casual acquaintances can be expected to exert little influence on each other's behavior.

As the web of groups becomes larger, members of a group at one corner of the web become more distant from persons at the other end. The strength of the rules governing behavior among members of the groups should weaken as the distance between groups, and therefore individuals, increases.

We also suggest that any change in conditions that reduces the reliance of people on one another would tend to lessen the incentive to develop interpersonal relationships. Accordingly, the interpersonal costs-and-benefit structure necessary to maintain ethical behavior in the small group setting, and consequently the web, will be weakened; we may expect a deterioration in the force of ethical and behavioral rules.

We have discussed how the prospects of individuals moving out of one group and into another affect the choice of ethical rules that may be developed within any given group; however, we must add that beyond some threshold, any increase in people's mobility can have a dampening effect on their willingness to invest in personal relationships and to maintain ethical rules. The change does not have to be generalized throughout the web in order for the entire web to be affected; the web insures the transmittal, in varying degrees, of any exogenous effects from one corner of the web to other parts.

The Relevance of Religion

A cornerstone of scientific economic inquiry is the a priori presumption that the private benefits of an action must exceed the private costs before individual action can be expected. This presumption has been intrinsic to the writings of Olson, Buchanan, and McKean and to the foregoing discussion. The costs and benefits may be real or imagined; the crucial point is that they must be viewed as relevant considerations. When the individual weighs subjectively each potential choice consideration, discounting it by the probability of its being realized, the distinction between what is real and imagined becomes blurred, if not irrelevant.

The conception of God as a universal force is a case in point. God may or may not exist. However, so long as the individual considers God to be a relevant factor, his subjective cost-and-benefit structure is different from what it would be otherwise.[10] The precise nature of this conception will have a corresponding reflection in behavior. In this way, the conception of God's existence will have a reinforcing influence on the viability of ethics. Changes in that conception will alter that viability.

It is easy at this point to become bogged down in a discussion of what God should or should not be or how people should or should not perceive him. To skirt these issues, however, I take as a point of departure several characteristics that may be generally, but, of course, not universally, attributable to the concept of God and then deduce the implications of such a concept for the viability of ethical codes. This concept can then be augmented with the purpose of determining changes in the viability of ethics. The force of the argument does not depend upon the readers' agreement with the description of God that follows. This description serves merely as a reference point for discussion.

To begin, God is a metaphysical concept by definition. An individual can believe with certainty that God does or does not exist but cannot prove that he does or does not in any objective sense. There is no scientific way to answer the question of "where did it all begin?" For this reason, most persons may attribute some, although in many cases very small, probability to God's existence.

He is normally considered to be omniscient and omnipotent; He pervades the total behavior of every individual, knowing his or her every thought and move. In this initial description, we assume that God is capable of imposing what may approach infinite costs (for example, eternal hell) for misdeeds and granting infinite benefits (for instance, eternal life in heaven) to those who hold certain values and behave according to certain rules. In most religious codes, these values and rules relate primarily to interpersonal group relationships and to the individual's relationship with God. Given this conception, the individual must attribute a small, if not zero, probability to any of his actions escaping God's knowledge. He must also attribute some probability to his actions affecting the benefits received or costs imposed by God on the day of reckoning.

In the context of some critical group size and structure, ethics, because of the externalities, may have no force in the absence of a conceptualized God. However, if God possesses the above attributes, then the externalities described above are internalized. The omniscience and omnipotence of God ensure this. If the costs of abiding by the ethical rules endorsed by God are less than the costs that may be imposed by others and God, the rational man will choose to behave ethically and contribute his small part to the public welfare. In short, ethics have force in part because of the religious costs of violations.*

Ethics and Marginal Man

We have discussed to this point only the basics of what is involved in a rational economic act. Marginal economic man will, given his or

---

*These points were developed in greater detail in the original journal version of this chapter. Religious beliefs can be self-reinforcing. The improvement in social welfare that may be attributed to belief in God and that may result from ethical behavior can reinforce belief in God, regardless of whether God exists. See Richard B. McKenzie, "The Economic Dimensions of Ethical Behavior," *Ethics* (April 1977), pp. 208–221.

her conception of God and the associated present values and probabilities, extend his ethical behavior up to the point where the marginal benefits equal the marginal costs. In this context, changes in the relevant probabilities and present values alter the level of ethical behavior. Even from an economic perspective there is, in other words, an optimum level of ethical behavior for each individual.

This view of human behavior provides a basis for postulating reasons for what many perceive to be an ethical crisis in contemporary society. First, there has been a decrease in emphasis that religious groups give to heaven and hell. This means that the costs and benefits of ethical behavior have been reduced. Second, there has been a greater emphasis on forgiveness, which effectively lowers the costs of short-term unethical behavior.

Third, there has been a growing emphasis on personalized religion; "God is what you make him" is not an uncommon attitude. This reason, combined with the other two, may have resulted in a reduced inclination to behave according to a commonly held set of ethical rules, which, if obeyed, generate the public good that has been the heart of all that has been said. God's presence is not as clearly seen and the perceived probability of God's existence has been accordingly lowered. This in turn can lower the optimum level of ethical behavior. Through such reasoning one can postulate a snowballing effect on ethical behavior. The level of ethical behavior can drop asymptotically to a level that can be supported by the cost and the benefit structure of interpersonal relationships and the remaining belief in God.

Belief in God has one additional ramification that needs to be noted. The usual conception of God establishes certain values, ethical precepts, and behavioral rules as *absolutes* (or almost nearly absolute rules and values, subject to changes only under extreme conditions and in the very long run). Without such reference points, everything becomes relative to the conditions of the time, including the physical environment, human institutions, and the bargaining and other abilities of the relevant persons. Nothing is determined; everything must be determined and redetermined in the light of changes in conditions. This suggests that substantial costs must be incurred in establishing and re-establishing norms for behavior. By making certain forms of

behavior absolute, God effectively reduces, but by no means elimi-
nates, those types of costs; they are just not up for negotiation; they
are fixed and must be assumed to be a part of nature that constrains
behavior. Again, a public good is provided that can be shared by the
relevant group. Personal interaction is facilitated, and to this degree
the size of the workable group can expand. Still, a limit to the size of
the workable group is implied, and the functional relationship between group size and the viability of the ethical code remains.

Expanding Human Cooperation

One of the more difficult questions in social philosophy is how to
expand human cooperation and production beyond that which would
be permitted by adherence to commonly accepted ethics and other
social norms.

The fact of the matter is that even Adam Smith explicitly recognized that enlisting people's good will was often costly. Smith is
renowned for having elevated the role of self-interest in guiding
markets, but he also wrote immediately prior to making his famous
statement on the self-interest of butchers and bakers that the individual "has not the time, however, to do this upon every occasion
[that is, seek others' good will]. In civilized society he stands at all
times in need of the cooperation and assistance of great multitudes,
while his whole life is scarcely sufficient to gain the friendship of a
few persons."[11] It was, in other words, when the individual's need for
cooperation extended beyond the bounds of his friendships that the
appeal to another's self-interest was useful. Markets economize on
virtues like love, good will, altruism, and ethical precepts, and at the
same time rely on them.

Granted, markets have all kinds of imperfections, which was
stressed in chapter 1 in the review of Frank Knight's classic statement
on "The Ethics of Competition." However, markets also provide
incentives and disincentives for people to do more of what people
other than themselves perceive to be right and proper. (Markets
would be hard to justify to the vast majority of people if all they
accomplished was the wholesale expression of self-interest and
greed). Markets may, at the same time, encourage wrong and improper behavior; but the real issue is what happens on balance over

the course of time and many areas of human interaction. Proponents and opponents of markets often disagree over policies partly because of differences in basic values but also because they often disagree over how that social balance sheet is assessed.

The Irrationality of Ethics

The whole of the foregoing discussion presumes that ethics can be largely explained by resort to rational means, a clearly dubious proposition to most noneconomists. While the costs and benefits of people's actions offer some insight about ethical behavior, the most amazing thing about ethics to the strict economist, imbued with rationalistic models of behavior, is that they exist at all and persist with the force that they do have in shaping human action. The fact that remnants of ethical behavior remain with considerable force is startling to the person who thinks only in rational terms for two reasons. First, it is a mystery why people do anything other than free ride (or fail to cooperate) in helping to produce the public good associated with ethical behavior far more than they do. The logic of the free rider so dear to the theoretical hearts of economists would appear to be so powerful that opportunism would appear to be the norm.

Second, it is not clear that any group of people living under the force of accepted behavioral rules, including ethics, would understand or appreciate with reasonable clarity the practical value of any given commonly accepted ethical rules. This is because the established commonly accepted behavioral rules would have to emerge from the interactive process of generations of people. Rules tend to emerge in modified form because they seem to work better than their alternatives that have been tried and found deficient in one respect or another. They often result from a form of Social Darwinism, not always through human design or intended action by anyone or any group of people.[12] What is amazing is that individuals who do not understand the basis for existing rules and who do not have a direct private stake in the maintenance of rules of behavior act as if they do believe the rules count. Human society should consider itself blessed that people are not as rational as economists' theories would have us believe.

Concluding Comments

This chapter has attempted to introduce additional economic and noneconomic considerations in the discussion of ethics. Many issues have, understandably, gone unexplored. Much more thought needs to be given to other factors that may affect the individual's ethical-choice calculus, including changes in how ethics evolve and how structural and technological changes in the economy and the larger society affect the relative prices of pursuing ethical and nonethical behavior.

One major factor may be the expanding role of large-scale organizations, for example, governments and businesses, that can destabilize the tenuous state of commonly accepted ethics and other norms of behavior. Government enforced rules are one alternative way of potentially increasing and decreasing social welfare through controlling behavior, and they may be an imperfect substitute for ethical rules and norms.

Government's growth, which includes taxation, may distort the incentive structure in such a way that unethical acts may become more reasonable and lucrative. This is particularly true of governments or businesses that are protected from competition by barriers to entry. As opposed to dealing with one another on an interpersonal basis, people through governments, for example, are effectively thrown into a large-group structure in which all deal impersonally with a massive government superstructure that may not be easily identified with other persons. For that reason, people may be induced to a much greater extent to cheat on their income tax reporting and on their collections of government benefits. Such behavior can feed on itself in people's other dealings with many others, the result of which can be the weakening, if not dissolution, of norms of behavior and the social benefits that go with them.

These, however, are the more general concerns of social institutions that must be kept in mind when debating the desirability of markets, and the resulting decentralization of decision making, on fairness and ethical grounds. The fairness case against reliance on markets is often founded on less elevated charges, one of the most prominent of which is that trade, especially international trade, is unfair. That charge is evaluated in the next chapter.

Notes

1. David Hume, *An Inquiry Concerning the Principles of Morals*, included in *Hume: Selections*, ed. by Charles W. Hendel, Jr., (New York: Charles Scribner & Sons, 1927), p. 228.
2. Mancur Olson, *The Logic of Collective Action: Public Goods and the Theory of Groups* (Cambridge, Mass.: Harvard University Press, 1971); James M. Buchanan, "Ethical Rules, Expected Values, and Large Numbers," *Ethics* 76 (October 1965): 1–13.
3. Buchanan, "Ethical Rules, Expected Values, and Large Numbers," p. 8.
4. Ibid.
5. Ibid.
6. Armen A. Alchian and Harold Demsetz focus on the increase in monitoring and shirking cost of larger organizational units ("Production, Information Costs, and Economic Organization," *American Economic Review* 62 {December 1972}, 777–795).
7. Graphically, the overhead and moral cost function would be summed vertically. The graphical representation of the relationship would tend to parallel the construction employed by James M. Buchanan and Gordon Tullock in their *Calculus of Consent* (Ann Arbor: University of Michigan Press, 1972, p. 71.
8. Roland N. McKean, "Economics of Ethical and Behavioral Codes," mimeographed (Charlottesville: Department of Economics, University of Virginia, 1974), p. 6 (preliminary draft).
9. For a discussion of the various possible motives for charitable behavior, which is a part of what is at stake here, see Thomas R. Ireland and David Johnson, *The Economics of Charity* (Blacksburg, Va.: University Publications, 1970), particularly pp. 17–25.
10. See McKean, "Economics of Ethical and Behavioral Codes, p. 25.
11. Adam Smith, *An Inquiry into the Nature and Causes of the Wealth of Nations*, ed. by Charles W. Hendel, Jr. (New York: Charles Scribner & Sons, 1927), p. 14.
12. This Darwinistic conception of rule development is sketched in F. A. Hayek, *Law, Legislation, and Liberty*, 3 vols. (Chicago: University of Chicago Press, 1973, 1976, and 1979). The theme will be more fully developed by Hayek in *The Fatal Conceit*, a book that at this writing is under development.

Part II
Fairness and
the Freedom of Markets

———

3

The Fairness of Trade
and Protectionism

[T]here is a certain tendency on the part of short-sighted people to see only the . . . possible troubles that may arise in some localities and some industries as the result of our lowering of our trade barriers. . . . The increase in ·competition from abroad will be a challenge to American producers, but it will also bring benefits to consumers in the way of greater variety of products and some reductions in prices. . . . By substantially lowering the economic barriers that we have all erected against one another in the past we can assure for all broader markets, greater efficiences in production, greater economic stability, and faster economic growth. . . . The future of the automobile industry and the job security of its workers cannot be assured by a retreat to economic isolationism and the building of high tariff barriers.

—Walter Reuther[1]

T he trade-off between efficiency and equity has long been a sticking point in resolving major public policy debates. However, equity or fairness concerns have been elevated to a new prominence in current political battles over measures to protect American industries from foreign competition. While economists and other opponents of trade restrictions continue to articulate the efficiency arguments against protectionism, congressional and industry advocates of protection herald the fairness of their proposed restrictions.*

---

*Antiprotectionists point to the economic rents that will be reaped by special interests, the loss of consumer purchasing power, and the destruction of domestic jobs directly attributable to the proposed legislation. If it had been enacted, the proposed Textile and Apparel Trade Enforcement Act of 1985 alone may, according to antiprotectionists, cost American consumers a minimum of $23 billion annually and may wipe out 62,000 jobs in the retail industry, making the cost of each job saved in the textile and apparel industries several times textile workers' average wages [Laura Magna Baugham and Thomas Emrich, "An Analysis of the Impact of the Textile and Apparel Enforcement Act of 1985" (Washington: International Business and Economic Research Corporation, June 1985)]. Opponents of protection maintain that political interest in

Nowhere is the concern for fairness in trade more evident than in the debate over import protection for the domestic textile industry, which, according to the industry, has lost more than 300,000 jobs since 1980. "The essence of the bill [the Textile and Apparel Trade Enforcement Act of 1985]," writes Ellison McKissick, president of the American Textile Manufacturers Institute, "is to restore fair trade, to make the table level again. Our markets are overwhelmed by imports of yarn, fabric, clothing and home furnishings from foreign manufacturers whose low wages and working conditions would be unlawful in the U.S."[2]

Concerned about textile mill closings in his state, caused in part by imported shirts that can be made "in downtown Shanghai, China, for 18 cents an hour," Senator Fritz Hollings has impassionately called for "sensible protection," charging that

> [T]he Constitution provides for the protection of trade. But editorial writers are constantly carping "free trade, free trade," "protectionism, protectionism," "trade war, trade war." While the United States sits in the grandstand shouting, "We may start a trade war," down on the field the trade war is in the fourth quarter.
>
> We are losing our shirts. We are losing our shoes. We are losing our telecommunications equipment, our machine tools, our copper. We are losing our automobiles, our sporting goods, our TV's, our steel, our shipping. More recently we are losing our agriculture.[3]

Echoing Senator Hollings's sentiments, textile executive Roger Milliken maintains, "We are sacrificing our industrial base on the altar of free trade—a god no other nation worships."*

---

protectionist bills can be explained in large measure by the fact that the benefits of protection are concentrated on a relatively small number of well-organized groups of workers and firm owners, whereas the costs of protection are hidden in price increases and are spread thinly over a relatively large number of consumers who, individually, have little or no incentive openly to oppose protectionist measures. For an example of the efficiency arguments tendered against protectionism, see Murray L. Weidenbaum, "A 'Dutch Uncle' Talk on Foreign Trade," (St. Louis: Center for the Study of American Business, Washington University, October 1985).

*As quoted in "Look Who's Working with the Unions," Business Week (September 16, 1985), p. 52. This line of argument has been developed at length by James Clifton, who has also concluded, "What we are gaining from free trade policies as consumers we are losing as a working populace, and real wages have been declining since 1972 as a result. Because our products are no longer competitive, we are now consuming beyond our means. Only our military strength and financial acumen are enabling us to continue this course, but it cannot go on indefinitely" ["Are Free Trade Sentiments Still Applicable to the U.S. Economy?" (Washington: Washington Legal Foundation, 1986), p. 6].

And the protectionist political movement has had its impact. It has caused a free-trade president reluctantly to adopt some of the rhetoric, if not the substance, of protectionism. While acknowledging that history teaches that "the freer the trade, the stronger the tides of human progress," President Ronald Reagan has warned that he would not "stand by and watch American businesses fail because of unfair trading practices abroad. I will not stand by and watch American workers lose their jobs because other nations do not play by the rules."*

Although often couched in terms of lost jobs and closed plants, the continuing protection debate in Washington is not simply political. It is, to a significant extent, intellectual and philosophical, concerned with fundamental normative issues of whether the government should pursue a policy course of free trade or fair trade or even whether "free trade is fair trade," as the president maintains is the case.[4]

Advocates of protectionism, such as Hollings, McKissick, and Milliken, fervently maintain that free and unfettered international commerce is fundamentally unfair, founded on rules that favor other countries that are awash with cheap labor, that are unfettered by government controls on working conditions, and that are uninhibited in their efforts to subsidize and promote their export interests.

Besides, they contend, the United States has the most productive industrial firms in the world, which could compete if given the opportunity to do so on a playing field that is not tilted against them. The fact that many highly productive American industries cannot compete is often offered as prima facie evidence that trade is unfair.

Clearly, the conventional efficiency-based arguments of economists can affect, as they have affected, the political support for protectionist measures.[†] However, such arguments are also ignored by

---

*Ronald Reagan, "Transcript of Speech to Business and Government Leaders," New York Times (September 24, 1985), p. 48. In September 1985, Reagan called primarily for more aggressive investigations of unfair trading practices, greater efforts to liberalize trade through bilateral negotiations, and $300 million in additional export subsidies.

†The potential impact of economists' efficiency arguments is revealed in survey findings. A Roper poll found that more than 65 percent of Americans polled in October/November 1984 favored restrictions on "goods from other countries that are priced lower than American-made goods of the same kind" [as reported by Kevin Phillips, "The Politics of Protection," Public Opinion (April/May 1985), p. 42]. However, another poll undertaken by the New York Times and CBS found that while 63 percent of those polled favored import restrictions on Japanese goods, only a third of those (one-fifth of the total sample) said that their position would be unchanged if the restrictions resulted in higher prices and diminished product choice ["Democratic Delusions on Protection, New York Times (September 9, 1985), p. 18 (editorial).]

many supporters of protection who subscribe to the view that trade fairness is a more important human goal than economic efficiency.

Perhaps bridging the intellectual schism between protection's opponents and proponents is impossible, given the private interests at state. The fairness arguments of protectionists may simply be a political smoke screen intended to obscure public scrutiny of the income transfers inherent to protectionist legislation.* However, the debate over protectionism is too important for the future economic health of the country to dismiss out of hand the social objectives of proponents. The debate must be joined by economists on both efficiency and fairness grounds.

This chapter seeks to make the case against much protectionist policy by departing from conventional economic commentary and critically evaluating the fairness claims of advocates of restricted trade. It accepts as authentic the fairness concerns expressed by protectionists and assesses the validity of the protectionists' policy claims first by defining fairness in a way that might be acceptable to protectionists and then by asking if protectionists themselves would agree that their proposed trade restrictions are consistent with the agreed-upon definition of fairness in public policy.

Fairness as a Policy Criterion

The debate over free trade versus fair trade can only be advanced by constructing a definition of fairness that can be used to evaluate protectionist measures, for saying which policies are fair and which unfair. Any definition offered is unlikely to be definitive. Nonetheless, a working definition is necessary, and three elements of any useful definition appear essential:

First, fairness in policy requires that the factual and logical contentions undergirding appeals to fairness must be correct. A policy founded on misrepresentations or misstatements is a policy designed for a state or circumstance that does not, to one extent or another, exist. The policy might reasonably be judged fair for the state or circumstances as represented, but not for the state or circumstance to which the

---

*Surely this is not the case for all supporters of protectionist measures, some of whom have nothing to gain directly from the protectionist measures they support.

policy is actually applied. In concrete terms, textile protectionism is arguably unfair if it is passed based on representations by the textile industry to the effect that protection from textile imports will increase national employment when in fact, on balance, it will not or will increase jobs in the textile industry at the expense of jobs in other industries.

Second, fairness in policy is what all people would agree to if they were tolerably well informed about the consequences of the proposed policy. Policies that are acceptable to all can hardly be the subject of meaningful criticism by anyone. In the jargon of economics, such policies are "Pareto efficient," as well as fair. Clearly, where unanimous consent prevails, fairness and efficiency are fully compatible. Policies that are not agreeable to some, or even most, may be fair, but they still are arguably unfair to those not in agreement.

Third, fairness in policy is what should be made available to all similarly situated people or groups. The textile industry, for example, may believe that it is more deserving of government protection from foreign competition than other industries. The issue in such circumstances cannot be broadly defined as free trade versus fair trade, a conceptual distinction under which what is traded remains undefined in the sense that the category(ies) of goods and services are not specified.

The very generality of the concepts of free trade and fair trade implies a search for principles that are applicable to all, or virtually all, categories of goods and services produced and consumed by people with similar characteristics and in practically the same circumstances. Fairness in policy is, in other words, an appeal to principles that can be generalized beyond the individual circumstances of those who make the appeal.* In the case of international trade policy, a fair policy is necessarily one that neither intentionally favors nor

---

*An appeal to differential treatment must, because of private interests involved, remain suspiciously corruptible, if not corrupt. Even if the appeal to fairness were a disguised appeal for special treatment, the issue of special treatment could not be answered here solely by logical arguments. The test of the appeal would be the extent to which those making the appeal could convince others of the legitimacy of their claims for special treatment, given the precise circumstances under which their claims are made. Specific claims cannot, by definition, be considered in the abstract.

caters to the interest of, for example, the textile industry to the automatic exclusion of other similarly situated industries.

A fair policy is, therefore, one that is consistent with a broader principle or rule that is also considered fair. Rules are considered fair as long as they are designed to relieve problems that all agree should be relieved independent of who actually encounters the problems and benefits from the relief.

F. A. Hayek has developed in much greater detail this concept of fairness, illustrating his point with the fair rules used in parlor games. Parlor games are considered fair so long as the rules are selected independent of the players and their individual skills at playing the game. The rules are designed to ensure that someone can win, but not that a particular person will win. If the rules can be devised or changed to insure particular winners, then the people making the rules can ensure that they are the winners, which means that the contest may be arguably unfair.

The game is potentially rigged in the sense that the outcomes are predetermined. The outcome of a rigged game may simply reflect the interests of the people devising the rules.[5] A fair game is, therefore, one in which those who make the rules do not have an advantage because of their position as rulemakers.

A claim of fairness as an appeal to the fairness of a general principle is attractive in part because it represents a check on the arbitrariness and capriciousness of government policy. Thwarting arbitrariness and capriciousness in government policy may in itself be desirable, but it can also be attractive because it reduces the waste of resources implied in undirected and misdirected policies.

Fairness in rules, as a policy criterion, is also appealing because it is consistent with another fundamental norm for government, namely that each person should have equal protection under the law, which also means in effect that laws will not be tailored to meet the special needs and demands of identifiable people. In addition, it is consistent with the principle that justice should be blind to individuals who appeal for decisions on how government power will be employed. In this context, fairness as fair rules represents a check on the competitive employment of the concentrated coercive powers of government.

The Fairness of Restricted Trade

The fairness of protectionist proposals to consumers has long been questioned by economists, who have pointed out that protection is a hidden form of consumer taxation. If they were well informed on the consequences of protection, consumers would presumably object. The more interesting question is, Would the advocates of protectionism agree to their own restrictive proposals if they were reasonably well informed on the direct consequences of their proposals? Would they also agree if the advocated restrictions (or similar use of government powers) were immediately made available to all in comparable situations and if the advocates were reasonably well informed on the consequences of immediately elevating the restrictions to the status of principles? In other words, are the advocated restrictions fair, as judged by the consent of all (or almost all), including the advocates of restrictions?

The answer is most likely not. Granted, the advocates of restrictions would prefer special treatment to no trade restrictions.* However, when the proposed trade restrictions are subject to generalization, it is reasonably clear that their advocates would not recommend them. The textile industry, for example, might benefit from restricted trade so long as the restrictions were imposed on only textile imports (and, perhaps, a few other products). The textile import restrictions would restrain total market supply, raise textile prices, and increase the economic rents garnered by the textile firms and their workers, owners, and suppliers. The textile industry would gain to the extent that its income is, in the instance of its own protection, transferred from the rest of the citizenry to the textile industry. The transfer itself would hardly make the policy proposal fair to all, particularly those who are subjected to the implied taxation and diminished consumer choice through trade restrictions.

In addition, it should be stressed that if the textile trade restrictions were immediately generalized, the textile industry might not

---

*We might agree that special treatment is, as a rule, allowable, but not that a given case of special treatment is allowable. But there is no way for us here to say that special treatment (for the textile industry, or any other industry) is fair. The special case, by its nature, requires more information than is obtainable at the abstract level of discussion.

come out as a net gainer from its own advocated protectionist policy. Other industries would also be granted the privilege of having their import competition restricted. As a consequence, the textile industry would have to pay higher prices for imported machinery and materials used in production. It would also have to pay higher prices for the raw materials and intermediate inputs from other domestic producers whose costs are raised because of the restrictions on many other imports. And textile owners and workers (and their suppliers' owners and workers) would see their real income lowered by the higher prices they must pay for textiles and an exceedingly wide range of other goods and services.

The trade protection would necessarily have to extend beyond those industries that initially have to face foreign competition. The extended trade restriction would reduce the demand for foreign currencies on the international money markets, which would appreciate the dollar, exposing other industries to foreign competition.

These other industries newly exposed to the threat of foreign competition would also have access to the protective power of government. They, too, could be expected to seek protection, a process that could further harm the textile industry as well as expose other domestic industries to foreign competion. Conceivably, the generalization of any restriction granted the textile industry could encompass virtually the entire domestic economy.

The damage from the import restrictions to the domestic textile industry could be deepened through a reduction of textile exports and other domestic products that incorporate domestic textile products. Unless the protected industry faced peculiarly favorable supply and demand conditions, it would probably oppose its own protection, so long as others were also precluded from obtaining import restrictions.* Opposition to trade restrictions would appear to be unanimous, or virtually unanimous. Support for the rule of free trade (which

---

*At the abstract analytical level, there is no reason why protectionist restrictions conceptually accorded one industry in the current time period—the current textile industry—could not be extended, only for analytical purposes, to other industries in earlier time periods. That is, the relevant fairness question is whether or not a given industry seeking protection would agree to its own protection if that meant that industries in earlier periods could have the same protection. Protection in earlier time periods could mean a reduction in economic growth that would reduce the well-being of people in the current time period.

amounts to a rule against special treatment) would have similar broad-based appeal.*

Opposition to governmental obstructions to trade would be particularly strong if the principle of restricted trade were extended to the domestic market and if domestic competitors being beaten up on by their domestic rivals could also appeal to government for protection equal to the benefits accorded the textile industry. The cost incurred by the textile industry would most likely be enormous. Without knowing the exact outcome of such a generalized protectionist scheme, the textile industry could easily reason that its expected net benefits would be higher under a regime of free trade than protected trade. Protected trade would, in an ex ante sense, quite likely be perceived by all, or virtually all, as a negative sum game.

Nevertheless, in the absence of a firm constitutional prohibition against special treatment or for the free-trade rule, individual interest groups can be expected to push politically for their own protection from imports, as if they were actually against the rule of free trade. Each interest group can reason that if it does not seek protection, then others will, and the interest groups that do not seek protection (in the name of their free-trade ideals and any other social principle) will have to shoulder the burdens of protection granted others with no offsetting benefits for themselves. The drive of competitive politics can force all to digress from principle for their own protection from the political maneuvering of other interest groups (as well as from foreign imports). A constitutional prohibition against protectionism may, from this perspective, be seen as an institutional device for interest groups to protect themselves from each other.

The Fairness of the Law of Comparative Advantage

As noted, proponents of import restrictions contend that international trade is unfair because firms in the United States have to compete with companies in, for example, Shanghai that can pay their

---

*Seen as a rule, free trade is not a principle designed to leave private producers unconstrained in what they do. Indeed, they may be highly constrained in their competitive markets. Rather, it is rule designed as a constraint on the use of government powers, which means it is a rule that constrains the use of government power by business or other interest groups.

workers pauper wages, whereas U.S. firms cannot. As a consequence, international trade will lower American wages, if not impoverish American workers. The fairness argument has major flaws. First, it is not accurate. Wages are typically low across the board in low-wage countries, suggesting that low wages do not explain why such countries export given products to high-wage countries. The low wages also explain nothing about why these countries import goods from countries whose wages are much higher.

The low-wage argument also ignores or overlooks worker productivity. Wages tend to reflect workers' productivity: the higher the productivity, the higher the wages, meaning that high wages do not necessarily spell a cost disadvantage in production. Trade restrictions based on the low-wage argument can be construed as unfair to the extent they are misrepresentations and are not necessarily applicable to real-world trade.

On the other hand, low wages not fully offset by low productivity can spell a cost advantage for a foreign country. But then the law of comparative advantage says absolute cost levels do not determine trade, only comparative costs do. That is to say, what is important in determining the direction of trade—what is imported and exported—is a comparison of costs of various goods in one country with the costs of those goods in another country. The important comparison is relative costs of goods and services within each of two or more countries.

This means that the textile industry may not have to face import competition because of the low wages abroad or even its own absolute level of wages and productivity (it might be quite productive and pay relatively low wages, as the textile industry does in the United States). Rather, the textile industry may have to compete with imports because of the relatively more cost-effective methods of production achieved by other industries in the United States. The textile industry, in other words, does not necessarily have to face import competition because of its own absolute failures, but because of the relative successes of other U.S. industries.

Given our working definition of fairness, the relevant question is whether the textile industry itself would favor a policy rule that would provide protection to all industries that confront a comparative cost disadvantage, not necessarily just the textile industry and its political allies. For several reasons, the answer is, again, not very likely, especially if the rule were fully generalized.

As in the discussion of the previous section, protection based on comparative costs could mean that the textile industry would benefit to the extent that textile imports are restricted, but it would lose to the extent that its imports of resources and machinery are restricted. The textile import restrictions would shift the burden of the comparative cost disadvantage to other domestic industries, which could then be expected to seek protection on the same comparative cost grounds, to the detriment of the textile industry. The textile industry might also object to restrictions based on comparative costs because, in the abstract (not knowing its true economic position),* it might have a comparative cost advantage, in which case it would be penalized directly by a reduction in exports caused by the import restrictions. Import restrictions on other goods and services would restrict the dollar earnings of other countries and, thereby, the ability of other countries to buy U.S. goods, including textiles.

More important, however, the people in the textile industry may have agreed implicitly or explicitly to a prior rule that permits free and open competition that can include competition for a country's comparative cost advantage. The textile industry might have agreed to such a rule because free and open competition can result in efficiency improvements in a wide variety of industries that can be directly beneficial to people who may or may not be in the textile industry when restrictions are considered.†

A comparative cost advantage does not mean that anyone, or any industry, with the comparative cost advantage has acted unfairly. Indeed, by the nature of comparative costs, someone or some industry must have a comparative advantage while someone else or some other

---

*Implicitly a "Rawlsian veil of ignorance" is assumed in this discussion. See John Rawls, *Theory of Justice* (Cambridge, Mass.: Harvard University Press, 1971), chapter 4. Behind the Rawlsian veil of ignorance, the individual participant in the decision-making process must judge rules fully knowledgeable about the general features of society (for example, how the income is distributed) but without knowing anything at all about his or her absolute or relative position in the society.

†An appeal for protection on the basis of an unfair cost disadvantage can be an argument for the violation of the agreed-upon rule of free and unrestricted competition. Such an argument for restrictions may be considered no more fair than a proposal made in the third quarter by the losing football team that competitive handicaps should be imposed on the winning team. The fairness of such a proposal would be particularly questionable when in fact the rules of the game had been agreed to by all before the game began.

industry has a comparative disadvantage. And who or which industry has the advantage or disadvantage is as much dependent upon the competitors in the domestic economy, where proponents of protection rarely dispute the level of the playing field, as it is dependent upon competition from abroad, where the competitors have allegedly tilted the playing field against American industries.

When comparative costs are the basis for trade, there is no way that the international playing field can be level for all American industries in the sense that all industries will be winners. Level playing fields produce both winners and losers. Losers may believe they lost because of an uneven field, although the rules make it inevitable that there will be losers as well as winners. A claim by domestic firms of unfair competition from foreign firms in the same industry based on comparative costs is tantamount to a claim of unfair competition from firms in other domestic industries. Again, domestic competition can be just as much responsible for a given domestic industry having a comparative cost disadvantage as foreign competition is. Basing trade on comparative costs is, per se, neither fair nor unfair; comparative costs reflect existing preferences and production capabilities. As such, comparative costs can be no more nor no less fair or unfair than gravity, weather conditions, ocean currents, harbor sites, or the amount of sunlight available in different areas.

The fairness of trade based on comparative costs depends on the fairness of agreed-upon rules of trade. However, it is important to note that comparative costs may be construed as a fair basis for trade simply because it is virtually impossible for anyone or any interest group to know for very long what the comparative costs in the United States and other countries are. This is the case not only because costs are largely subjective (and thereby not knowable by outside observers), but also because the information requirements of intelligently knowing what comparative costs are, and will be in the future, far exceed the capacity of individuals assisted by even very large computers to absorb and comprehend information. Comparative costs may therefore be an attractive basis for trade for two reasons: First, trade based on comparative costs enhances economic efficiency and income. Second, trade based on comparative cost cannot (for very long) be intentionally designed to favor any identifiable persons or groups; it is fair to the extent it cannot be rigged.

The Fairness of Foreign Subsidies
and Domestic Policies

Proponents of protectionism maintain that foreign competition is unfair because of foreign governments' subsidies to their industries or because our government's regulations (for example, environmental regulations, minimum wage laws, and health and safety requirements) impose price-distorting costs on American industries. Free trade, they say in effect, is not trade free of government intervention.

Protectionists seem to be saying government policies here and abroad distort prices, causing some industries to face competitive pressures they would not otherwise have to face. The international trade game is unfair as it is being played because, after having played by the rules of the game, American firms are not permitted to benefit from the comparative cost advantages they have rightfully realized. The foreign competition, in other words, has effectively changed the rules of the game in the middle of the game to ensure that American firms are losers. Implicit in such contentions is the assumption that trade conducted on the basis of true, as opposed to distorted, comparative costs is more or less fair.

Admittedly, foreign competitors may benefit from subsidies. Some trade may indeed be unfair in the sense that the direction of trade, or the extent of trade, may reflect violations of agreed-upon trading rules. People and interest groups, like the textile industry, may agree to restrictions based on foreign subsidies simply because of the violations, because restrictions can return comparative prices to what they would have been in the absence of subsidies, and because there is, potentially at least, an external check on the scope and extent of protection granted. Protection in this country will be limited to what other countries do.

However, for several reasons it does not follow that the mere existence of subsidies for foreign firms is sufficient reason to conclude that the international trade is unfair. First, the foreign subsidies may correct for some other inefficiency in the foreign economy (due, for example, to monopoly power and externalities). When the full facts of the subsidies are understood, they may be fair as defined by agreement.

Second, the foreign subsidies may have been instituted in response to subsidies already in existence in the American economy. The domestic subsidies may be granted in the direct forms of government payments for product developments and in the indirect forms of government expenditures on roads, bridges, and sewer systems and of tax relief through investment tax credits and accelerated depreciation schedules. The foreign subsidies may have been instituted to make the playing field level again.*

Third, while the point of the discussion is that subsidies may be a necessary argument in any claim of fairness, it is not a sufficient argument. A sufficient argument would entail, at a minimum, a comparative analysis of subsidies in foreign and domestic economies.

Fourth, even if it were proved that foreign governments subsidize their industries more than the domestic government, the claim of unfair trade may not be fully justified. Again, the foreign subsidy may correct for some inefficiency in the allocation of resources in the foreign country. In addition, the foreign subsidy may have been longstanding and more or less permanent and may have been a part of the international trading rules that were implicitly accepted. In this regard, the comparatively greater foreign subsidy may be no more unfair than favorable climate or fertile soil that can also affect the direction and extent of trade.†

Still, foreign and domestic regulatory and industrial policies can be unfair in the sense that they are a violation of agreed-upon rules. However, it does not follow that the offended domestic industry would agree to institutional procedures that would allow government to shape international trade barriers based on charges of unfair competition that are themselves founded on claims of foreign and

---

*Furthermore, it is important to understand that subsidies affect trade by changing relative, not absolute, prices in the trading countries. A foreign subsidy that is matched by a comparable subsidy in the domestic economy can cause the relative prices, and the direction and volume of trade, to be what they would have been in the absence of all subsidies. In that case, foreign subsidies would be fair because they would not affect trade. Trade based on offsetting subsidies would be no more nor no less unfair than trade based on comparative costs.

†Government regulations in the domestic economy that are not imposed with an equal burden in foreign countries also do not necessarily make the resulting international trade unfair. This is because the regulations can be considered fair in the sense they are reasonable and acceptable to all. They may not distort domestic prices; indeed, they may correct for domestic price distortions.

domestic subsidies and regulations that distort relative prices. This is because the process that provides restrictions could get out of hand.

The textile industry might benefit directly from protection granted on a proven case of unfair subsidies. However, other industries and interest groups would also have the right to appeal for protection on fairness grounds. If the foreign subsidies are broad based, the domestic textile industry may be no better off after the protection has been extended to all offended domestic groups than it would have been without the appeal process. In addition, other domestic industries may exploit the protection procedures to obtain unwarranted and unfair protection, all to the potential detriment of the textile industry.

Clearly, what is needed in the protectionist political battle is some control over the extent to which protection is granted. Protection based on proven claims of unfair subsidies represents a check on the granting of protection. However, such proof may not provide sufficient control, meaning that one form of institutionalized domestic unfairness is ultimately substituted for other forms of institutionalized foreign unfairness.

Concluding Comments

Critical analysis of the fairness of free trade leads inextricably to one central conclusion: When trade is based on comparative cost advantages, it is arguably fair in the sense that industrial interests who often support trade restriction would not agree to their own protectionist measures if the kinds of restrictions obtained were simultaneously made available to all other similarly situated people and interest groups. In this regard, and as a general but not universal proposition, free trade is fair trade; restricted trade is unfair trade.

A central point of this chapter is that in order to be persuasive, the case for unrestricted trade must encompass more than an assessment of a larger economic pie, which has been its conventional focus. The case for free trade is predicated on a prior dedication to a more fundamental principle, namely that government market powers will not be arbitrarily employed, that is, will be controlled by principles that extend beyond particular circumstances and appeals for the use of government powers. The case for free trade is, in other words, founded on the proposition that government's market powers should be used when they can be generally applied in nondiscriminatory manners. When trade policies are guided by that governmental tenet, it is doubtful that proponents of protectionism would support their own legislative agenda.

Finally, the fairness of free trade is necessarily a relative concept. Free trade will always have elements of unfairness, as does every other aspect of life. So will efforts to control trade. The relevant question is which is more or less fair. Free traders are typically skeptical of protection based on fairness claims, not because they cannot imagine situations in which fairness would be promoted through isolated cases of protection, but because the process by which protection is provided will be insufficiently controlled—itself insufficiently restricted to ensure that the resulting world trade climate is actually fairer than a climate of free trade. Opposition to a regime of restricted trade is founded on distrust not of government, per se, but of the people and interest groups who would misuse and abuse government powers in pursuit of their own narrow interest, ultimately to the detriment of all, including themselves.

Notes

1. Statement of Walter Reuther, president of the United Automobile Workers of America, before the Committee on Ways and Means, U.S. House of Representatives, May 20, 1962, pp. 2, 4, and 10; as quoted by Thomas F. Walton, "Trade Strategies for the Automobile Industry," a paper presented at a conference held at the University of Michigan, March 15, 1985.
2. Ellison S. McKissick, Jr., "Sweatshirts and Sweatshops," *Wall Street Journal* (September 4, 1985), p. 23.
3. Fritz Hollings, "We're in a Trade War," *Reports* (Washington: U.S. Senate, July 1985), back page.
4. Ronald Reagan, "Transcript of Speech to Business and Government Leaders," *New York Times* (September 24, 1985).
5. See F. A. Hayek, *Law, Legislation, and Liberty: Rules and Order*, vol. I (Chicago: University of Chicago Press, 1973).

4

The Fairness of Economic Failure

A system—any system, economic or other—that at *every* given point of time fully utilizes its possibilities to the best advantage may yet in the long run be inferior to a system that does so at *no* point of time, because the latter's failure to do so may be a condition for the level or speed of long-run performance.

—Joseph Schumpeter[1]

S uccess is the professed goal of every economy, and the U.S. economy has had its successes. Those successes are vividly portrayed in statistical terms through the historical records of growth in gross national product, industrial production, employment, personal income, and labor force participation, and in more human terms through the emancipation of many Americans from the grip of poverty and in the elevation of many others to riches.

But failures are also endemic to the U.S. economy. A continual flow of news reports on bankruptcies, plant closings, layoffs, stock market slumps, industrial accidents, financial losses, and persistent poverty makes the fact of pervasive failures indubitably clear. The failure of American firms to compete successfully with their foreign rivals, the topic covered in the preceding chapter, is only one dimension of the problem of failure that pervades any market economy. After acknowledging the successes of the new-found capitalistic policies in contemporary China, Charles Krauthammer in a *Washington Post* column lamented that in the United States,

however, many hands are wringing. They belong to steelworkers, farmers and, now, savings-and-loan depositors. The ravaged steel towns, the bankrupt farmers, the locked-out savers evoke Depression images. When seventy-one Ohio S & Ls were closed last week by order of the governor, pointed reference was made to the fact that this is the biggest bank closing since the thirties."[2]

In 1983, more than 31,000 commercial and industrial businesses failed in the United States. In 1985, the number of business failures was above 57,000 (one every nine minutes). And the number of business failures during that year and the previous two or three years was up dramatically from the level of the 1970s.* Thousands of farms also went under in 1983 as well as in 1985, while tens of thousands more teetered on the brink of bankruptcy during each of the years.

However frequent they may be, business and farm failures represent only a minor fraction (less than 6 percent) of the legally acknowledged bankruptcies in the country, which in 1983 totaled more than a half a million.† In the early 1980s, bankruptcies were also substantially up, running at more than twice the rate of the late 1960s and 1970s. Clearly, business failures during the first half of the decade were a serious problem that was getting worse.

The prevalence and consequences of economic failure can also be captured in the number of unemployed and dislocated workers. A rising trend in the number and percentage of American workers unemployed has emerged over the past two decades. Although the unemployment rate was falling in the mid-1980s, there were still more than 8 million Americans unemployed at the end of 1985. And the unemployment rate at the peak of the recoveries during the 1969–1981 period was edging upward. The unemployment rate still hovered close to 7 percent in December 1985 (more than three years after the latest trough).‡

Between 1979 and January 1984, 11.5 million Americans lost their jobs because of "a plant closing, an employer going out of business, [or] a layoff from which . . . (the worker in question) was not recalled."§ Over 5 million of these workers had significant

---

*These figures are based on a Dun & Bradstreet Corporation study reported in March 1986. The number of business failures was just over 52,000 in 1984 ["Bankruptcies Increase 9.6%," *New York Times* (March 3, 1986), p. 31.

†An additional 350,000 bankruptcies were still pending in 1983 from previous years.

‡During the four recessions between 1969 and 1981, the following unemployment rates were measured at the cycle peaks:

Cycle Peak	Lowest Rate
Dec. 1969	3.4 percent
Nov. 1973	4.6 percent
Jan. 1980	5.6 percent
July 1981	7.2 percent

See Henry F. Meyer, "The Rising Natural Rate of Unemployment," *Wall Street Journal* (February 25, 1985), p. 1.

§Meyer, "The Rising Natural Rate of Unemployment," *Wall Street Journal*, p. 1.

tenure (more than three years) at their jobs, causing them to be officially characterized as "dislocated." And a quarter of these dislocated workers were still looking for work in January 1984.*

For most of the dislocated workers, their employment troubles probably were not the direct consequence of their own actions; most were dislocated for reasons beyond their individual control. Most were, in other words, involuntarily unemployed, meaning most had clearly failed in a very real and personal sense in the complicated process of skill and job selection.†

While flawed to one extent or another as descriptions of misguided economic decisions, all such statistics reported incessantly in the daily press speak eloquently of the pervasiveness of individual and collective failures. Most such failures, however, have economic consequences, sometimes dire ones.

Unfortunately, it is all too easy to dwell on the dark side of the force of failure—that is, on the pain that people feel when faced with failures. Such pain is brought to life on the television screen when fired or laid-off workers, the homeless, foreclosed farmers, and airline crash victims are interviewed for the nightly news programs. The emotional appeal of these failures for governmental remedies is indeed intense and compelling, so much so that policymakers can hardly overlook them for both humanitarian and opportunistic political reasons. Confronted with the facts of failures, they are frequently driven to do something or to stall for time in the hope that the observed pain of these failures will fade with time.

My purpose in this chapter is not to dispute the economic hardship and personal pain that is felt when failures occur. Nor is my

---

*Generally, displaced workers are workers "who have lost jobs in which they had a considerable investment in terms of skill development and for whom the prospects of re-employment in similar jobs are rather dim" [Paul O. Flaim and Ellen Sehgal, *Displaced Workers of 1979–1983: How Well Have They Fared?* Bulletin 2240 (Washington: U.S. Department of Commerce, Bureau of Labor Statistics, July 1985), p. 2. Seven percent of the displaced workers were in agriculture and government.

†Failures that have important economic consequences are, of course, rampant throughout the U.S. social structure. In 1981, there were more than 100,000 deaths from accidents, nearly 21,000 suicides, 70,000 unwanted births, 1.2 million divorces, and almost a quarter of a million court cases brought before the U.S. district courts (the vast majority of which involved disputes over contracts and property). Only about a third of high school graduates that year went on to college, and a mere 30 percent of the eighteen-year-olds four years earlier graduated from college in 1981. In 1984, 435 congressional candidates and 35 senatorial candidates lost their elections, and consumers bought millions of products that were defective, unsafe, or unusable. In 1985, a streak of unprecedented airline crashes claimed the lives of more than 2,000 passengers.

purpose to suggest that all failures are deserved, just, or fair. Of course not. Rather, I intend to balance public discussions of failures by recasting past arguments that lead to an important but frequently overlooked point: While failures may often be undeserved, unjust, and unfair, the system that spawns them may still be just and fair.[3] Nevertheless, democracies have a built-in political bias toward mitigating short-run failures and, in the process, creating long-run mischief. I make these points by first observing that many failures not only have a rational foundation but are often, but not always, expected by economic agents, private citizens and consumers, private investors, and government policymakers.

So while failures are avoided wherever and whenever possible, many failures remain unavoidable and often accompany successes. Indeed, failures often inspire future successes. In other words, contrary to what is suggested in the media and public policy debates, failures cannot be reasonably isolated from successes. This bright side of the force of economic failure is the central concern of this chapter.

The Economy of Failure

To imagine any advantage at all to observed failures, it must be understood that failures arise because of the basic human condition of scarcity, because of the human search for rational results and greater rewards, and because of the capitalistic system. These sources of failures are considered in turn.

The Failures of Scarcity

Economists have long noted that because peoples' wants far outstrip their abilities to produce, choices involving the allocation of resources are unavoidable. That point, while patently obvious, is fundamental because it acknowledges that not all goods and services can be produced. Nor is it reasonable to expect that all goods currently produced will continue to be produced. Some producers will fail to secure the necessary resources to start production. Others, already in production, will fail to retain the resources they have. In other words, choice and the necessity of allocation make failure absolutely certain, absolutely unavoidable. However, it cannot be forgotten that while some firms fail (those that do not obtain or cannot retain the limited resources), others will succeed.

The pervasiveness of scarcity ensures the pervasiveness of failure. This is because of the pervasiveness of success, that is, the ability of some to secure resources and, at the same time, deny resources to others. Firms fold, plants close, and workers are unemployed because strategic resources are reallocated to other, more successful firms, plants, and workers. Indeed, the failures of some increase the probability of success for those remaining in the market. The failures cause a release of resources that can then be employed (at possibly lower resource prices) by the remaining competitors and a reduction in the supply of the goods and services produced that can then be sold at higher prices and, thus, on more profitable terms.

The growth in the number of business failures during the early 1980s is, without question, partially a product of the twin recessions, spawned in large measure by government policies to reduce inflation. However, many failures were also spurred by the emergence of new firms and the expansion of established ones. There has been, for example, substantial growth in new incorporations, although the number of new incorporations, admittedly, is only a rough measure of the emergence of new businesses.* In 1983, 600,000 businesses were incorporated, more than twice the number of 1970.

The businesses that emerged in the 1970s and 1980s caused the failures of others by driving up the price of resources to the point where some firms were no longer competitive.† The textile and apparel industry, centered primarily in the Carolinas, has been racked by plant closings and layoffs for the past decade. Part of the industry's problem has been the expansion of nontextile and apparel sectors in the Carolinas that has forced up labor prices paid by the textile firms. In addition, textile firms have become more productive with the introduction of new technology, putting downward pressures on textile and apparel prices.

---

*Many businesses arise that are never incorporated and many new incorporations are established businesses. Also, many companies are incorporated for legal and tax reasons, not to produce a new good or service.

†We can also anticipate that an increase in the number of business failures will accompany, with a lag, an increase in the number of business formations because of the lack of experience of the businesses that emerge.

Relative Performance and Failures

The economic source of failure cannot, in a world of scarcity, be a matter of absolute performance levels. The firms that fold may be well organized, the plants that close may be very efficient, and the workers unemployed may be quite productive in what they do. They can still fail because others are even better organized, more efficient, and more productive. The fundamental goal of every economy is presumably to overcome scarcity, and the process of failure is driven by people's efforts to get the most possible from the available resources.

Policymakers often lament the impact of foreign imports on domestic production and relate the imports to plant closures and unemployment. As noted in the previous chapter, textile and apparel trade restrictions, for example, have been proposed on the theory that expanding imports caused the closure of as many as 250 textile and apparel plants between 1980 and 1985, robbing American textile and apparel workers in the United States of hundreds of thousands of jobs.[4] The unemployment and plant-closing problem faced by the textile industry is presumed to have been solely created by imports (made competitive by low wages paid foreign workers).

In fact, economists have long argued that the direction of trade (what is imported and exported) is predicated on comparative, not absolute, cost advantages. While the textile and apparel industries blame foreigners, the industries probably have failed in their competition with other domestic producers for control over the available and limited resources in the domestic economy.* We stressed in the last chapter, however, that other American producers are, in effect, the competitive culprit because they are the ones that were relatively more cost effective in production than the textile and apparel industries. They are more successful in capturing the country's comparative advantage in production and in being able to export (and not face import competition).†

---

*If the textile and apparel industries are at all in competition with foreign producers, the competition is with foreign producers who seek U.S. resources or U.S. goods, or, in other words, foreign importers.

†Actually, the textile and apparel industry sales have continued to expand, although irregularly, over the past two decades. However, the thrust of the argument still holds: the textile industry has failed to capture the country's comparative advantage on the margin of production.

Information and Failures

The process of failure is greatly aggravated by the scarcity of one critically important resource that ties economic activity over time together: information on what consumers and other producers want and on how, where, and when they want what they do.

The information problem is made more complex—and more subject to the constraints of scarcity—by the amounts and kinds of information that can be useful in achieving successes and avoiding failures. Regrettably, such information is not readily accessible. Information on the availability of resources (for example, on the amount of labor) is widely scattered among thousands, if not millions, of people and must somehow be induced from its holders. It is influenced by the amount of resources applied to gathering information, meaning the amount and quality of the information flow will depend much on its cost. And even that kind of information is not always readily available in usable form.

To say the absence of adequate information is a source of failures is to state the obvious, but it is such obvious points that are often overlooked when policymakers consider remedies for failures, especially remedies that themselves fail to address the information problem. The information problem may not always be correctable simply because it is the result of scarcity. Public policy solutions may accomplish nothing more than a reallocation of resources, a redistribution of successes and failures. Indeed, changing people's incentives to provide and acquire information may aggravate the problem of failure.

Much has been made of the information problem in a market economy. The central criticism is that the multitude of market participants have only limited information, that is, their own individual plans, which are not coordinated with the plans of all others in the market. In effect, the left hand in the market does not know what the right hand is doing. Housing, for example, goes through cycles of booms and busts because individual contractors, who are uncertain of each other's plans, overbuild, which causes precipitous price drops, bankruptcies, and contractor failures.

Many critics presume that centralizing the decision-making process will solve the information problem. Central planning of production may solve some information problems—for example, how much is planned—but it can run headlong into other information problems, such as exactly how many resources (hours of work and energy expended) are available to individual producers.

The proposed solution is plagued by the limited capacity of planners to gather and assimilate manageable, available information. One of the great virtues of markets is that they divide responsibility for obtaining and handling information among a host of market participants, especially information that can minimize the chance of failures. Centrally directed economic activity can impose superhuman demand on the limited capacity of the planners to handle information. Increases in the complexity of production processes that may emerge with the integration of the world economy and with technological development only increase demands that would be imposed on planners.*

Risk, Uncertainty, and Rational Failures

Information deficiencies ultimately translate into problems of risk and uncertainty about future economic events, which also spell failures. Risk, which is grounded in probability, means that some ventures will not go as planned. That is to say, risk is a statement about the distribution of successes and failures over a series of ventures. For example, seven out of ten restaurants will fail. The missing information is exactly which ventures will succeed and which will fail. The information is missing because of its cost or simply the cost of acting on the available information.

Uncertainty, on the other hand, amounts to a lack of information about the distribution of how ventures will turn out, meaning as successes or failures. Uncertainty is simply unsureness about what to expect and, as such, represents less information than exists with risk. Uncertainty emerges because of lack of experience and the difficulty

---

*The limited capacity of planners to handle the necessary information required in efforts to centrally direct an economy, or a major sector, has been a lifelong theme of F. A. Hayek, who once wrote prophetically, "The more men know, the smaller the share of that knowledge becomes that any one mind can absorb. The more civilized we become, the more relatively ignorant must each individual be of the facts on which the workings of his civilization depends. The very division of knowledge increases the necessary ignorance of the individual of most of this knowledge" [F. A. Hayek, *The Constitution of Liberty* (Chicago: University of Chicago Press, 1960,)', p. 26].

of obtaining the requisite information on the probability of successes or failures. The cost of information no doubt plays a role in establishing the degree of uncertainty.

Risk and uncertainty ensure failures. Not everything can turn out right. Eliminating failure in the face of risk and uncertainty would be counterproductive because the costs of doing so would be higher than the costs endured through the failures.* In other words, firms will fold, plants will close, and workers will be unemployed, not necessarily because of anything wrong they may have done. Even though everything may be done correctly, justly, and fairly, or as correctly and justly and fairly as economically reasonable, risk and uncertainty militate against the success of all firms, plants, and workers.†

In their most raw form, risk and uncertainty imply that many failures are planned and expected—that is, are no less founded in rational tests than are production and consumption decisions that do not always match expectations. Less than perfectly suitable goods and services are produced because the benefits of improving them would not be worth the cost. Plants close because the cost of preventing their closures through the acquisition of more market information and insuring against closure would be greater than the costs associated with their closures. Failures may be bad, which no one can deny; but a reduction of failures, especially if legislated, can be even worse because such a solution could increase the costs endured and decrease the net income received by people.

In a limited but analytically meaningful sense, failures ironically are sought to increase income (through production cost reductions). Failures can be looked upon as one of many costs of doing business. And if the rational firm were truly interested in maximizing profits, it would simply extend its operations to cover progressively more risky ventures until the additional income received no longer exceeded the additional costs incurred from failures and the use of all resources.‡

---

*If this were not the case, why would risk and uncertainty remain in the first place?

†Granted, many failures in risky or uncertain endeavors (and the attendant costs) may be avoidable. We can only reason that they will be avoided, unless the costs of doing so are too great. If that is not the case, then we can only inquire as to why cost-effective avoidance of failures is not undertaken.

‡This statement is nothing more than an application of the general principle that firms should extend production level until the marginal (or additional) cost from expanded production equals marginal (or additional) revenue received from extended production. In the process of accepting more risk in the search of profits, in other words, firms will inevitably encounter failures.

In each instance of failure, there is an economic cost, of course; and as with any other cost, the cost of failure would preferably be reduced, if not totally avoided. However, most failures are not isolated ventures but are part and parcel of a whole complex of ventures, all of which combined have some risk and uncertainty of not working out as planned. Risky and uncertain ventures typically carry the greatest rewards, partially to overcome the costs associated with failures and partially to compensate for people's natural or learned inclination to avoid risky and uncertain outcomes. (In the jargon of economists, many people are "risk averse.") If an outcome is more risky and uncertain, the reward tends to be greater.*

To accommodate risk and uncertainty and to increase income, people protect themselves through the purchase of insurance policies and through self-insurance. They play the field—that is, play the probabilities—and expect greater returns in the process.

The paradigm analogy is the stock market investor who understands that the purchase of stocks entails risk and uncertainty along with the prospect of rewards. The investor typically assembles a number of different stocks in a portfolio, understanding that one or more of his purchases occasionally, perhaps even frequently, will not meet profit expectations. The investor evaluates the selections by how the entire portfolio does on balance. In this sense, failure is planned, expected, and even sought. To insure that no stock ever fails probably is a prescription for minimizing the return on the portfolio of stocks.† However, because expected income is increased through the development of a portfolio of stocks, the investor is better able to buy stock—better able to suffer failures and more likely to suffer a greater number of failures.‡

Firm managers and workers typically deal with risk and uncertainty through what amount to portfolios of activities. Firms produce several products and run several plants knowing that some products will fail in the market or that several plants will have to be closed. In effect, they rationally develop portfolios of products and plants and

---

*If that were not the case, risk and uncertainty would mean little, economically speaking.

†This may be especially true when the cost of the information on stocks is considered.

‡The greater income permits the purchase of a greater number of stocks, and the greater number of stocks purchased will increase the absolute number of failures (although the rate of failure over stock purchases is reduced).

rationally plan for failures, although they simultaneously will do what they can (or what is economically reasonable) to avoid failures, termination of product lines, and plant closings. By developing portfolios, they expect to increase their production incomes on balance. Their ability to spread their risks and increase their incomes means more products will be developed and more plants opened. But it also means a greater number of failures, although the failure rate may be reduced through greater experience with more products and plants and through a greater capacity to absorb the costs of avoiding failure.

Workers and consumers also engage in portfolio management. Workers often develop a variety of skills (or keep their skills general, applicable to many different work environments) and engage in a variety of activities, one of which is a job. They understand that through time and over the course of a number of activities and jobs, they will at times fail, that is, become unemployed or find their skills and abilities of less value than planned. Many consumers also buy appliances that they know are not "top of the line" and that will occasionally fail, but they buy what they do in anticipation that their portfolios will yield them a greater net return than if they bought more expensive appliances with a lower chance of failure.* The important point is that in spite of the failures, consumers and workers manage their portfolios with the intent of raising their incomes.

Learning from Failures

It is all too easy to think solely of failure as tragedy. After all, we do expend considerable energy seeking to avoid individual failures wherever and whenever possible.

Nothing could be further from the truth, for failures are highly instructive and necessarily productive. They help, perhaps more than successes, to outline the bounds of profitable and productive economic activity. Failures instruct those who fail on what they should not do the next time, if there is a next time; more important, they tell many others in the market what can be done wrong and what will have to be done to become or remain successful. They are, in other words, a critically important source of information. As such, they

---

*We assume that the more failure-prone appliances are less expensive; otherwise, everything else equal, few would buy them.

provide market participants with the necessary incentives and disincentives (instructions) on what people, acting independently of one another, should and should not do.

Past failures of many grocery stores have informed other stores that they could not remain content to offer only groceries but must expand to accommodate the demands of their customers for cosmetics, books, video tapes, prepared meals, and even restaurant services. The failures of computer companies have taught remaining computer companies that they cannot afford to hold back, for example, on the expansion of their computers' internal memory, to resist making them compatible with IBM computers, or to refuse to accommodate the needs of the business-computer markets. From books and articles that are turned down by publishers, writers learn where and how they should direct their future writings.* From the rash of business failures in the first half of the decade, caused in part from superior and more aggressive Japanese firms, businesses in the United States have learned that they must rethink their management practices and investment strategies. The performance of the U.S. economy will most likely show the feedback effects in improved growth during the 1990's, if not sooner.[5]

Failures are a part of an organic process that has both a past and a present, as are successes. "[S]ince we are dealing with an organic process," Professor Schumpeter reminds us, "an analysis of what happens in any particular part of it—say, in an individual concern or industry—may indeed clarify details of mechanism but is inconclusive beyond that. . . . It must be seen in its role in the perennial gale of creative destruction; it cannot be understood irrespective of it or, in fact, on the hypothesis that there is a perennial lull."[6]

Risk Management through a Market Economy

Arguments for a market economy abound, and the conventional case for the market on grounds of efficiency and individual freedom has

---

*As an aside, it may be useful to note that professors generally find their acceptance rate on articles submitted to journals going up as their career progresses. One explanation is that the professors improve their research and writing skills. Another, perhaps more important, explanation is that the professors know better from their "turndowns" what should not be written and where manuscripts should and should not be submitted.

been developed in some detail elsewhere.[7] We need only note here that the logic of risk and portfolio management can also be applied to entire economies. The ultimate goal of societies is welfare improvement through human endeavors. In framing any economy, we know that not everyone has the capacity—the willingness as well as the ability—to succeed, to find welfare-enhancing (profitable) opportunities through alertness and innovation. We understand the risk of failure, but we also understand that we do not know exactly who will fail and who will succeed.

The market system is a grand portfolio of people that is devised for determining the critically important missing information on people's capacity to succeed and fail. One justification for the market system is that over time, and over the course of many people and circumstances, the vast majority of people's welfare will on balance be enhanced through combinations of individual successes and failures.* A critically important force in minimizing failures is the pricing system, which contributes to welfare by providing people with necessary market information and by coordinating people's individual activities. Markets tend to economize on failures.

The Justice of Failure

Clearly, not all failures are just or fair. Some failures are the consequence of violations of contracts. Banks have failed because employees have embezzled funds. Real estate deals have failed because contractors did not build buildings as they said they would. And manufacturing plants have folded because supplies have not been delivered as promised or strategic employees did not fulfill their contracts. The injustice of these instances of failures is interesting because they represent behavior that violates "rules to which one has given prior consent."[8]

However, many failures may be just in the sense that no previously agreed-upon rules have been violated. All contracts may have been honored; all rules obeyed. The firms failed simply as a consequence

---

*This theme is developed in detail in chapter 11.

of problems associated with scarcity, namely risk and uncertainty. Indeed, the failures may have been anticipated, and no loss of income may have resulted.

Individual instances of failures, isolated from successes, may appear to be unjust or unfair, but this does not mean that the system that spawned the failures is unjust or unfair. Again, no previously agreed-upon rules may have been violated. In addition, the failures may mirror an increase in income for those who experience the failures. People may be hurt by their own failures, but they can be helped by their other successes and by the failures and successes of others that result in improved goods and services. The result can be a greater income from a system that allows failure than from one that deliberately attempts to contain them. The prospects of greater income, in spite of the prospects of failures, can be the impetus for the consent of those within the system.

Still, not everyone is likely to gain from a market system that permits unchecked failures. There will be those who fail at everything or practically everything and end up as net losers from the system. The question of whether net losers should be helped by public means is a difficult question, one that cannot be fully treated here.[9] The net losers may have implicitly or explicitly agreed to the system, and they may simply have been unfortunate or unlucky.

On the other hand, there is no reason why the participants might not have agreed to a system that allowed for compensation be paid to the net losers just to ensure that no one is made worse off from the operation of the system. The compensation could be extracted from the greater incomes of those who, on balance, gain from the system.* If it were, it is hard to see how the system could be viewed as unjust.

The Samaritan's Dilemma

Those who seem to object frequently to public efforts to help the businesses that go bankrupt, farmers whose farms are sold at auction,

---

*The taxes imposed on those who gain on balance from the system could be less than the increase in their incomes from operation of the system, meaning that everyone's position could, after transfers, improve. The inherent difficulty of granting government transfer authority to help the net losers is that it might be exploited by net gainers, a point that is developed in chapter 9.

and workers whose plants close are viewed as unable to empathize with the economic difficulty, if not misery, encountered by others. Differences on public policy arise because some people do not really care about the fates of others, while others do care. However, differences on what should be done to remedy failures arise even between those who care. This is because of the ever-present Samaritan's dilemma that will very likely remain a central component of public welfare discussion: Should those in need be helped by public means? The answer is not nearly so obvious as might be presumed.

If public aid had no consequence beyond relief of failures, the debate would not be nearly so intense as it often is. However, as with failures, relief also has consequences. It can encourage the very problem that is the object of the public remedy. Relief can make failures more palatable and, thereby, more likely. It can, in other words, reduce the tendency of a market economy to economize on failures and to learn from them. When this point is recognized, it does not follow that those who object to public remedies necessarily object to helping others. Objectors can be concerned about those future groups who will suffer from failures that are encouraged by policies adopted today.*

Concluding Comments

In the Charlotte, North Carolina, airport, there is a wall poster that sums up in a very few words a theme of this chapter: "No one ever accomplished anything without risking something." The same thought is aptly captured by the old adage "Nothing ventured, nothing gained." That simple point is all too frequently forgotten in public discussions of policies that are myopically concerned with observed failures in our economy.

To those who understand the message on the airport wall, it comes as no surprise that the more dynamic, venturesome, and

---

*One of the more interesting, and frequently overlooked, analytical issues surrounding public relief efforts is whether or not democracy encourages too much or too little aid. Geoffrey Brennan and James Buchanan contend that democracy has a built-in bias toward too much aid because people acting in their public role as voters would be more likely to provide more aid than they would in their private dealings. This is because people as voters will have a small probability of having to cope with the consequences of decisions made currently. See Brennan and Buchanan, *The Reason of Rules*, pp. 75–81.

growth-oriented a market economy is, the more it will be fraught with failures. This simple understanding is what caused Marx to praise capitalism.[10] It is also what Joseph Schumpeter meant when he characterized capitalism as "a process of Creative Destruction" and when he suggested that the long-run performance of any economy often depends upon the economy not fully utilizing its possibilities at every point in time—that is, on its being willing and able to endure passing failures and resist the temptation to prevent failures and the distress they individually cause.[11] It was also that simple understanding that *Washington Post* columnist Charles Krauthammer must have had in mind when continuing his commentary on the bad economic news of the early 1980s:

> These disasters are the product not of capitalism's failure but of its success. In 1984 the American economy grew faster than any time since 1951. The paradox of capitalism is that it is most successful when most dynamic, and when most dynamic, it is most destructive. . . . It is the first system in history to lift the mass of men out of economic misery. But to keep the engine going, it randomly visits misery on selected groups. Instead of searching for villains, it might be more humane for the rest of society, which benefits from that mighty engine, to devote some of its vast surplus to cushioning the fall of its victims.[12]

Notes

1. Joseph A. Schumpeter, *Capitalism, Socialism, and Democracy*, 2nd ed. (New York: Harper & Brothers Publishers, 1947), p. 83.
2. Charles Krauthammer, "One Cheer for Capitalism," *Cutting Edges* (New York: Random House, 1985), p. 91 [reprinted from the *Washington Post* (March 22, 1985)].
3. While their arguments may not have been cast in justice or fairness terms, Joseph Schumpeter and Frank Knight have articulated many of the points repeated and recast here. See Schumpeter, *Capitalism, Socialism, and Democracy* and Frank H. Knight, *Risk, Uncertainty, and Profit* (Chicago: University of Chicago Press, 1971).
4. U.S. Congress, Senate, "Textile and Apparel Trade and Enforcement Act of 1985," S. 680 (February 26, 1985).
5. For a review of the ways U.S. businesses have adapted to their new competitive environment, see Murray L. Weidenbaum, Richard E. Cook and Richard E.

Burr, *Learning to Compete: The Feedback Effects of the Non-Linear Economy* (St. Louis: Center for the Study of American Business, Washington University in St. Louis, 1986).

6. Schumpeter, *Capitalism, Socialism, and Democracy*, p. 84.

7. The most prominent of the defenders of the market economy is Milton Friedman. See his and Rose Friedman's book *Free to Choose* (New York: Avon Books, 1981). This author has made the case for the market economy in Richard B. McKenzie, *Bound to Be Free* (Stanford, Calif.: Hoover Institution Books, 1982); and *Competing Visions: The Political Conflict over America's Economic Future* (Washington: Cato Institute, 1985).

8. The concept of justice employed has been developed in Geoffrey Brennan and James M. Buchanan, *The Reason of Rules: Constitutional Political Economy* (Cambridge, Mass.: Cambridge University Press, 1985), especially chapter 7.

9. This question has been considered in some detail elsewhere by the author. See Richard B. McKenzie, "The Conservative Case for the Contained Welfare State" (St. Louis: Center for the Study of American Business, Washington University working paper, 1985).

10. See M. M. Bober, *Karl Marx's Interpretation of History* (New York: W. W. Norton & Co., 1965), especially pp. 18–19.

11. Schumpeter, *Capitalism, Socialism, and Democracy*, p. 83.

12. Krauthammer, "One Cheer for Capitalism," pp. 91–92.

Part III
Justice in
the Labor Market

5
Justice as Participation in the Workplace: The Religious Foundations of Democracy

> The nation's founders took daring steps to create structures of participation, mutual accountability, and widely distributed power to ensure the political rights and freedoms of all. We believe that similar steps are needed today to expand economic participation, broaden the sharing of economic power, and make economic decisions more accountable to the common good.
>
> —U.S. Catholic bishops[1]

The twin recessions of the early 1980s, coupled with increased international competition, have raised many concerns about our current labor and management practices. Some people, especially religious leaders, truly believe that greater equity and efficiency, which can contribute to enhanced competitiveness, can only be achieved in the United States by making private enterprise more democratic. That is to say, workers should have a greater voice in planning the national economy and in making the production and investment decisions of their firms. Owners of capital and their principal agents, managers, should, accordingly, have less unilateral control over the employment of resources and labor, as well as capital.

In the depth of the latest recession, these reformers advocated the creation of a "tripartite planning council," composed of representatives of labor, business and government, that would chart the future economic structure of the economy. They also proposed resurrecting the Reconstruction Finance Corporation (giving it the more up-to-date label Economic Development Bank), first established in the 1930s, to "allocate sacrifice" and to disburse federally subsidized and guaranteed loans following the democratic dictates of the tripartite council.*

Meanwhile, in order to achieve greater democratization of the workplace, labor-management councils would be developed. Workers would "participate in company decisions about physical capital, helping choose the direction and magnitude of new investment in research, plant and machinery."† Others believe that workers at the enterprise or plant level should be responsible for setting wages and fringe benefits, establishing production standards, hiring managers and setting worker-management wage differentials.[2]

"Greater democracy," write "economic democrats" Martin Carnoy, Derek Shearer, and Russell Rumberger, "means that those with jobs will have much more to say about the way those jobs are organized; those who live in communities will have more to say about what happens to those communities—even whether a plant can simply up and leave after thirty years."[3] These writers conclude that "the main goals of a democratic planning system are to develop innovative solutions to unemployment, set norms for corporate behavior, and develop new kinds of products and more democratic work organizations."[4]

Economic democrats fervently maintain that through greater participation, or a more complete economic democracy, cooperation will, at least marginally, replace conflict among competing economic interest groups, economic welfare will be enhanced, and society will become more just and fair, as well as more efficient. In the words of Harvard business professor Robert Reich, "[I]n the emerging era of

---

*These policy proposals are evaluated in Richard B. McKenzie, *Competing Visions: The Political Conflict over America's Economic Future* (Washington: Cato Institute, 1985), chapters 4 and 5. A frequently cited objective of a new Reconstruction Finance Corporation would be "to rebuild the national infra-structure and revitalize basic industries; and insure the ability of the United States to compete in the world economy." [U.S. Senate, ninety-eighth Cong., S 265 (introduced January 27, 1983, by Sen. Fritz Hollings), pp. 1–2]

†Robert B. Reich, *The Next American Frontier* (New York: Times Books, 1983), p. 248. Professor Reich adds, "Such employee participation in company strategy will be necessary to ensure that capital adjustment and labor adjustment are well coordinated and also take full advantage of the knowledge and skills of the company's work force." (Reich, *The Next American Frontier*).

productivity, social justice is not incompatible with economic growth, but essential to it. A social organization premised on equity, security, and participation will generate greater productivity than one premised on greed and fear."* While admitting that comparisons between stockholders and employee-managed firms have only been rarely made, Yale political science professor Robert Dahl concludes that "participation by workers in decision-making rarely leads to a decline of productivity; far more often it either has no effect or results in an increase in productivity."[5]

The Catholic bishops have joined their voices to the advocates of economic democracy. Reflecting on the political experiment forged by the country's Founding Fathers more than two hundred years ago, the bishops wrote in late 1984 in the first draft of their pastoral letter on the economy:

> We believe the time has come for a similar experiment in economic democracy: the creation of an order that guarantees the minimum conditions of human dignity in the economic sphere for every person. By drawing on the resources of the Catholic moral-religious tradition, we hope to make a contribution to such a new "American experiment" in this [pastoral] letter [on the social economy.][†]

A common philosophical and religious theme running through various economic reform proposals is the belief that justice can be approached, if not fully achieved, through increasing worker democratic participation in economic decisions (beyond the level of participation that would be freely negotiated by the contracting parties,

---

*Reich, *The Next American Frontier*, p. 20. This point is echoed by others. "We think mainstream economists are fundamentally wrong about the trade-offs between efficiency and democracy. More democracy does not have to mean more inefficiency and waste." [Samuel Bowles, David M. Gordon, and Thomas E. Weisskopf, *Beyond the Waste Land: A Democratic Alternative to Economic Decline* (Garden City, N.J.: Anchor Press/Doubleday, 1983), p. 264.]

†Catholic bishops, "Pastoral Letter on Social Teaching and the U.S. Economy" (first draft), *National Catholic Reporter* (November 23, 1984), p. 16. In their outline of their policy agenda, the bishops write, "In an advanced economy like ours, all actors of society, including government, must actively and positively cooperate in forming national economic policies. Catholic social teachings support the need for society to make provisions for overall planning in the economic domain, but it must be done in such a way that strikes a balance between individual initiatives and the common good." ("Pastoral Letter," p. 10.)

employers and employees). The purpose of this and the following chapter is to explicate and evaluate this "justice-as-participation" theme and its foundation as a theory of rights. This chapter presents the case for affording workers greater participation rights, while chapter 6 develops a critique of that case.

Our discussion relies heavily on the first draft of the bishops' letter on the economy for two reasons. First, while the published views of the bishops have changed substantially in subsequent drafts, the first draft is still instructive because it shows how many people, including some bishops and other religious groups, conclude that worker participation is no ordinary social value or goal. Second, through examining in some detail the bishops' first draft, we can understand why they changed their thinking and adjusted the positions assumed in published form.

A major conclusion is that greater economic democracy, especially when it is imposed by government mandate, does not lead to an unambiguous increase in worker participation (or in the extent to which the varying and diverse views of workers are represented) in economic decisions at the national or firm level. While the economic and political interests of some workers may be more fully reflected in policies adopted in an economic (or industrial) democracy, the interests of others will be less represented. This conclusion casts doubt on the justice of the participation that is imagined by economic democrats.

The Foundations of Justice as Participation

We begin our assessment of "justice as participation" by presenting the moral, religious and economic justifications for elevating participation to a standard of social morality. Then, in chapter 6, the justifications are critiqued.

Moral Underpinnings

In their 1984 pastoral letter, the Catholic bishops conclude that "In line with our insistence on the indispensability of human dignity and social solidarity, it is clear that *justice demands the establishment of minimum levels of participation by all persons in the life of the human community.* The ultimate injustice is for a person or group to be actively treated or passively abandoned as a non-member of the moral community which is the human race" (emphasis in the original).[6] They continue:

> Justice demands that social institutions be ordered in a way that guarantees all persons the ability to participate actively in the economic, political and cultural life of the community. In the words of the 1971 synod of bishops: "Participation constitutes a right which is to be applied in the economic and in the social and political field." The level of participation in these different sectors of social life may legitimately be greater for some persons than for others, but there is a minimum level of access that must be made available to all.[7]

Similarly, citing the social and economic order that prevailed in Old Testament Israel, the Ecumenical Great Lakes/Appalachian Project (Ecumenical Project, for short) maintains that "the purpose of such law and such economic policy was to enable a just and inclusive community. Justice in such a context becomes justice-as-participation, not justice by rules alone or justice by calculated economic contract."[8] Justice as participation, as a moral criterion, is founded partly on religious teachings, partly on concern for the poor, and partly on economic analysis.

Religious Teachings

As for the religious teachings underpinning justice as participation, the Ecumenical Project concludes that

> God's redemptive covenant not only addresses a whole people but demands the energetic and conscientious response of each individual. Because each of us is related to God, we must have access to the decisions affecting our capacity to live according to God's promises. Therefore, the right to participation arises as one of the most fundamental claims of faith itself. Through it we participate in the communal response to God's action and call in our own time. Through it we testify to our conventional bond with our Creator and Redeemer.[9]

Participation, in other words, is a mechanism for holding the community (of believers?) together. In seeking biblical support for the ethical norm of justice as participation, the Catholic bishops, while acknowledging the sanctity of individuals (meaning the special place the individual has in God's eyes), stress that individuals are necessarily social beings whose individual lives are ordered and made livable "in communion with others who are called to love the same God and who are themselves recipients of God's love."* While "the bondage in Egypt provides a paradigm of oppression," which should not, the bishops argue, be forgotten in structuring any economy, the exodus from Egypt "was the birth of a people truly unified with each other as recipients of God's saving gift. Their status before God is ultimately connected with the wholeness of the community. Individuals are responsible before God both to and for the community."[10] A wealth of other biblical teachings, including Christian baptism, "calls us to a sense of community and solidarity as strong as that experienced by the people of the Exodus."[11] "This union," the bishops maintain, "transcends the division of sex, race and social status since there is neither Jew nor Greek, there is neither slave nor free, there is neither male nor female; for you are all one in Jesus Christ."[12]

A variety of complementary resources (including the Bible, the Christian tradition, and philosophical reasoning) have caused "modern Catholic social teachings . . . to insist that economic ethics rests on the bedrock principle that the dignity of the person can only be realized and protected by nurturing and strengthening the bonds of solidarity. Communal solidarity is at the heart of the biblical understanding of the human condition."[13]

While the Council of Bishops emphasized that "technical progress must be fostered, along with a spirit of initiatives, an eagerness to create and expand enterprises,"[14] the Second Vatican Council of Bishops also made it clear that "increased production is not an end in itself but a contribution to the common good of society, which Pope John XXIII defined as 'the sum total of those conditions of social living, whereby human beings are enabled more fully and more readily to achieve their own perfection.' "[15] Judgments about economic prosperity cannot be divorced from the social institution on which it is built (and thereby measured in output or efficiency terms alone). This is the case because

---

*"Pastoral Letter," The bishops write, "Far from being arbitrary restrictions on the life of the people, these codes [as developed in *Exodus*] made life in community possible." (p. 12).

> Man's social nature makes it evident that the progress of the
> human person and the advance of social life itself hinge on each
> other. . . . This social life is not something added on to man.
> Hence, through his dealings with others, reciprocal duties and
> through fraternal dialogue, he develops all his gifts and is able to
> rise to his full destiny.*

Concern for the Poor

More important, justice as participation is viewed as a criterion
founded on a morally imposed concern for helping the poor, who
lack the economic power to participate adequately in decisions that
affect their economic fates and to share in the output of economic
systems. The bishops stress that their logic leads to one "fundamental norm": "*Will this decision or policy help the poor and deprived
members of the human community and enable them to become more active
participants in economic life?*" (emphasis in the original).[16] The bishops
express considerable concern for the "marginalization" of people,
"which can result from the patterns of institutional organization and
distribution of power in contemporary society."[17]

The bishops note that marginalization can take a political form
when, for example, people are denied their right of free speech or the
vote; but it can also take economic forms, with even more severe
effects on the inclusiveness of the community—for example, when
men and women fall victim to recession, when workers are "thrown
out of work as a result of plant closings or national policies they are
too weak to change precisely because they are unemployed or unor-
ganized," when farm families "are driven off the land" or when the
elderly are forced to give up their homes to condominium conver-
sions.[18] Overcoming these patterns of marginalization and power-
lessness through democratic participation is seen by the bishops as
the "most urgent demand of justice."[19]

Helping the poor with direct aid, giving them a job that is secure
and sufficiently well-paying "to guarantee one's family 'a standard of

---

*Pastoral Constitution, No. 20, as quoted in "Pastoral Letter," p. 15. The bishops add, "Men
and women cannot grow to full self-realization in isolation. This realization takes place in
interaction, interdependence, communication, collaboration and—in the fullest form—communion and love. . . . This Christian and human vision grounds our conviction that communal solidarity and mutual responsibility must characterize an economy that truly respects
persons" ("Pastoral Letter," p. 15).

living in keeping with human dignity,' " and acknowledging their rights to participate in their firms' economic decisions that affect their livelihood are fundamental rights that "set moral constraints on the institutional order of the economy."[20] Creating a just society will carry its own rewards. By observing God's laws, people will form a "faithful community," one that will allow them to accomplish more than if they followed largely unrelated and noninclusive lives. "When a society is just," the bishops maintain, "prosperity and blessings result. As Isaiah says: 'Justice will bring peace; right will produce calm and security.' "[21]

The Ecumenical Project also emphasizes the plight of the poor who are oppressed and marginalized by human sin, fueled in part by greed and the unbridled search for profits. Thus, to the extent that people are impoverished, human society (or covenant community), which is "at core relational," is partially destroyed. According to the Ecumenical Project, community destruction is cause enough for God to call a community "to healthy anger, not turned inward against the victim, but focused outward on those values and systems that destroy covenant community and oppress the poor."[22] Community destruction is also cause enough to declare that it is a sin

> to take away a person's work and their means of production so they cannot participate in community or share in God's creativity.
>
> to exploit employees by paying wages too low to allow them a decent, secure place in the community.
>
> to hide away from the dispossessed.
>
> to be apathetic about the exclusion of persons from meaningful work.
>
> to destroy communities for the sake of greater profits or even higher productivity.[23]

Economics and Participation

The case for justice as participation is, as shown, founded on deeply held religious convictions that people should be able to participate in firm and rational economic decisions, partially because those are God's instructions. However, the case is also based on the view that participation, including the process that makes the community more inclusive, yields good results: prosperity, security, peace, and individual morality.*

Professor Dahl cites two reasons why he believes economic democracy will promote moral responsibility on the part of workers. First, workers would have a stake in the welfare of the firm. Second, the managerial decisions of workers would more closely reflect the preferences of the general population. This is because managers represent a minuscule proportion of the population who escaped the social consequence of their decisions and because workers represent a much larger proportion of the population and are, as a consequence, much more likely to bear the costs of their decisions.[24]

In addition, it must be understood that work and community are also seen by proponents of economic democracy as "goods" typically left out of the conventional economic calculus of costs and benefits. Proponents of justice as participation do not see work as merely a means to an end (production or consumption of goods and services, per se), but an end in itself, something that gives meaning or definition to life and to what is obtained through work.

Similarly, community, which adds value to people's lives, is a delicate, interconnected web of relationships that can be unsettled, if not destroyed, by unbridled movements within. The drive for cost savings, productivity improvement, and profits (all interrelated objectives) are seen by secular, as well as religious, industrial policy advocates as forces that may (but often will not) lead to a more efficient allocation of resources as judged by the narrow perspective of people's preferences for the normal goods and services (excluding work and community) that are produced within the covenant community.

However, that drive can also lead to community destruction, the costs and benefits of which should also be taken into consideration,

---

*Professor Dahl notes: "Workplace democracy, it is sometimes claimed, will foster human development, enhance the sense of political efficacy, reduce alienation, create a solidarity community based on work, strengthen attachments to the general good of the community, weaken the pull of self-interest, produce a body of active and concerned public-spirited citizens, within the enterprises, and stimulate greater participation and better citizenship in the government of the state itself" [A Preface to Economic Democracy, p. 95]. The empirical support for this position is also reviewed by Walter R. Nord, "Participation in the Workplace: Issues of Process and Substance in the Attainment of Justice," a paper presented at a conference on "Justice as Participation: Should Workers Be Given Managerial Rights?," sponsored by the Liberty Fund, Inc., and held in St. Louis (September 11–13, 1986).

especially when work and community are viewed as moral imperatives. For example, proponents of restrictions on industrial closures
suggest that closing decisions, "often made in distant power centers,"
are like bombs dropped by "pilots at 30,000 feet who never see the
devastation" on the ground.[25] Again, the closing decisions may be
efficient from the (myopic) view of professional economists, but not
when viewed in the context of social systems themselves.

The economic case for justice as participation goes beyond the
acknowledgment of additional goods, work, and community, which
society seeks to maximize. The economic case also hangs on the very
practical concern over how economic efficiency can be achieved
when work and community are viewed as social goods, how to get
the economy moving again to produce jobs (as well as the things that
can be produced through jobs), and how economic rights should be
distributed or redistributed, especially in the workplace.

Making Everyone Better Off

In their arguments for new economic institutions, founded on democratic principles, proponents of justice as participation concentrate
on the social consequences of economic decisions made by individuals or firms. For example, proponents of restrictions contend that
plant closings destroy jobs, create unemployment, and depress the
"social wage." Unemployment can undercut worker self-esteem and
lead to family financial problems, including alcoholism, child abuse,
murder, suicides, and mental disorders.* Plant closings, in other
words, have external, or "spillover," effects that, in terms of free-
market economists' own efficiency-based models, can justify government intervention.

---

*In the words of the Task Force on Theology and Economic Justice: "The effects of sustained
unemployment are well-documented. Workers lose their sense of personal worth. Child abuse
and spouse abuse, suicides, separation, family disorganization, ill health, and mortality rates all
increase. The effects are equally disastrous for communities heavily dependent upon production industries, from Youngstown to Detroit to South Chicago to West Virginia mining towns.
Businesses, schools and local governments lose their economic base. Churches and social
agencies no longer have the resources to meet escalating family and personal problems. Unemployed youth become a threat, not a resource. And as people lose their sense of worth and
retreat into themselves or television, the social network—including both taverns and churches
—[falls] apart. People grow cynical about all forms of organization and all leaders." ["Doing
Theology in the Economic Crisis," pp. 2–3]. The case for plant closing restrictions has been
developed at length in Barry Bluestone and Bennett Harrison, *The Deindustrialization of America*
(New York: Basic Books, 1982).

Closing restrictions (such as prenotification, severance pay, and community restitution requirements), which carry costs, have been seen by their advocates as means of "internalizing externalities," that is, of making firms compensate workers and communities for the costs they necessarily suffer when plants close down. The restrictions will result in fewer and more rational plant-closing decisions and a more efficient allocation of resources, or so the proponents of restrictions contend.

The case for plant-closing restrictions (as well as the case for import restrictions or business subsidies that can prevent or delay plants from closing) has been developed in much the same way as the case for government controls on pollution. When firms are able to emit pollutants into the atmosphere at or near zero cost, the prices of the products produced will be understated in the sense that not all costs will be reflected in the market prices. As a result, the products will be overproduced in the sense that the total marginal cost to society of producing some units will exceed their marginal value to consumers. When paper plants do not have to abate the smells from their plants or to compensate local residents for enduring the smells, paper will be underpriced and overproduced. To that extent, resources will be misallocated—production will be inefficient.

Similarly, when firms do not have to consider the social costs of their plant-closing decisions, plant closings will also be underpriced and overproduced, resulting in too little economic stability or community cohesiveness. Looked at from a rights perspective, closing decisions result in community residents having their rights taken from them without their consent and without compensation. Participation, from this perspective, becomes a practical means (a social solution between what the bishops call realism and hope) by which those who are affected by the economic decisions can give their consent and, if appropriate, extract compensation, making the closing decision Pareto efficient (or mutually beneficial to all involved).

Participation and Flexibility

According to economic democrats, democratization of the national economy and the workplace is needed for American industries to recoup their international competitiveness. Professor Reich has sought to lay a historical foundation for this view. Between 1870 and 1920, the "era of mobilization," Professor Reich recounts how "a major new invention made its appearance in America, on average, every fifteen months,"[26] enabling firms to expand their operations to scales "never before imagined."[27] However, the economies of scale achieved led to overproduction and "ruinous price competition," making personal initiative, which characterized the era of mobilization, "inconsistent with the needs of an emerging economy grown suddenly more complex."[28] The scale economies also gave rise to price fixing, protective government controls over markets and, most importantly, improved management techniques.[29]

During the following "era of management," which ran from about 1920 to 1970, management science supposedly flourished, enabling firms to reduce their costs by further expanding their control over larger numbers of people and larger operating scales. However, it was during this period that "market competition ceased to be the main force behind the evolution of American industry" and that the main economic policy debate became "centered not on the choice between free market and planning, but on whether business leaders or government administrators would take the lead in planning."[30]

Since about 1970, so this thesis contends, the American economy has entered a period of relative decline for two basic reasons. First, changes in the competitiveness of world markets have made obsolete many standardized production processes to which some American industries have become wedded by decades of thinking in terms of long production runs and of not having to concede to competitive market pressures. Second, American managers have become bogged down in "paper entrepreneurialism," which is the "bastard child of scientific management" and amounts to elaborate corporate paper shuffling that seeks bookkeeping (as opposed to economic) profits through mergers, acquisitions, and tax avoidance and evasion, not through the creation of new productive assets.*

Worker participation thus should be a right unto itself, on par with other basic political rights, partially justified by the evil of monopoly power. Greater participation is also necessary if the American

---

*Reich, *The Next American Frontier*, pp. 121–145. Paper entrepreneurialism, according to Reich, relies on financial and legal virtuosity: "Through shrewd maneuvering, accounting and tax rules can be finessed and the numbers on the balance sheet and tax returns manipulated, giving the appearance of greater and lesser earnings . . . . Huge profits are generated by these ploys . . . . But they do not enlarge the economic pie, they merely reassign the slices." [Ibid., p. 145.]

economy is to break the stranglehold that large, inflexible, and monopolistic corporate structures have on entrepreneurial initiative and is to adapt to the challenges of the competitive international economy.

In addition, government officials, along with workers, must become involved in the details of economic planning, in this view, not because they are "wiser or more far-seeing than private managers," but because a return to prosperity depends upon social investments that private executives "cannot be expected to undertake and on a broader economic perspective than private managers can attend to."[31] A part of this broader economic perspective is the need of the whole community to hold together. In other words, worker and government participation in economic decisions at the firm and national levels is seen as adding flexibility to the calcified economy and ordering the pace of transition so that communities may continue to cohere in the face of change.

Job Rights and Participation

Economic democrats also reason that participation is an outgrowth of rights that workers have in their jobs. Professor Judith Lichtenberg starts her assessment of the morality of unilateral plant closing decisions, a major concern of industrial policy advocates, by quoting Staughton Lynd, a longtime proponent of plant-closing restrictions:

> "Workers in Youngstown and elsewhere are beginning to ask: Why is the company allowed to make shutdown decisions unilaterally? Since the decision affects my life so much, why can't I have a voice in the decision? . . . The communities in which shutdowns occur are starting to ask the same question."[32]

"The thrust of these questions is moral, not practical," declares Professor Lichtenberg.[33] The suggestion is that workers have a moral right that should be made a legal right to participate in such decisions as plant closings.

Why or how do workers acquire these participation rights? Several economic democrats cite John Locke's labor theory of value, which is founded on the proposition that the source of all value is ultimately labor. Locke argued that "property rights are acquired by

'mixing one's labour' with, and thereby, adding to, external objects,''
a conception of the world that necessarily means that "having worked
on an object and transformed it into a socially valuable commodity
gives one *some* claim to the fruits of one's labor."[34]

Similarly, others who support justice as participation maintain
that Locke's labor theory of value cannot justify the ownership of a
corporation by stockholders.* The argument goes on to suggest that
the question at issue in the ownership debate is not totally practical,
involving efficiency concerns alone, but "whether any alternative to
ownership and nominal control by stockholders would necessarily
violate some fundamental moral claim."[35]

This line of thinking appears to apply with equal force to workers'
property rights to their jobs as well as products, both of which they
help create. According to this viewpoint, the proposition that investors' control of firms is justified by their sacrifice of consumption is
"laughable, given the concentration of corporate ownership in the
hands of institutions and wealthy investors . . . . [T]he argument
from sacrifice would at most justify a return for the sacrifice, it
would not justify control. . . . [W]orkers sacrifice more of their
lives by working than investors sacrifice by investing."†

The integration of the firm's activities with the community over a
period of time can also cause a shift of decision-making rights to
employees.‡Why or how the company loses its freedom of mobility

---

*Professor Dahl writes: "For on Locke's justification, only those who labor to produce goods
and services, the workers and employees, would be entitled to own the goods and services
produced by a firm. Moreover, no one would be entitled to own land or to gain rent from land;
at most, those who labored to improve it would be entitled to the fruits of their labor." [*Preface
to Economic Democracy*, p. 78.]

†Dahl, *Preface to Economic Democracy*, p. 80. This perspective on job rights can be found in
decisions of the National Labor Relations Board. After noting that plant-closing decisions are
important to the employer, because of the investment involved, the National Labor Relations
Board points out that: "For, just as the employer has invested capital in the business, so the
employee has invested years of his working life, accumulating seniority, accruing pension
rights, and developing skills that may or may not be saleable to another employer. And, just as
the employer's interest in the protection of his capital investment is entitled to consideration in
our interpretation of the [National Labor Relations] Act, so too is the employee's interest in
the protection of his livelihood." [Ozark Trailers, Inc., 161 NLRB 561, 63 LRRM at 1267.]

‡Professor Lichtenberg argues: "The second argument for workers' rights to a say in shutdown
decisions expresses the idea that when a company has dug deep over generations into people's
lives, perhaps affecting a whole community, it incurs obligations to those people and that
community. Although the company may have entered freely, it is no longer at liberty simply to
withdraw from relationships that have developed over years or generations." ["Workers,
Owners, and Factory Closings," pp. 9–10.]

is not clear from the arguments of economic democrats. What is clear, however, is that they do not believe that shifting decision-making rights to workers will cause any inefficiency. This position relies on the "Coase theorem," which says, in effect, that so long as bargaining between workers and owners is permitted, the more efficient outcome will result: "For whichever side stands to benefit most will simply buy out the other side's entitlement, if it doesn't possess the entitlement itself."[36]

Professor Lichtenberg illustrates the point with an example of a plant that could be moved from Ohio to South Carolina with a cost saving to the firm of $4 million and a loss of income to the workers of $3 million. If the plant owners have the entitlement to the plant, they will move because the workers would only pay, at maximum, $3 million to keep the plant owners from moving, whereas the owners could gain as much as $4 million by moving. If, on the other hand, the workers have the entitlement, then management would be willing to pay more, up to $4 million, than the workers would lose, $3 million, by the move. A deal would be struck to move the plant.

Similarly, Professor Lichtenberg surmises that the plant would stay in Ohio if the workers would lose more, for example, $5 million, than the owners would gain by the move, again $4 million. She then concludes, "There is, then, no merit to the claim that allowing workers to have some control over shutdown decisions is bad for the economy because it is inefficient."[37]

Such economic arguments might be on shaky moral grounds, however, given the bishops' "fundamental norm," the welfare of the poor. If relocating factories shifts employment and income from relatively high income workers in Ohio to relatively lower income workers elsewhere in this country or the world, the moral imperative would indicate that the plant should be moved. The counter-argument goes as follows: "Even though in the short run workers in South Carolina or Korea might benefit from Ohio plant closings—and might benefit from them more, economically, than Ohio workers are harmed—over time, corporate autonomy in shutdown decisons is a setback for labor, not an advance."[38] Capital mobility, in other words, suppresses the long run wages of all workers because of movements or the threat of movements.

Concluding Comments

The case for a new economic democracy encompasses a variety of moral and practical concerns. Efficiency, profit, and production are not the only virtues by which social institutions should be judged because they are not the only "goods" people seek. Community, concern for the poor, and work are broad economic objectives that are normally overlooked, or intentionally excluded, from conventional economic analysis.

Even if efficiency, narrowly conceived, were important, the allocation of resources would not be affected by reassignment of entitlements, that is, by giving workers rights of participation (which they are due anyway, because of their investment in their jobs and communities). Since efficiency in the assignment of rights is of no particular consequence, ethical or moral arguments should guide public policy in institutional design. Indeed, the transfer of participation rights to workers should lead to an expansion of the national economic pie, or so the thrust of the argument goes. These arguments are critically evaluated in the following chapter.

Notes

1. Catholic Bishops, "Pastoral Letter on the Social Economy," third draft (duplicated, 1986), p. 80.
2. See Robert A. Dahl, *Preface to Economic Democracy* (Berkeley, Calif.: University of California Press, 1985), chapters 3 and 4.
3. Martin Carnoy, Derek Shearer, and Russell Rumberger, *A New Contract: The Economy and Government after Reagan* (New York: Harper and Row Publishers, 1983), p. 2.
4. Ibid., p. 3.
5. Dahl, *Preface to Economic Democracy*, pp. 285–93.
6. "Pastoral Letter," p. 16
7. Ibid.
8. "Building Justice in Communities: Doing Theology in the Economic Crisis" (Cleveland, Oh.: Ecumenical Great Lakes/Appalachian Project on the Economic Crisis, December 7–9, 1984), p. 7.
9. Ibid.
10. Ibid., p. 13.
11. Ibid.
12. Ibid., p. 13.
13. Ibid., p. 15.

14. Ibid.
15. Ibid.
16. Ibid., p. 12.
17. Ibid., p. 16.
18. Ibid., p. 16.
19. Ibid., p. 16.
20. Ibid., p. 15.
21. Ibid., p. 14.
22. "Doing Theology in the Economic Crisis," p. 8.
23. Ibid.
24. Dahl, *A Preface to Economic Democracy*, p. 100.
25. "Doing Theology in the Economic Crisis," pp. 3–4.
26. Reich, *The Next American Frontier*, p. 26.
27. Ibid., p. 29.
28. Ibid., p. 33.
29. Ibid.
30. Ibid., p. 57.
31. Reich, *The Next American Frontier*, p. 14.
32. As quoted from Staughton Lynd, *The Fight Against Shutdowns* in Judith Lichtenberg "Workers, Owners, and Factory Closings" *Report* (College Park, Md.: Center for Philosophy and Public Policy, Fall 1984), p. 9.
33. Ibid.
34. Ibid., p. 9.
35. Dahl, *Preface to Economic Democracy*, p. 79.
36. Lichtenberg, "Workers, Owners, and Factory Closings," p. 10
37. Ibid., p. 11.
38. Ibid., p. 12.

6
Justice as Participation in the Workplace: The Economics of Participatory Markets

Employee participation in management decisions is indispensible to the management of a modern corporation. Those that have it and use it possess *one* of the absolute prerequisities of business success today. Those that don't court disaster.

—James Child[1]

T he preceding chapter developed a number of core arguments in the case for giving workers greater participation rights in management decisions. This chapter offers criticisms of those arguments, primarily to the extent that they support the imposition of participation rights on workplace contracts. The criticisms developed may help explain why the Catholic bishops have modified their position substantially in subsequent drafts of their pastoral letter on the economy.

Evaluating the Argument: Markets and Community

A critique of economic democracy as a moral criterion could be developed in a number of ways. For example, the biblical and church

authorities on which the theory of justice rests could be disputed.*
This has been done by several critics, including a thirty-member lay
commission chaired by former secretary of the treasury William
Simon and organized specifically to provide an alternative, market-
oriented perspective on the issues raised in the bishops' "Pastoral
Letter."[2] Many references could be made to passages in the Bible
connecting moral behavior with individual and voluntary actions, as
opposed to collective and coerced behavior. For example, the lay
commission makes the following references to what is termed "clas-
sical papal documents":

> Any human society, if it is to be well-ordered and productive,
> must lay down *as a foundation this principle, namely, that every
> human being is a person*, that is, his nature is endowed with intelli-
> gence and free will. By virtue of this, he has rights and duties of his
> own, flowing directly and simultaneously from his very nature.
> *Pacem in Terris*, 9 (emphasis added).

> The cardinal point of this teaching is *that individual men are neces-
> sarily the foundation, cause, and end of all social institutions*. We are
> referring to human beings, insofar as they are social by nature, and
> raised to an order of existence that transcends and subdues nature.
> *Mater et Magistra*, 219 (emphasis added).

> [I]t is a fundamental principle of social philosophy, fixed and
> unchangeable, that *one should not withdraw from individual endeavor
> and commit to the community what they can accomplish by their own
> enterprise and industry*. So, too, it is an injustice and at the same time
> a grave evil and a disturbance of right order, to transfer to the larger
> and higher collectivity functions which can be performed and
> provided for by lesser and subordinate bodies. Inasmuch as every
> social activity should, by its very nature, prove a help to members

---

*In his criticism of the biblical foundations of the bishops' letter, University of Washington
professor Paul Heyne wrote: "The bishops want to transform institutions and structures; they
are therefore wise to focus on gaining control of government policies. When they do so,
however, honesty requires that they give up the authority of the New Testament as support for
what they are doing. It is the enlightenment, not the Gospels, that provides the 'theological'
framework for the debate that the bishops have initiated. It might be considerably easier to
conduct the debate, with the civility for which the bishops call, if all parties stopped claiming
that the battle is between God and the devil and admitted frankly that we are contrasting the
social visions of such mere mortals as Adam Smith and Karl Marx." [Paul Heyne, "The U.S.
Catholic Bishops and the Pursuit of Justice," Policy Analysis (Washington: Cato Institute,
March 5, 1985), pp. 17–18.]

of the body social, it should never destroy or absorb them. *Quadragesimo Anno*, 79 (emphasis added).[3]

The lay commission then concludes, "The first principle of Catholic social thought, the *individual dignity of every single human person*, flows from the fact that every human being is created in the image of God and is called in accordance with this image to make free choices of immortal consequence."[4]

However, as some critics of this debate over religious precedents point out, Catholics have been making so many diverse pronouncements on social policy for so long that it would be a surprise if reputable critics could not reference church doctrine for virtually any set of preconceived views, a point equally applicable to Protestant social thought. "Finding [authoritative] support for any position," write two of these observers, "must by now be largely a matter of diligence in library search."[5]

A more fruitful critique, on the other hand, can be marshalled by first acknowledging the commonality that exists between proponents of justice as participation and their critics. All, proponents and critics alike, appear to agree on the sanctity of the individual, the need to develop an economic system that promotes human dignity (through, for instance, a reduction in unemployment), the contribution that work and a sense of community can make to individual lives, and the need for people to be conscious of the special needs of the "marginalized" poor.

Where goals are concerned, especially when they are stated in broad, general terms, agreement is the rule. Disagreement, however, is the rule in assessment of the degree and importance of participation in markets and democracies. There is, therefore, much disagreement over the relative extent to which the two decision-making processes contribute to, say, community. More importantly, while it may be agreed by all that some form of participation in the workplace is desirable from a noneconomic, as well as an economic, perspective, much disagreement remains over whether a level of participation greater than that which is freely negotiated would improve the justice of labor markets.

The bishops, participants in the Ecumenical Project, and other economic democrats, as proponents of justice as participation, seem

to envision markets as social mechanisms intentionally and exclusively designed to promote self-interest (or private profit) at the
expense of the common good. They see markets as institutional
arrangements for ensuring the continued fragmentation of society
through competition and conflict. While the bishops tip their philosophical hats in deference to individual initiative and private property, they also take a dim view of the profit motive. They suggest that
"society must make provision for overall planning in the economic
domain," meaning that "all actors of society, including government,
must actively and positively cooperate in forming national economic
policies."[6]

They apparently believe that since the market system is not centrally directed, it remains effectively unplanned. Interestingly, in the
course of their "Pastoral Letter" on the religious and moral merit of
markets and democratic institutions (which covers more than thirty
newspaper-size pages), the bishops never once mention relative prices,
except to the extent the low wages of the poor are discussed.

If markets fail to coordinate people's individual actions (and,
therefore, are in radical conflict with human nature, which is at its
core relational), the case for greater participation of workers (or
consumers or government officials) through democratic institutions
would be difficult to dispute. In the absence of any coordinating
mechanism, virtual chaos would reign. The common good would
rarely, if ever, be served. And people's sense of community would be
severely restricted, if not totally destroyed. A call for the pursuit of
social justice through greater democratic participation in economic
decisions would go largely unchallenged, or so it would seem.

However, the debate over justice as participation centers on differing views of the extent to which markets do allow for individual
and group participation in economic decisions while simultaneously
coordinating individual activities. Market advocates have very entrenched views on how individual activities are coordinated in markets—through the pricing system, a major point of earlier chapters.
Evidence of this coordination can be seen by the extent to which
resources are moved to where they can be used productively. From
this perspective, cooperation abounds in markets, even if it is private
interest that is the motivating factor.

The production and distribution of computers, for instance, requires the cooperation of millions of individuals. Indeed, markets are institutional devices for extending people's cooperative efforts (and relevant community) beyond the cooperative limits set by such socially motivating forces of love, family ties, and altruism. Rather than being unplanned, markets abound with plans at the individual, family, cooperative, and firm levels. Plans can be made, revised and revised again to meet changing market circumstances, many of which cannot be foreseen outside of the market process.[7] This is partly because the full constellation of people's wants and reactions to the behavior and wants of each other cannot be known with much precision outside the market process.[8]

Participation in the market processes is evident from the trillions of decisions made annually by billions of people in millions of markets that extend across the globe. Of course, as the bishops and others protest, problems do abound in markets and emerge because of markets. Plants close down, sometimes unnecessarily; involuntary unemployment persists; and families separate because of the financial burdens of unemployment. We discussed in some detail in chapter 4 the inevitable pervasiveness of economic failures in any market system. Such problems, however, may demonstrate the prevalence of scarcity and the sheer magnitude of the coordinating problems posed for markets rather than provide evidence on the deficiencies of markets vis-a-vis tripartite councils and collectively set national plants.

The public good may not be the overriding motive of participants in market processes, but that does not mean that the public good is not served by the market system. Markets can also be assessed in terms of the freedoms they offer people to pursue their own interests (which can also be construed as a part of the public good, perhaps no less important than "work" and "community"). They can just as easily be evaluated in terms of the public good that is achieved through the participation of people who seek their own interests.

Seen in the light of this vision of the market, as opposed to the vision that undergirds the bishops' "Pastoral Letter," the case for justice as participation through economic democracy is not nearly so persuasive. Clearly, a portrayal of problems is a necessary component of any case for institutional change, but it is not a sufficient component. There are several reasons to question whether or not workers would gain from an imposed level and form of participation in management decisions or whether a national planning process will add to people's sense of community or solidarity or will be more inclined to serve the public good.

First, critics point out that labor-management councils at the firm level and tripartite councils at the national level do not dispense with, or even modulate, people's conflicting and competing interests. They fear that instituting economic democracy would merely shift the setting in which the conflicts and competition will be realized from markets to political arenas and may even exacerbate the breakdown of community. (One prominent proponent of economic democracy acknowledges that more democratic workplaces have at times increased the alienation of some worker groups, especially the worker representatives who sit on the labor-management councils.[9]) Because politics generally requires agreement among only a majority, each side of many political contests can frequently reason that their political objective should be to minimize their own net costs from political decisions. To do so, the coercive powers of government are used to spread the costs of government decisions to others, many of whom do not share the same views. People can vote for policies that benefit them extensively and for taxes that are covered by others. Proponents of economic democracy view their proposal as a means of "internalizing externalities," but their proposed system may actually encourage the opposite result, giving rise to "political externalities."

Each side in a political contest can, accordingly, be expected to engage in much political posturing and defensive maneuvering, shrouded often in inflammatory debate peppered with the rhetoric of justice, fairness, and goodness, just to promote and protect their interests. Indeed, because the political spoils of policy decisions often go to those who protest the loudest and with the greatest vigor, political decisions can exaggerate and aggravate divisions in communities, a not uncommon phenomenon in defense, environmental, and budgetary debates at all levels of government.[10]

By their confidence in the solidifying quality of political discussion and votes, proponents of justice as participation appear to assume that broad-based political agreement exists naturally, at least among workers. (If workers are not in agreement, then they can reach a consensus at modest social costs through open debate in which all are allowed to participate.) Is this likely to be the case in decisions over the future structure of the industrial economy? After all, picking winners can also amount to picking losers; protecting industries from foreign competition (steel, for example) can mean higher costs for other industries (farm equipment); and establishing plant closing restrictions can also mean reducing the likelihood of plant openings.

Second, economic democrats decry the greed and self-centeredness of markets, but they fail to explain how their proposed institutional changes will alter fundamental human motivations or how greed and self-centeredness will be tamed by political institutions. Given the interest groups that constantly ply the streets of Washington, one must wonder whether greed and fear will be any less important forces in a more inclusive economic democracy than in the current market economy in America.

Proponents of greater workplace democracy counter that workers will become more responsible in their managerial decisions since they will then more likely bear the burden of irresponsible decisions.[11] This is a highly dubious point, however, since individual worker groups at the enterprise level will also constitute a minuscule proportion of the population and since rights of participation can be effectively used to shift the costs of their decisions from the workers to the owners of capital and to consumers.*

Third, proponents of justice as participation seem to envision markets being supplanted, at least marginally, by democratic institutions in which everyone's views would be fully represented. The presumption is that workers speak with one voice on such issues as wage rates, fringe benefits, absenteeism, and reinvestment policies.[12] Complete democracy is unattainable, at least in large plants, simply because it would involve too many people and would be too cumbersome and costly to make decisions. Except in relatively small firms, workers never speak with one voice. Representative democracy necessarily means that some people's views will be heard and acted on, while others' will not; some people will have participation rights, while others will not.

---

*Worker-managers would also not be residual claimants, a source of inefficiency that will be considered more carefully later [Dahl, *Preface to Economic Democracy*, p. 140].

The justice of such an incomplete participatory social system must be scrutinized just as closely as the justice of a market system, which is also, admittedly, a social system that is not fully participatory. The relevant issue is which system is more participatory? Which system best represents the diverse views on what and how things should be undertaken by people constrained in the availability of resources—industrial markets or industrial tripartite councils and labor-management councils?

People may well be marginalized through markets that pay little or no attention to their preferences and needs, a point that bishops and others have made with force. But people can be just as easily marginalized by a participatory political system that rarely, if ever, votes their way, an issue never seriously entertained by the bishops and other economic democrats.

The points raised are not intended to make the comprehensive case for the continuance of a market economy; rather, they are raised simply to demonstrate that the case for economic democracy is not as complete as the Catholic bishops, the members of the Ecumenical Project, and others would have us believe. The debate does not, in other words, hinge on one social system offering participation rights while the other does not. Instead, both offer participation rights that are expressed in different ways.

Markets offer participation through the right to devise individual agreements between individual buyers (or employers) and sellers (or employees). Economic democracy offers participation through votes on collective positions to be adopted by groups of buyers and sellers.

It is true that individual buyers and sellers in markets may have very restricted influence on the terms of their agreements; individual choices may not count for very much because of their inconsequential impact relative to the entire market. However, the same argument can be leveled against economic democracy: The individual's vote may be one of many and, therefore, may have precious little influence on the actual collective decisions made.

The critical question in the debate is not whether one participatory system is just and the other one unjust; both are just in the sense that they offer participation rights and both are unjust to the extent that they are not fully participatory.* Instead, the critical question is

---

*Since it is difficult, if not impossible, to say which social system offers more participation, the relative justice of the two participatory systems is equally hard to assess in the abstract.

what types of participation give the most useful coordinating signals to people, all of whom may highly value normal goods and services, community and work, and all of whom are concerned about justice and the welfare of the poorest people within the community.

The bishops appear to believe that the poor will benefit from making institutions more democratic if for no other reason than that the poor will then have a greater say over how the nation's economic pie is divided. However, not all of the people whose participation rights are enhanced will be poor; many will have relatively high incomes. Is there reason to believe that the resulting participation of all workers will necessarily lead to a welfare improvement of the poorest among us? The poor will certainly be trying to use their participation rights to obtain more income, but so will the higher income workers.

In other words, the very characteristics held by some people, for example, managers and owners or the rich, are also the very characteristics that would make the same people adept in the political process. To give people equal access to any participatory process should not be construed as giving them equal effectiveness and power in that process.

For example, whose interests are likely to be represented to a greater degree on tripartite labor-management councils? Can we expect the poorer workers to be more effective than other worker groups in swaying collective decisions? What about the poor of the future? Will their interests be more or less represented in current industrial policy decisions if the economy were to be converted to an economic democracy? Are the economic interests of the current poor, who might have an understandable concern about current consumer goods, fully compatible with the economic interests of the future poor, who would have a greater interest in investment that affects future economic well-being? These are important questions that the bishops' "Pastoral Letter" and similar social statements on justice as participation leave unaddressed, and for good reason. The answers to these questions hit at the difficulty of elevating both participation and aiding the poor to moral imperatives.

The Evil of Monopoly

Support for a more participatory economy rests in part on the perceived social inefficiency, if not evil, of monopoly power. Worker and government participation in the formulation of policies at the firm and national levels is necessary because too many very large firms have too much economic power; that is, they can dictate the products produced and the prices charged. Economic democrats assert that the monopoly power of many large firms has not only resulted in much inefficiency in the allocation of resources and inflexibility in production processes, but has also meant that consumers have, over the decades in which scale economies and management science have developed, lost much of their right to participate, by their buying decisions, in how resources are allocated. Firms, mainly large ones, now control markets, as opposed to the other way around. Participatory economic democracy may, from this perspective, be seen as a means of returning to consumers their past rights of participation (and control).

This line of argument can be contested on several grounds. First, the presumed distressed current and future states of the American economy are highly debatable.[13] Second, the growing monopolization of the American economy is an issue that has been sharply disputed.[14] Third, the growing inflexibility of American industry to adapt to economic incentives is also questionable. (From discussions of growing paper entrepreneurialism, we learn much about the ability of entrepreneurs to adapt to economic incentives, namely tax incentives.) Fourth, the emergence of smaller, more flexible foreign competitors should reduce the monopoly power of large and inflexible American companies.

More important, however, while we might all agree that monopoly is an evil, we can be at considerable odds over the extent to which making the economy more democratic through the creation of planning councils will alter the monopoly power of established industries. Opponents of economic democracy fear that tripartite councils will seek to protect established industries with considerable political clout from emerging domestic and international competitive pressures. Much of the recent policy debate in Washington has centered on protecting and supporting the basic industries in the country, for instance, the automobile, textile, and steel industries. Most of the attention has been directed at seeing how the policy principles underlying the Chrysler bailout and the voluntary restrictions on car imports can be extended over time to other industries. The fear is that a greater number of people will be marginalized through politics, and the economic system will, to that extent, become more unjust.

The Lockean Perspective on Property

The bishops and other advocates of justice as participation share John Locke's view on the original "state of nature." They both agree, in Locke's words, "[I]t is very clear that God, as King David says (Psalm 25:16), 'has given the earth to the children of men,' given it to mankind in common."[15] Both the bishops and Locke seem to elevate the integrity and dignity of the individual person to that of a moral standard. However, their philosophical views appear to diverge from that point onward, for Locke's central concern was the extent to which one could mix his or her labor with things that "nature hath provided," effectively privatizing the common property and enhancing the value of the common property: "To which let me add that he who appropriates land to himself by his labour does not lessen but increases the common stock of mankind."[16]

Granted, in Locke's world a person acquires property through his labor: "It being by him removed from the common state nature hath placed it in." Locke writes, "It hath by his labour something annexed to it that excludes the common right of other men. For this labour being the unquestionable property of the labourer, no man but he can have a right to what that is once joined to, at least where there is enough and as good left in common for others."[17] According to Locke, in the state of nature, common property has little or no value, a condition that is radically changed when a worker removes it from the common property state by "annexing" his labor. Consequently, since labor is responsible for the overwhelming value of the property, the property annexed belongs to labor.

Note that in Locke's theory of property, the property extracted from nature is private, meaning no longer subject to collective control. Also, contrary to what economic democrats contend, it does not follow in Locke's property rights theory that the laborer cannot transfer the rights of his labor or property he has acquired, or that capitalists do not also have claims to property. Locke acknowledges several kinds of labor, including "the labor of his body, and the work of his hands," but he also suggests that private property can emerge from "the grass my horse has bit, the turfs my servant has cut, and the ore I have digged in any place I have a right to them in common with others, become my property without the assignment or consent of others."[18] Thus, a person could, as a capitalist and employer, acquire ownership rights through capital (the horse) and employees (servants). How does that happen? The worker negotiates a contract, giving up his or her claim to what is produced in return for a wage.*

The fact that support for justice as participation cannot be found in Locke may leave proponents unimpressed. They may still maintain that Locke has inappropriately extended his theory. They may contend that workers should, as a matter of justice, still have rights of participation because they have mixed their labor with the good produced, have helped create and define their jobs, and have contributed to their firm's profits. The presumption underlying such a contention is that ownership rights to profits have not been traded for other presumably more valuable rights such as wages and fringe benefits.

Without looking at the details of worker contracts, it is hard to understand how proponents of justice as participation can actually say what rights have been traded or that workers still retain participation rights, regardless of what the explicit or implicit employment contracts have been. If worker participation rights have been traded, then to declare that workers still have those rights is tantamount to declaring that past trades are invalid. A move toward greater justice would then, presumably, require that employers give back the participation rights and that workers give back the benefits acquired from giving up these rights. Could we then conclude that the would-be traders' welfare would be improved?

Perhaps proponents of justice as participation believe that participation rights should not be tradeable simply because of the declared moral status of participation. Such an intellectual posture abridges

---

*George Mason University professor Karen Vaughn maintains that in Locke's view: "A servant is originally a free agent who chooses to make a contract with his employer to do as the employer wishes (insofar as his employer does not ask him to do anything immoral), in return for a stated wage. What he subsequently does, then, is at his employer's direction and is the result of his employer's initiative, and since he has voluntarily agreed to trade a title to property, he is in no way harmed or exploited. Locke describes the relationship very precisely: 'for a Free-man makes himself a servant to another, by selling himself for a certain time, the service he undertakes to do, in exchange for wages he is to receive: and through this commonly puts him into the family of the Master, and under ordinary discipline thereof; yet it gives the Master but a temporary power over him, and no greater, than what is contained in the contract between 'em.'" [*John Locke: Economist and Social Scientist* (Chicago: University of Chicago Press, 1980), pp. 83–84.]

commonly acknowledged rights of ownership achieved through the mixing of one's labor—the right to trade what is owned. It also devalues the rights of labor, one of which is to trade off things that are owned (for instance, participation rights) for things perceived by the workers to be more valuable, namely wages and fringe benefits (or a host of other beneficial job characteristics). In the process, the capital value of labor is reduced.

Seen from this perspective, a declaration of justice as participation requires substantial moral arrogance on the part of the advocates who implicitly maintain that they know better than the multitude of people working under diverse conditions what is good for them. Arrogance aside, one must wonder how participation rights will, in the name of justice, be transferred. Will they be taken from firm owners by force? Or will the owners be compensated, especially for the rights that they have justly purchased through the payment of higher wages? How, too, can workers who have been given full participation rights, which they themselves would otherwise have traded away, be prevented from using their newly acquired participation rights to change the rules of participation—to re-establish their rights to trade away participation privileges for other forms of compensation?

This is, of course, a fundamental democratic dilemma: Does democracy entail the right of the electorate to destroy the democratic process by democratic means? Professor Dahl says no:

> If it is desirable that a people should govern itself democratically, then it cannot be desirable that it be governed undemocratically. If people believe that democracy is desirable and justified, logically they cannot simultaneously believe that it is undesirable, and thereby justify the destruction of the democratic process.[19]

This in effect means that acquired democratic rights must be non-tradeable, in spite of what individual worker groups may think to the contrary and in spite of the fact that tradeable democratic rights might improve workers' welfare, as they, the workers, not proponents of economic democracy, assess their own welfare.

One must wonder how economic democrats would react if workers refused, through political democracy at the national or state level, to adopt economic democracy at the national, state, enterprise, or plant level, especially if the economic democracy up for vote included nontradeable voting rights. Would economic democrats in the name of justice, morality, and fairness be willing to impose their views on workers, who by their own admission constitute an overwhelming representative majority of the citizenry? These are heady questions that economic democrats have chosen to ignore or sidestep by claiming that the accumulation of wealth has led to the political subjugation of worker interest.

Perhaps advocates of participatory economic decision making are really concerned that workers have never been compensated for the participation rights they have given up. It would appear, however, that such a question could be handled under current legal institutions, under contract law and through the courts. In addition, we must wonder how labor could remain uncompensated, at least in the long run, for not retaining these rights. If workers truly value rights of participation, then it should follow that the supply of labor would be restricted in those markets that did not offer them, and workers' wages would be pushed upward, at least in competitive labor markets.

Granted, not all labor markets are fully competitive. However, even in monopsonistic labor markets, a labor supply restricted by the absence of participation rights should lead to wages and fringe benefits that are higher than they would otherwise be. In such markets, a declaration of worker rights of participation can be expected in the long run to lead to a reconstituting of the worker benefit package, but not necessarily to an improvement in worker welfare. This is because the participation rights they are forced to retain can be less highly valued than the wages and fringe benefits they will be forced to forego.

Community Obligations

Economic democrats are also concerned that firms have, by their tenure in a given place, incurred "obligations to those people and that community,"[20] that is, to remain in place or at least to give up some management discretion over relocation and closure decisions to workers and community officials. Does this apply in all cases, regardless of circumstances? Does justice as participation amount to a proposal to scrap the whole of contract law and to deny the rights of communities to devise their own contracts to meet their varying circumstances?

The obligations firms have incurred would appear to depend on what they said they were going to do or how they intended to act and on what they gave up to retain discretion over relocation and closing decisions. Again, if labor and communities value participation rights in plant relocation and closure decisions, we would expect firms to have to pay for retention of discretion over disinvestment and reinvestment decisions.

In general, it might be true that many, but by no means all, workers, communities, and firms value participation rights, but surely they value them differently. In addition, the usefulness, effectiveness, and productivity of worker and community participation in firm decisions probably varies across firms, industries, and communities. Hence, we might expect to observe differing degrees of worker and community participation in firm decisions across the economy, which is what is observed.

Admittedly, the economy (especially in the industrial sectors) is not perfectly fluid and competitive. Nonetheless, considerable latitude exists over how firms and industries can be organized. Firms that are fully labor-managed and those that are owner-managed represent the extremes of an organizational continuum.

It should be no great surprise, given the diversity of production processes and circumstances, that successful labor-managed firms that give workers considerable voice in company policy decisions have emerged. However, if greater participation at the firm level is as valued and is as productive as suggested by its advocates, we must wonder why more labor-managed firms have not emerged or voluntarily altered their decision-making structures to allow greater input by workers and community officials.* Competitive pressures should extend the prevalence of worker participation among firms.

Indeed, it appears contradictory for economic democrats to contend that participation is profitable and that profit-seeking capitalists

---

*As a matter of fact, worker buy-outs of their firms have expanded over the past decade as an organizational form, partially encouraged by tax benefits. For a recent discussion of worker buy-outs, see Peter Young, "Privatization: The Worker Buy-Out Option," *Policy Analysis*, No. 76 (Cato Institute, July 1986).

would run their companies without some form of participation. As businessman-turned-philosopher James Child suggests in the quotation that heads this chapter, it would appear to be folly for managers to deny their workers some rights of participation, since firms depend upon the interplay of their people in order to be successful. Nevertheless, economic democrats would appear to be arguing, in essence, that a level of participation be imposed on managers that is greater than that which the managers, given constraints, would negotiate with their workers.

In assessing community obligations and the role of justice as participation, several points should be kept in mind. It is one thing to suggest that justice can be achieved by democratic participation. It is quite another thing to assert that the justice of a given level of participation under standardized rules for the entire economy is superior to the diversity of levels of participation that would exist in the absence of a legislated degree of participation.* The construction of such rules may give workers certain specified participation rights, but it can also snuff out worker and owner rights to experiment with alternative sets of participation rights that could yield more benefits to particular workers and communities. In the long run, communities can be more inclusive and more stable with a variety of participation agreements, including nonparticipation, than with one set of participation rights established collectively (in Congress) that is acceptable to some but not to others.

As noted much earlier, economic democrats agonize over the plant-closing decisions of absentee owners who do not have a personal stake in the communities where their plants are located. In effect, they say local workers and community officials should be given a voice in the closing decisions for large plants especially, to prevent the community from being destabilized. Admittedly, giving workers a say in closing decisions could lead to fewer closings or delayed closings.

However, granting workers and communities participation rights in such decisions will likely lead to higher costs of doing business, reduced investments in such places, and lower community stability.[21] For this reason, using the participation rights at their disposal,

---

*Professor Dahl recommends following the one employee–one vote rule and ensuring that the voting rights are nontradeable. [*Preface to Economic Democracy*, pp. 148–149.]

communities might understandably agree that firms will not be required to give up their management discretion.

Proponents of participation might see the arguments just posed as part and parcel of the case for national standards for the participation of workers and communities in closing decisions (or other policy areas). However, such standardization means denial of participation rights of individual worker groups and communities. Nationalization of standards can be an affront to individual dignity, a professed concern of the reformers. Standards can also be a restriction on the social welfare of the losing, diverse minority of workers and communities that prefer a different set of participation rights. To the extent that the national participation rights are suitable to some but not to others, they are discriminatory, very likely making the competitive tasks of retaining and attracting stable employment opportunities for some worker groups and communities all the more difficult. Because of their discriminatory nature, the debate over the specifics of national (or regional) participation rights will most likely be resolved by politics, which will reflect the prevailing power structure.

More fundamentally, giving workers at a given plant a say in the plant's closing and relocating can be an indirect means of disenfranchising other workers in other locations who would want the plant to close and move. If all workers, those in the prospective as well as in the old location, were given participatory rights, it is not at all clear how the decisions would come down.

Capital Mobility and Worker Poverty

Economic democrats echo a familiar theme of the economic reform movement when they argue that capital mobility represents a threat to worker welfare. By pitting workers across regions of the country and globe against one another in a competitive struggle for jobs, owners of capital are able to suppress workers' social wages—to erode the benefits workers have struggled to achieve over the decades in which capital has not been so mobile. To retain these gains or to slow the erosion of them, workers need the right to participate in their firms' investment and, especially, disinvestment decisions. Granting participatory rights (which actually can be interpreted in this application as rights to retard or block the movement of capital) is justified on the grounds that low-income workers do not ultimately benefit from the threat of capital mobility. Their wages are suppressed just as are the wages of higher-income workers. Thus, a part of the value created by workers is transferred as a surplus to owners of capital, or so it is argued.

Clearly, capital mobility has improved with the reductions in the cost of transportation, and capital mobility can suppress the wages of workers directly affected in individual instances of plant closings or relocations. If capital mobility did nothing more than suppress worker wages across the income spectrum, an institutional shift toward a more complete economic democracy would again be hard to challenge.

Concern for the poor is not really the issue, however. What is disputed is the impact of restricting capital mobility across time and space. For several reasons, it does not necessarily follow that workers across the labor force are damaged as a consequence of capital mobility.

First, labor mobility often parallels capital mobility, and the ability of workers to move offers workers a bargaining position to raise their wages.

Second, perhaps as often as not, capital follows labor, meaning capital moves to where labor wants to go, rather than escaping from labor demands. Democratic restraints on capital are not simply restrictions on the owners of capital (whose rights do not seem to count for much to the advocates of justice as participation); they are also restrictions on workers who desire to move (whose rights are of paramount importance to those advocates).

Third, in the process of moving or threatening to move, production costs and prices are lowered, and the real value of any given social wage is raised.

Fourth, growing capital mobility can mean an increase in the ability and willingness of capital to move into a given labor market (and expand in that market), as well as an increase in the ability and willingness of capital to move out (or contract).

Fifth, much of the capital that moves out does so because wages in its initial location are rising owing to expansions of other industries. Many movements of capital, therefore, reflect expanding, rather than contracting, job opportunities and wage rates for labor.

Still, some capital moves because the wages and fringe benefits of workers exceed competitive levels, in which case the affected workers are forced to accept lower pay in their next best employment alternatives. However, if we are to take the bishops' concern for the poor seriously, there remain two important questions. Can or should anything be done through the transfer of participation rights that would keep these workers' wages from falling? If workers refuse to allow their firm to relocate and take advantage of more profitable opportunities, then other firms will spring up to exploit them. Are the workers who earn wages above competitive market levels likely to be poor? Not necessarily. The poor typically earn their living in markets virtually unrestricted to entry and exit.

Without question, some workers lose when their plants close or relocate, but they often gain by the closures and relocations of many other plants. Most American workers have, over time, experienced rising real income. This means that, on balance, they have gained from capital mobility, a central point of the lay commission's critique of the bishops' "Pastoral Letter."[22] This point was critical to chapter 4. At the same time, because of the sheer numbers of people involved, it is also clear that there have been and will continue to be net losers from capital mobility, those whose losses from their own inability to obtain and retain useful and stable employment are greater than their gains through greater efficiency in other sectors of the economy. Any social system that seeks to avoid all prospects of net losers from the market system is utopian. Certainly, such concerns do not lead inextricably to a case for economic democracy. Economic democracy could create a greater number of net losers, a point directly related to our discussion of the economic legitimacy of the contained welfare state (see chapter 9).

Participation and Industrial Policies

While the bishops and others concerned with the changing industrial structure seek justice through worker participation in firm and national policies, they also advocate a variety of more or less specific policies designed to remedy observed economic problems, such as unemployment, poverty, displaced workers, disinvestment, capital mobility, and foreign competition. Maintaining that the "distribution of income and wealth in the U.S. is so inequitable that it violates the minimum standard of justice,"* the bishops also propose a number of welfare reforms, support the union movement, advocate comparable pay for comparable work, and suggest that the government

---

*Bishops, "Pastoral Letter," p. 10. Professor Dahl sidesteps the fairness issue in transferring participatory rights to workers by asserting "[I]t would be very hard to develop a reasoned argument that the prevailing distribution of wealth and income in the United States satisfied defensible standards of equity. Few people attempt to justify economic inequality as equitable." [Dahl, *Preface to Economic Democracy*, p. 138.]

ought to rededicate itself to guaranteeing full employment.[23] The
institutional changes are promoted, as is participation, in the name of
social justice, basic human morality, and concern for the marginalized poor. They are founded on a particular assessment of the current
and future states of the economy.

The potential for conflict between greater participation and specific policy proposals should be self-evident. Greater participation,
in and of itself, may not yield the proposed morally based policies.
Suppose the economic system is made more participatory, but the
representatives of workers, management, and government, after much
deliberation, do not assess the state of the economy to be as serious
as the bishops and do not adopt the recommended policies—either
because the state of the economy does not require them or because
they will not work or may not even be counterproductive.

Indeed, suppose that the new representatives seek policies that
contract the welfare system, eliminate minimum wages, or dissolve
import protection for basic industries. Does it follow that economic
democracy is unjust? Does it mean that the democratic institutions
will need to be adjusted until the right or just policies, as the bishops
conceive rightness and justice, are adopted? If so, then perhaps the
recommended democratic institutions are superfluous; we could simply follow the recommendations of the bishops or other groups who
believe they know how justice can be achieved through government
policies. But then we do not have justice as participation, except to
the extent that we have participation by the bishops or those who
believe they know the moral public policy course. In addition, when
we adjust the rules of participation to achieve preconceived outcomes, the justice of the participatory system becomes suspect,
simply because participation then becomes an endogenous variable
in the social system, not a moral standard.

Matters of Principle

We have in past chapters maintained that fairness is, at least to some
extent, related to the willingness of proponents of policy changes to
generalize their proposed reforms. Granting workers participation
rights is advocated on the grounds that workers are meaningfully
affected by workplace decisions, but so are many other groups—for

example, consumers of the goods and services the workers produce and other workers outside the firm who supply parts and whose livelihoods are, in this and other, more indirect ways, affected by the firm's investment and disinvestment decisions.

Fairness as generalized principle would mean that these other interest groups should also be given participatory rights. It is not at all clear that workers in a given plant would be willing to accept such constraints—and the participation of other groups would represent constraints on any given set of workers, just as the participation of workers in a given firm represents constraints on the firm's management. Their agreement to participation as generalized principle is especially doubtful, since the workers in a given plant might, because of their limited numbers, then have little real control over the decision-making process. In addition, the participation of the other groups might be rejected simply because the decision-making process would be too complicated—rather, too costly and inefficient.

Advocates propose that workers be given greater participation rights in management decisions than would be freely negotiated. Generalization of principle would require that workers acknowledge they also have spheres of activities in their jobs over which they have some discretion. Although often highly constrained, worker discretion is often highly meaningful, especially in nonroutine jobs. Generalization of principle would require that workers grant to management greater participation rights in their spheres of activities than would be freely negotiated. When a reform is advocated on the grounds that workers should "get something (rights) for nothing," their full support can be expected. Their support may wane significantly when the reform is transformed into a generalizable principle, which means that identifiable worker groups are treated like everyone else, neither better nor worse.

Markets versus Democracy

In summary, the case for economic democracy in the United States is founded in part on a number of contentions about the U.S. economy, not the least of which are that:

U.S. industries are highly concentrated and noncompetitive.

Capitalism has resulted in the accumulation of massive amounts of wealth in the hands of relatively few people.

Economic power has been transformed into political power.

U.S. firms do not now allow, to any meaningful extent, for worker participation in managerial decisions (except where strong unions have established such rights).

Large modern corporations are only loosely controlled, if at all, by their stockholders, who have little or no incentive to pay attention to what the managers do on a day-to-day basis.

The accumulation of wealth in the United States has been to the detriment of the poor, and the poor will continue to suffer unless a major shift in the distribution of managerial rights is made.

Workers truly want the brand of economic democracy that is advocated.

While most economic democrats write as if these points are settled conclusions, virtually all of them are highly contentious, if not dubious, propositions.* But the key claim is that economic democracy is just because it is a better system, even from the perspective of a conventional political economy that puts great weight on production and consumption of goods and services. As noted, proponents of economic democracy maintain that giving workers the right of participation in managerial decisions will not only foster moral responsibility and political justice, but will also give rise to greater productivity.

Proponents of participatory economic decision making claim that implementing their ideas would: 1) vastly reduce the adversarial and antagonistic relations that foster moral irresponsibility on both sides;[24] 2) greatly reduce the inequality of income and wealth, and enhance people's appraisal of the fairness of the economic system;[25] and 3) stimulate saving, investment, and growth, since workers typically

---

*Such empirical issues have been considered in Simon, et al., *Toward the Future*, especially part II.

would stand to incur severe losses from the decline of a firm.* Because more would be expected of workers and employment would be more stable,[26] and because workers would benefit more directly from their own and their firms' investment in human capital,[27] economic democracy should "heighten—not diminish—efforts to improve a country's human capital." In general, worker productivity would rise because "self-governing enterprises are likely to tap the creativity, energies, and loyalties of workers to an extent that stockholder-owned corporations probably never can, even with profit-sharing plans."[28]

Such claims of obvious superiority raise the simple question: If worker-managed firms are so productive, why are they not tried more frequently than they are?† Why aren't workers given more rights of participation than they are? Proponents attribute past failures of such organizations to a lack of "credit, capital, and managerial skills," and to the fact that they have been attempted almost exclusively when firms were on the verge of collapse.[29] Although we cannot conclude that what exists in the way of industrial organization is necessarily more efficient and effective than forms of business organization that do not exist, still, what does exist is suggestive. We must wonder why there has been a shortage of credit, capital, and managerial skills under normal market conditions or why worker-managed firms have not been formed under normal healthy economic conditions.

Surely, profit-hungry capitalists should be able to see that worker-managed firms offer an opportunity for making greater profits. If capitalists are as greedy and self-serving as economic democrats suggest, it should follow that they would eagerly seek to invest in worker-managed firms. If, for some reason, conventional capitalists are blinded by ideology to the benefits of worker-managed firms, then workers (or even economic democrats) could use their special knowledge to organize such firms and outperform the conventional stockholder-managed firms—thereby putting competitive pressure

---

*Dahl, *Preface to Economic Democracy*, p. 123. Setting interpersonal utility comparisons aside, Professor Dahl suggests that "the losses from the decline of a firm are normally much greater for the workers than the owners of the firm, because it is ordinarily much easier and less costly in human terms for a well-heeled investor to switch in and out of the securities market than for a worker to switch in and out of the job market." [Ibid.].

†Professor Dahl reviews a number of cases in which worker-governed enterprises have been tried, some of which have failed and some of which have succeeded. See *Preface to Economic Democracy*, chapter 4.

on stockholder-managed firms to follow suit. To argue the contrary is tantamount to a contention that all capitalists and workers are intractably stupid and/or are not as greedy as economic democrats suppose.

Clearly, not all worker groups have the needed financial capital to start worker-managed firms or to take over their firms and reorganize them according to democratic principles. However, this is not true for all worker groups: automobile and steel workers, who are often the objects of economic democrats' concern, earn substantially higher-than-average manufacturing wages. Wealthier worker groups could buy at least parts of their firms, reorganize them, and enjoy the benefits of the resultant productivity gains. Such worker groups would then be in the vanguard of competitive change. They could demonstrate to conventional capitalists how firms can and should be reorganized to be more productive and profitable.

Admittedly, not everyone is interested in greater profits. But more profits, garnered through greater productivity, can be sacrificed for any number of other labor objectives, including more meaningful and varied work experiences, greater fringe benefits, or even more relaxed production environments. According to economic democrats, these benefits should be more readily available, if they are available at all, to those worker groups that voluntarily (meaning without government mandate) take the lead in organizing their firms along democratic lines.

Advocates of justice as participation tell us that workers want democratic workplaces. Do they really mean all workers? Unless they do, it is hard to understand why economic democrats talk of worker participation in workplace decisions as a moral standard. On the other hand, if they mean all workers, then how have they come to such a sweeping conclusion? Given the extraordinarily wide variety of production circumstances and worker preferences for rights to wages, fringe benefits, participation, production standards, and so on, how can economic democrats know that all workers wish to participate in economic decision making?*

---

*Perhaps Professor Dahl was reflecting the rationale of many economic democrats when he wrote: "If democracy is justified in governing the state, then it is also justified in governing economic enterprises. What is more, if it cannot be justified in governing economic enterprises, we do not quite see how it can be justified in governing the state. Members of any association for whom the assumptions of the democratic process are valid have a right to govern them-selves by means of the democratic process. If, as we believe, those assumptions hold among us, not only for the government of the state but also for the internal government of economic enterprises, then we have a *right* to govern ourselves democratically." [*Preface to Economic Democracy*, p. 135.]

The proposition that workers have a self-evident right to self-government can be disputed on several grounds, not the least of which is that the body polity, including workers, may never have created or delegated such a right. The body polity may organize a state along democratic principles simply as an instrument of distributing political power; as a means of making decisions on issues that affect all, or almost all, of the body polity; or as a means of restricting the capacity of the body polity to make collective or joint decisions.*

When government bodies direct economic decisions, we need to be concerned with the distribution of decision-making power because of the breadth of the coverage of collectively made decisions. Concentrated decision-making power is a major concern primarily because citizens have relatively few places to go to escape the impact of such collective decisions.

At the firm level, however, people have many more places to go to escape the consequences of decisions that are taken. The threat of people avoiding the consequences of decisions made by managers should, therefore, place far more constraints on management.

Economic democrats start with the assumption that decision-making power at the firm level is highly concentrated in the U.S. economy. They write eloquently of the economic and political power of giant and dominant corporations. But, if it is only these corporate giants who possess undue authority, then this is an argument for installing economic democracy in large, dominant corporations, not for the entire economy.

But, once again, partial democracy may be no solution for the affected workers in the dominant corporations, unless economic democracy is truly a more efficient method of organizing firms. If not, large firms will be placed at a competitive disadvantage with respect to smaller nondemocratic firms. Financial capital can be expected to flow to the smaller firms, giving them the opportunity to expand and take over the markets of the larger, democratically run firms. Again, however, if economic democracy is truly more efficient, then the large firms can be expected to take these initiatives voluntarily.

---

*Obstructing the decision-making power of democracy was a central concern of James Madison, as well as a number of other federalists and antifederalists. See Alexander Hamilton, John Jay, and James Madison, *The Federalist* (New York: Modern Library, n.d.), no. 51.

Economic Democracy and Investment

Economic democrats often charge that corporate managers in a market economy are short-sighted, driven by profits, and directed too much by the bottom line of a firm's current income statement. While it may be conceded that capitalists are concerned with profits, it does not follow that they are exclusively and myopically concerned with current profits.

Capitalist owners of firms can also be expected to be concerned with the value of their stock, which should reflect current profits but also prospective future profits. If firms take actions (such as closing a plant) or fail to take actions (such as refusing to introduce technological improvements in their operations) that sacrifice future profits for current profits, the value of the firms' stock will fall. This financial constraint should temper, although not eliminate, any inherent shortsightedness on the part of management.

By proposing to give workers nonsalable voting rights, economic democrats propose to take from firm owners some of the incentive for focusing on their firm's wealth. Workers who manage their firms, by virtue of the nonsalability of their voting rights, will not benefit as much as stockholders would from resisting the very real temptation to sacrifice future profits for current profits.* (Workers who expect to be in their jobs for a relatively short period of time should be especially prone to vote for current wages over future profits.) As a consequence, we should expect worker-managed firms to shift somewhat from using their income for investment and reinvestment to paying wages and fringe benefits. Contrary to what the economic democrats contend, the result should be a marginal reduction in the rate of economic growth (meaning the accumulation of income-generating wealth).

If worker voting rights could be bought and sold, then economic democrats would run headlong into a social problem they seek to avoid: namely, that the voting rights held by workers of successful firms would become so expensive that new entrants might be unable

---

*Arthur Denzau, who pointed out to me the line of analysis taken in this section, stresses that if workers with nontradable voting rights do not raise wages above competitive levels to absorb would-be profits, then the stockholders will gain, through dividends or an appreciation of the firm's stock, at the expense of workers—just as in conventionally organized firms. If workers vote to sacrifice profits for wages, then their firms will be noncompetitive in the capital market, stunting growth that would have been possible through capital accumulation. To attract the necessary capital, the workers may have to concede some of their management discretion, subverting the intent of enterprise democracy.

to purchase these rights—that is, unable to obtain employment with successful firms. Economic democrats also must confront the charge that the creation of tradable voting rights is little more than a surreptitious means of transferring firm wealth from stockholders to workers, which may be all that is really intended.

The justice of such a transfer must be questioned, given the breadth and haphazard method of transfer. Many workers—some poor, some not so poor—are stockholders either directly through their own stock purchases or indirectly through the purchases of stock by their life insurance policies and pension funds. Many stockholders are quite rich, but many do not fit the well-worn image of the rapacious capitalist. Charitable organizations, educational institutions, and so on also invest in the stock market. Many current stockholders sit on substantial capital gains, some of which may be the product of luck and may be "unearned" (as some describe profits), but other stockholders have paid the current market value for their shares. Granting workers managerial discretion and tradable rights that affect the current and future income of the firm can mean that wealth is effectively stolen from many people who, even by the standards of the bishops, have justly acquired their wealth and who are as deserving as the employees who acquire the wealth.

Should stockholders be paid for what they give up? If so, how much? The current market prices of their stocks? The current market prices capture the expected discounted value of the future income stream, which means that workers would gain nothing financially and would be made worse off since they would then be forced to buy stock that they could have purchased voluntarily, but did not. Again, if the purchase of the ownership rights of a firm by workers was expected to be profitable, we would expect workers to purchase those rights and manage their firms, or we would expect entrepreneurs to organize firms that give workers managerial rights. If economic democracy is imposed on the entire economy, or just a major sector, society will lose the opportunity to learn the relative efficiency of worker-managed firms.

False Dichotomies

Words help us communicate and understand one another—most of the time. However, they sometimes help intensify misunderstandings. Such is the case in social politics. The debate is all too often couched in terms of contrasting extremes that amount to false dichotomies. Such is surely the case when we debate questions of the poor versus the rich, managers (or owners) versus workers, or participatory versus nonparticipatory firms. The fact of the matter is that questions are matters of scale or of continuum, with no sharp dividing lines. In the real world, there is no clear distinction between "poor" and "rich," "managers" and "workers," or "participatory" and "nonparticipatory" firms. To that extent, the presumption of conflict between or among classes and organizational forms is not nearly so evident as might be presumed from reading much social commentary.

Many "poor" people have been marginalized, but so have many of the rich. Most "managers" are in fact "workers" with interests in common with those they employ. And all workers are, to one degree or another, managers over some sphere of activities within the firm. Even workers have, within bounds, the authority to manage machinery and their own time. Finally, it would be clearly bizarre for people to organize firms—that is, combinations of capital and workers, each with specialties and abilities to contribute to the group's welfare—and not expect at least some limited degree of participation. The differences among firms are more in the degree rather than the participation.

Once we recognize that we at all times exist on social continuums, we can begin to see why there may be a far greater degree of coherence within society than might be expected from reading commentaries about societies that by necessity rely on sharply defined categories. Conflict can be expected to emerge in societies where groups can be readily identified. Conflict is not so evident when we don't know which group to join and whom to prevail against. Furthermore, when we acknowledge that we exist on social continuums, we immediately see the difficulty of designing one participatory system (or even a limited number of alternative systems) that is adaptable to the multiplicity of interests represented by the people around us. For all of these reasons, it is understandable why the bishops had, by the time they wrote the third draft of their pastoral letter, concluded quite responsibly, "Since there is no single innovation that will solve all problems, we recommend careful experimentation with several possibilities that hold considerable hope for increasing partnership and strengthening mutual responsibility for economic justice."[30]

Concluding Comments

Any debate over social organization is ultimately concerned with the distribution of power: how to disperse political and economic power. The challenging question is how to contain and direct the power that is dispersed for the betterment of people, individually and collectively. Participatory economic democracy is one means of dispersing, containing, and directing political and economic power; but it is not the only means. Neither is it necessarily the most effective means of all levels and types of decision making.

Participatory democratic institutions have proven quite effective for making decisions regarding goods that are necessarily consumed and financed jointly by broad sectors of the citizenry. Our government functions in this fashion. However, we should remember that we have opted for a representative form of government rather than a fully democratic form. Whether or not we will have a more inclusive economic democracy of the kind the bishops recommend is another such decision that must be settled jointly through the political process. However, it does not follow that economic democracy is the only just means of providing for participation in the economic sphere. Our current market system is another important social institution that disperses power, offers people rights of participation, and results in decisions.

Furthermore, we should not expect economic democracy to always be the most effective social institution for all segments of the population and for individuals. This is because people differ, their circumstances differ, and their interests can conflict. The majority can also run roughshod over minorities.

By developing their positions in the name of justice, proponents of economic democracy seem to suggest that those who do not support their proposed institutional changes harbor little or no concern for justice. Economists, who are prone to harp on the efficiency of markets and who deny any particular professional talent to comment on matters of social justice, seem to be unfeeling individuals of this type. However, it may be more accurate to say that all social philosophy is concerned ultimately with matters of justice.

The debate over justice as participation is really among people who differ over how justice can be more fully achieved. It is, at least in part, a debate over the relative moral worth of the individual, who can only have moral and legal meaning if he or she is viewed as a decision maker, someone who can—within limits—take actions that are not subject to approval or second-guessing by anyone or any group of people.

Contrary to surface appearances, the proponents of justice as participation seek to contract the sphere of individual decision making. Proponents of economic democracy would install an institutional design (approved, for example, by the federal government) for all firms, regardless of individual circumstances and preferences.

Opponents of economic democracy seek to retain the capacity of individuals to act through firms and worker groups to establish their own form of internal workplace governance. Nothing in the case for the retention of an open market system denies managers or workers the right to organize firms along democratic lines. Indeed, as has been repeatedly stressed, an open and free market system encourages experimentation with a variety of organizational forms. Seen in this light, people may reject economic democracy not because they seek to maintain economic injustice; but, rather, a system of private property and individual (or firm) decision making, although imperfect, is still more inclusive, effective, and beneficial for everyone, at least over the long run.

Notes

1. James W. Child, "The Operation of the Firm under Participatory and Non-Participatory Schemes," a paper presented at a Liberty Fund symposium on "Justice as Participation: Should Workers Be Given Managerial Rights?" (St. Louis, September 11–13, 1986), p. 1.
2. William E. Simon, et al., *Toward the Future: Catholic Social Thought and the U.S. Economy* (New York: Lay Commission on Catholic Social Teaching and the U.S. Economy, 1984).
3. Ibid., pp. 4–5.
4. Ibid., p. 5.
5. Armen A. Alchian and William H. Meckling, "Comments on 'Pastoral Letter on Catholic Teaching and the U.S. Economy (First Draft),' " a paper presented at a Liberty Fund symposium on national industrial policy organized by the Center for Research in Government Policy and Business, University of Rochester (Key Biscayne, Fla., February 28–March 2, 1985) p. 7.
6. Bishops, "Pastoral Letter," p. 10.
7. For a discussion of how market plans are devised and revised and the problems of replacing markets with central planning, see F. A. Hayek, "Theory of Complex Phenomena" and "The Results of Human Action But Not of Human

Design," *Studies in Philosophy, Politics, and Economics* (Chicago: University of Chicago Press, 1967), chapters 2 and 6. See also Donald Lavoie, "National Economic Planning: What Is Left?" (Washington: Cato Institute, 1985), especially chapters 3 and 5.

8. This point is discussed in some detail, with appropriate references, in Richard B. McKenzie, *Competing Visions*, chapter 5.
9. Dahl, *Preface to Economic Democracy*, p. 97.
10. For an extended discussion of this theme, see Dwight R. Lee, *Political Economy of Social Conflict or Malice In Plunderland* (Los Angeles: International Institute for Economic Research, 1982).
11. Dahl, *Preface to Economic Democracy*, p. 100.
12. Ibid., pp. 104–107.
13. See McKenzie, *Competing Visions*, chapters 2 and 3.
14. See, for example, G. Warren Nutter and Henry Adler Einhorn, *Enterprise Monopoly in the United States: 1899–1958* (New York: Columbia University Press, 1969).
15. John Locke, *Two Treatises on Government: The Second Treatise on Civil Government*, edited by Thomas L. Cook (New York: Hafner Publishing Company, 1947), p. 133.
16. Ibid., p. 139.
17. Ibid., p. 134.
18. Ibid., p. 135.
19. Dahl, *Preface to Economic Democracy*, p. 29.
20. Lichtenberg, "Workers, Owners, and Factory Closings" p. 9.
21. The economic consequences of plant closing restrictions are discussed in detail in Richard B. McKenzie, *Fugitive Industry: The Economics and Politics of Deindustrialization* (San Francisco: Pacific Institute, 1984); and Richard B. McKenzie, ed., *Plant Closings: Public or Private Choices?*, rev. ed. (Washington: Cato Institute, 1984).
22. Simon, et al., *Toward the Future*.
23. Bishops, "Pastoral Letter," pp. 10 and 16–17.
24. Dahl, *Preface to Economic Democracy*, p. 100.
25. Ibid., p. 105.
26. Ibid., p. 129.
27. Ibid.
28. Ibid., p. 132.
29. Ibid., p. 131.
30. Catholic bishops, "Pastoral Letter on Social Teaching and the Economy" (third draft; duplicated, 1986), p. 81.

7

The Unfairness of
Legislated Wages

I have always maintained that a minimum wage of zero is far too high.
This is because it would deny unskilled workers the right to pay for their
on-the-job training and lead to their continued impoverishment.
—Richard Epstein[1]

By almost any national standard, many workers in the United States make abysmally low wages. Their wages are so low that it is understandable why many concerned citizens worry that these hard-working Americans are only marginally better off than unemployed workers. Even when workers earn the legislated minimum wage (set at $3.35 an hour in 1986), they gross only $134 for a forty-hour week, an amount that is slightly less than $7,000 a year and slightly above the official poverty threshold for a single person.

If a minimum wage earner has a nonworking spouse or children, then poverty must be a constant companion. Understandably, many of these minimum wage earners may find little solace knowing that they are still fortunate to have a job that pays far more than many worse jobs in other countries around the world.

The apparent remedy for the low wages and poverty of many American workers is to boost the legislated minimum wage, especially now that the market value of the current minimum wage has been eroded by years of inflation. Indeed, according to supporters of an increase in the legislated minimum wage, "Policy makers should set the minimum wage at $4.33, because that is a level where only a few jobs are lost but where income and work-incentive effects are substantial."[2] It is also the level that would give the official minimum wage the same purchasing power it had in 1981, the last time it was raised.

In addition, a higher minimum wage would not materially affect the employment opportunities of those covered by the law. In the words of advocates of a higher minimum, "The Federal Minimum Wage Commission Study, appointed by President Jimmy Carter, estimated, in its 1981 report, that a 10 percent increase in that wage decreases teen-age employment by 1 percent, and concluded that the employment loss for adults is less than for youths."[3]

Clearly, a heart-wrenching ethical and fairness dilemma undergirds any political debate over legislated solutions to low wages for some Americans. The dilemma is not eased at all by economists' standard textbook argument that legislated minimum wages benefit some workers (those covered workers who retain their jobs) at the expense of others (those covered workers who lose their jobs or cannot find them) because fewer jobs are available.

Is it fair or ethical for government to institute policies, like minimum wages, that knowingly will hurt some while helping others— that will redistribute income among some of the lowest income workers in the country? That is not an easy question to answer. From the perspective of conventional economic analysis, the question poses social tradeoffs that must be politically debated and decided, and there is no particular reason to conclude that legislated minimum wages for the poor, blacks, women, or any other identified group are unfair or, for that matter, socially unwise policies. The question boils down to a question of whose welfare counts the most, those who retain their jobs or those who lose their jobs, and how many people's employment can be sacrificed in the pursuit of improved welfare for others. Aside from declaring that they side with the welfare of some favored group (for instance, those who retain their jobs), economists appear to have no particularly useful expertise in providing an answer.

However, the tradeoff presumed in this question is more theoretical than real. It is founded largely on conventional economic theory that is far more defective than generations of economists have been led to believe. If critical defects in conventional theory are corrected, as is done in this chapter, the perceived social tradeoffs in the minimum wage debate nearly evaporate.* As a result, legislated wages are unfair because everyone (or practically everyone) affected by them is made worse off. It is counterproductive to promote policy based on fairness (let alone efficiency) if legislated minimum wages do not help low-income workers. The following analysis helps to explain why the employment effects of minimum wage laws have been so inconsequential.†

The Effects of Legislated Wages: The Conventional Argument

There are many jokes about economists never reaching a conclusion or never agreeing on a matter—Harry Truman's search for a "one-arm economist" being one of the most familiar.‡ However, with regards to the effects of minimum wage laws, there is considerable agreement in the profession.[4] These laws are notorious for raising the wages of a subset of affected workers, reducing the job opportunities and wages of other workers, increasing the number of people searching for work, swelling the ranks of the unemployed, and causing inefficiency in the allocation of resources.

The predicted effects of minimum wage laws have generally, but not universally, been supported by empirical studies. Finis Welch has recently written, "If there is a general theme to the empirical literature on the subject, it is that the simple theoretical predictions are confirmed. Almost every serious scholar of minimum wages

---

*The qualification "nearly" is added simply because it is unrealistic to believe that a government policy would not benefit someone or some small group of affected workers. The point of the discussion in this chapter, which is that minimum wages do far more damage than is generally believed, still holds. That is to say, many of those people, who are conventionally believed to be better off because they retain their jobs and because they receive higher money wages, are made worse off by legislated minimum wages.

†The analysis will become unavoidably technical at times. Graphs are employed at strategic points in the discussion because they are the best way of making the argument fully convincing to those who have accepted the conventional view of minimum wage laws that has been developed and refined in graphical terms.

‡After hearing conflicting advice from his economic advisors who frequently talked in terms of "on the one hand . . . but then on the other hand," President Truman is reported to have declared in a fit of exasperation, "What this country needs is a good one-arm economist."

would argue (on the basis of available evidence) that wage minimums have reduced employment for those who would otherwise earn low wages, particularly teenagers."[5]

The loss of employment opportunities is explained in three ways. First, some jobs do not produce sufficient market value per hour to cover the minimum wage some workers must be paid.* Second, there are some workers who do not have the necessary skills that would enable employers to make a profit by employing them at the minimum wage. Third, by raising the cost of labor, the minimum wage will cause a substitution of machines for workers.

However, for many persons who oppose the laws on ideological grounds, the long-run employment costs of minimum wages have been uncomfortably small, as revealed by real-world data. Economists have explained the small impact of the laws by noting, for example, that (1) the legislated minimum wage, after all, applies only to a small portion of the total labor market, (2) the demand for menial labor tends to be unresponsive to wage hikes, and (3) the minimum wage is typically not all that far removed from the true market wage for most of the covered workers.

The Market for Menial Workers:
Important Revisions

The conventional line of analysis and policy proposals misses several important but relatively simple points. By its very nature, employment in any labor market is a complex phenomenon. Employment is based on a great variety of potential contract terms and a tremendous assortment of environmental conditions. The money-wage rate paid workers is only one of many dimensions of work. To develop the analysis in its starkest terms, consider an unscrupulous employer who is interested in draining as much profit as possible from his or her workers, and who, therefore, pays his or her workers as little as possible.

---

*A part of the explanation is bound up in the law of diminishing returns, which mandates that beyond some point in hiring workers the additional value of additional workers will begin to decline. At some point additional workers will not produce enough market value to justify the minimum wage.

Such a profit-maximizing employer will, before settling on a wage offer to workers, consider the entire work situation with an objective of minimizing costs and maximizing output. As is fully recognized in much highly sophisticated labor-market theory, the employer can be expected to seek a combination of capital (plant and machinery) and labor that results in the most profits. In addition, he or she will seek to adjust all of the implicit and explicit terms of the labor contract and the environmental conditions of the workplace to maximize the efficiency of labor, given the capital that is employed, and to minimize the effective total wage, including the money wage that may be paid on an hourly basis and the nonmonetary benefits of the workplace environment.*

In less technical terms, an employer can effectively pay workers with dollars, with normal fringe benefits such as prepaid medical care, and with pleasant working conditions that may arise from the installation of air conditioning, noise abatement systems, or those informal musical programs broadcast throughout the workplace. The worker can also be effectively paid with the location convenience of the workplace, the courteousness of the management, the safety of the workplace, chances for on-the-job training, and the production demands of supervisors.

To achieve maximum efficiency and profits from a given expenditure level, the last dollar of cost incurred on, say air conditioning (or any other fringe benefit or condition of work) must reduce the money wage bill or raise company revenues by one dollar. If this marginal condition does not prevail, then the employer can either expand or cut his expenditures on, say, air conditioning and reduce his labor cost, or he can increase his output with the same labor cost. The employer should, on the margin, be indifferent to spending an additional dollar on wages or an additional dollar on air conditioning or some other condition of work.

---

*Indeed, the profit-maximizing employers can be expected to adjust the conditions of work until the last dollar of cost incurred because of the adjustments is just equal to a dollar reduction in the money wage. Given the amount of capital employed and a competitive market, the firm's direct and indirect expenditures on labor (in a market free of government wage interference) can be expected to achieve maximum efficiency. [The mathematics of the relationship between the prices of one factor input and other variable factor inputs is developed in C.E. Ferguson *The Neoclassical Theory of Production and Distribution* (London: Cambridge University Press, 1969) chapter 6.]

The employer's expenditures on different working conditions or fringe benefits will have different effects on supply of and demand for labor. Expenditures on, for example, company picnics may not affect worker productivity. However, since picnics can increase the supply of workers, such expenditures can be offset by a reduction in the company's money wage bill. The profit-maximizing employer will extend the expenditures on picnics up to the point that the last dollar of cost incurred will be just offset by a dollar reduction in the total wage bill that is due to an increase in the supply of labor.

Other changes in working conditions or fringe benefits can affect worker productivity. Worker productivity, for instance, can be increased by the introduction of air conditioning. The firm's expenditures on air conditioning or other work-environment changes will be increased until the additional cost equals the additional revenue received by the productivity improvement plus the reduction in the wage bill. Since each worker will be worth more in terms of output per worker-hour and receive less in money wages, the number of workers demanded should increase, and the firm should be willing to hire more workers at any given wage rate.

When worker productivity rises owing to a change in the workplace or in fringe benefits, the firm's supply of labor may increase or decrease, depending on how the change affects workers' job satisfaction (or dissatisfaction). If the work experience is made more satisfying, more workers should be willing to work for any given wage, that is, labor supply should increase. For similar reasons, the supply of labor should contract with workplace changes that reduce workers' job-related satisfaction. The important points to remember are that an increase in the labor supply can be expected to lead to a reduction in the wage paid and that a decrease in the labor supply can be expected to lead to an increase in the wage rate paid.

This means that when the supply of labor increases, the cost of the change in workplace conditions can be offset by an increase in the productivity of labor or a reduction in the wage that the firm would otherwise have to pay. Alternatively, the supply of workers may be reduced by the workplace change initiated by the employer. However, the change will still be made so long as it adds more to revenue than it adds to cost.

It is also possible that the profit-maximizing employer could voluntarily (that is, without any government encouragement or requirement) make changes in the workplace that reduce the productivity of labor but increase the supply of labor. So long as the reduction in the value of worker productivity lost is less than the reduction in the wage bill, the change is profitable for the firm. Reducing the production demands on employees might also reduce productivity and the market value of workers to the employer. However, it might also increase the attractiveness of work—hence, the supply of labor—and therefore reduce the firm's wage bill.

The central point of the foregoing discussion is that, given all of the possible changes that can be made, the profit-maximizing employer will make those changes that enable him or her to minimize his or her labor cost and maximize profits. Indeed, firms in competitive markets will be forced to find a cost-minimizing combination of capital, labor, fringe benefits, and working conditions. If an employer in a competitive labor market does not achieve the cost-minimizing combination, he or she will be underpriced and the firm will be forced to contract its position or withdraw from the final product market.

The Impact of Minimum Wages

Minimum wage laws establish a legal floor for money wages; however, they do not suppress competitive pressures. These restrictions only cap the pressures in one of the multitude of competitive outlets, namely money wages. More to the point, they do not set a legal minimum for the effective wage (including the money and nonmoney benefits of employment) that is paid workers.

The impact of mandating minimum wages depends upon the ability of the employer to adjust the nonmoney conditions of work or fringe benefits in response to a required pay change. Conventional analysis of minimum wage laws, embedded in economics textbooks, implicitly assumes that money wages are the only form of labor compensation. Hence, when the money wage is set at a legal minimum, employment falls by some amount given by the demand for labor.

Consider the impact of wages as presented in a standard supply and demand graph in figure 7–1, which has the workers' wage rate on the vertical axis and the quantity of labor (or number of workers) on the horizontal axis. The demand for labor curve, labeled D_1, is downward sloping, based on the reasoned argument (implicit in the foregoing discussion) that employers will hire more workers if the wage is reduced. A decrease in the wage rate from a wage rate of, say, W_m to W_o will lead to an increase in the number of workers hired from Q_1 to Q_2. On the other hand, the supply of labor curve, labeled S_1, is upward sloping, based on the argument that more workers will be willing to work at higher wages than at lower wages. Therefore, an increase in the wage rate from, say, W_o to W_m will lead to an increase in the number of workers willing to work from Q_2 to Q_3.

If an acceptable minimum wage is set at W_m in figure 7–1, the quantity of labor demanded falls from Q_2 to Q_1 and the quantity of labor supplied expands from Q_2 to Q_3. According to the conventional view, a surplus of unemployed labor emerges in the market equal to Q_3–Q_1. This is because there is no assumed way employers can react to that surplus of unemployed labor. From this line of analysis, the conclusion is drawn that the effective wage for those who retain their jobs rises by the amount of the increase in their wage rate, the competitive market-wage rate, W_o, minus the minimum wage, W_m. The people who lose their jobs are pushed into lower-paying labor markets or onto the roles of the unemployed. (Again, the unemployment can be conceptually measured by the distance between Q_1 and Q_3.)

This line of analysis may still be fully applicable to those limited number of labor markets in which money is the only form of compensation and in which employers can do little or nothing to change the skill and production demands imposed on workers.* In such cases, minimum wage laws may still have the predicted effect, a labor-market surplus of unemployed menial workers caused by an above-market level of compensation.

---

*Clearly, many minimum wage jobs do not carry standard fringe benefits, such as life and medical insurance and retirement plans. However, most do offer fringes in the forms of the conditions in the work environment, attitudes of the bosses, breaks, frequency and promptness of pay, variety of work, uniforms, use of company tools and supplies, meals and drinks, and precautions against accidents. These fringes are subject to withdrawal when minimum wages are mandated.

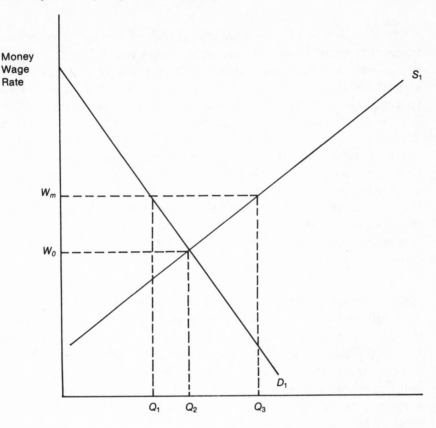

Figure 7-1. *The Conventional View of Minimum Wage Laws*

However, the previous analysis does not consider the possibility that profit-maximizing competitive employers will adjust to the labor market surplus created by the minimum wage law.* It seems highly

---

*Technically speaking, in the analysis that follows, the market demand for the labor curve is constructed, as is conventional, by appropriately summing the demand curves of individual firms. The firm's demand curve for labor is the locus of points obtained from shifts in the value of the marginal product curve, which in turn is due to changes in the variable factor inputs used in conjunction with labor. The market demand curve in the graphical analysis that follows is not, however, equivalent to the curve that represents the full marginal value of labor. The demand curve that is drawn in figure 7–1 is the relationship between the money wage rate and the quantity of labor employed and is the net of the cost per unit of labor of improved working conditions and fringe benefits that equals, on the margin, the value of labor to firms in the market. The demand curve described in figure 7–1, as a function of the money wage, is lower than the true demand curve for labor and is a function of the cost of the fringe benefits that are provided.

reasonable that employers who are capable of paying their workers wages that are too low, because of, for example, antisocial attitudes or competitive pressures, are also quite capable of adjusting other conditions of work in response to the labor market surplus. Indeed, to keep cost-competitive, employers in competitive labor markets will have to adjust to the labor surplus by cutting labor costs in nonwage ways—for example, eliminating workplace picnics, reducing fringe benefits, or increasing production demands.[6] Employers in such labor markets can be expected to reduce their labor costs in nonmoney ways until they are no longer confronted by a surplus— that is, until their labor markets clear once again.* Having said that, the labor market effects of employer nonmoney adjustments made in response to a wage minimum can be discussed briefly in terms of two general cases.

Case I. Changes in Fringe Benefits That Do Not Affect Labor Productivity. Employers can be expected to respond to a minimum wage law by cutting or eliminating those fringe benefits and conditions of work, like workplace parties, that increase the supply of labor but that do not materially affect labor productivity. By reducing such nonmoney benefits of employment, the employer reduces his labor costs from what they would otherwise have been and loses nothing in the way of reduced labor productivity.

Continuation of such nonmoney benefits that affect the supply is made uneconomical by the money wage minimum; they no longer pay for themselves in terms of lower wage rates. Furthermore, employers in highly competitive final products markets must adjust such work conditions to remain competitive and to survive. Otherwise, other firms will lower their labor costs (by contracting or eliminating fringe benefits) and force the employers who retain their fringe benefits and continue to pay the higher minimum wage rate out of their final product markets.

---

*More precisely, the labor markets should, after adjustments, clear more or less to the same extent as they did before the minimum wage law was imposed. Of course, employers are not directly concerned with ensuring that their labor market clears. They are, however, interested in minimizing their labor costs, a motivation that drives them to adjust the conditions of work until the market clears. The point is that if the employer is confronted by more workers than he or she needs, he or she can offer less or demand more until the surplus is eliminated.

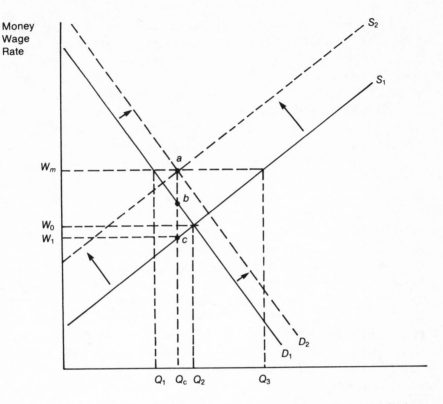

Figure 7-2. *The Revised View of Minimum Wage Laws*

Because of the changes in the work conditions, the supply curve of labor, whose position is partially determined by working conditions and fringe benefits, can be expected to shift upward. The effects of such a supply shift are shown in figure 7-2, which incorporates the supply and demand curves of the previous figure. The vertical shift in the supply curve will be equal to labor's dollar evaluation, on the margin, of the adjustments made in employment conditions. The demand curve for labor will shift upward to the right, reflecting the reduced expenditure per unit of labor on fringe benefits.*

---

*Remember that the demand-for-labor curve is the net of fringe benefits. A reduction in fringe benefits will thereby increase employer's willingness to pay higher wages, which explains the increase in (or shift outward of) the demand for labor.

As before, fringe benefits are provided so long as their cost to the firm per unit of labor is less than the reduced wage rate—so long as labor's evaluation of the fringe benefits lost is greater than the firms' costs. Therefore, the vertical, upward shift in the supply curve will be greater than the vertical, upward shift in the demand curve. In figure 7–2, the vertical shift in the supply curve is ac, and the vertical shift in the demand curve is less, ab.* It is important to note that the market clears, however, at the minimum wage because of secondary market adjustments in fringe benefits. But it is equally important to see that the market clears at a lower employment level, Q_c instead of Q_2.

In other words, the surplus of labor that conventional analysis suggests exists in face of a minimum wage law is eliminated by the shifts in the curves. However, labor is worse off because of the wage floor and adjustments in fringe benefits. After the vertical distance between the two supply curves, ac (which, again, is labor's dollar evaluation of the fringe benefits lost because of the minimum wage) is subtracted from the minimum wage W_m, the effective wage paid labor is reduced to W_1, or by W_0-W_1. In short, when labor is paid in many forms, a minimum wage reduces, not increases, the effective payment going to affected workers.

Conventional analysis suggests that a minimum wage of W_m will cause employment opportunities for labor to fall to Q_1. The adjustments that employers make to nonmoney conditions of work causes employment opportunities to fall by less, to only Q_c in figure 7–2.†

Case II. Changes in Fringe Benefits That Affect Labor Productivity. Because of the surplus that emerges when money wages are set at a legal minimum, employers can increase the production demands that are placed on their workers. The result can be an increase in the productivity of labor; hence, the demand curve for labor can rise.

---

*If the vertical distance of the shift in the supply curve were not greater than the vertical distance of the shift in the demand curve, then the change in fringe benefits would have been made even in the absence of the minimum wage.

†Indeed, if employers had an infinite number of ways to adjust nonmoney conditions of work and the market money wage were a small part of total labor payment, the minimum wage would not significantly affect employment opportunities. When employers have an infinite or even a very large number of ways to pay labor, a change in the money wage by law will not significantly affect the payment options open to employers and the ability of the employers to pay the effective market wage.

Workers who have to deal with the labor surplus must either accept the new demands placed on them or retire from the market. The supply curve falls by the workers' evaluation in money terms of the greater production demands.

The graphical analysis is the same as in the preceding case. The demand for labor, as a function of the wage rate, shifts upward, reflecting the greater productivity of labor. The supply curve contracts by the workers' marginal evaluation of the higher production demands. The employment opportunities for labor can be expected to fall on balance because the minimum-wage law increases the cost of labor relative to other variable resources and induces some substitution of other factors for labor and because the law increases the overall cost of production and reduces the quantity of the final product sold.*

If more of other factors of production are employed in lieu of labor, then a lower output can only be achieved with less labor. However, the lower employment level will, as before, be accompanied by a reduction in the effective wage going to labor.

Employers can also react to the higher wage minimum by making changes in workplace conditions such as air conditioning, which complements labor in production and which, if reduced in use, can lower the productivity of labor.† Firms will make such adjustments so long as the change in the money wage rate is greater than the dollar value of the change in labor productivity. These changes will cause the supply curve of labor to shift until it intersects the demand curve at the minimum wage rate. The effective wage and employment opportunities are then reduced as before.

Differences in Perspective

This analysis conflicts with conventional, textbook treatment of minimum wages in several important respects. First, conventional analysis holds that the effective wage rate increases for some workers,

---

*This assumes implicitly a constant money stock.

†It should be noted that the employer must be careful in cutting back on some fringe benefits like air conditioning. A reduction in air conditioning for workers affected by minimum wage laws can adversely affect higher-paid workers, forcing the firm to raise the wages of the workers who are paid more than the minimum wage. However, this qualification does not affect the thrust of the argument, which is that the employer will make adjustments that are made economical by a legal wage floor.

declines for others. As noted, this is because of the implicit assumption that an increase in the minimum wage rate is equivalent to an increase in the effective wage rate. I conclude, however, that the effective wage rate of all workers, including those who retain their jobs in spite of wage minimums, decreases; they are worse off to the extent that employers have the opportunity to adjust working conditions and fringe benefits. For that reason, minimum wages appear patently unfair to those who are covered by them (even by the standards of many of those who promote legislated wage minimums).

Second, conventional analysis predicts that the market does not clear. At any wage above the competitive wage levels, there will supposedly be an "army of unemployed" equal to the difference between the quantity supplied and the quantity demanded (Q_3-Q_1). From this perspective, some people who want jobs at the higher minimum wage will lose them. The analysis suggests that people who stop work because of the minimum wage do so because they do not want their jobs at the induced lower effective wage rate.

Third, standard textbook treatment of minimum wage laws suggests that measured unemployment from the imposition of wage controls should be in the range of Q_1 to Q_3. (Actual job losses should be the difference between Q_1 and Q_2.) Recognition of the various adjustments employers can make in response to any surplus of labor that develops leads to the conclusion that actual job losses may be quite small*; how small depends on the variety of adjustments that employers can make to fringe benefits, nonwage conditions of employment, and the productivity of alternative ways of paying labor and upon the amount of time employers have to adjust to the wage law.† From the perspective of this new way of looking at the impact of minimum wage laws, it is not at all surprising that

---

*Of course, dispute remains over how small is small, and empirical studies vary in their assessment of the estimated impact of the laws. James Ragan estimated that minimum wage in existence in 1972 resulted in lost employment for approximately 320,000 teenagers. The youth unemployment rate would have been, in the absence of the minimum wage law, 3.8 percentage points lower than it was. See James F. Ragan, Jr., "Minimum Wage Legislation and the Youth Labor Market" (St. Louis: Center for the Study of American Business, Washington University, 1976).

†As indicated in a foregoing footnote, if there were an infinite number of adjustments that employers could make in the nonwage conditions of employment, then an increase in the minimum would, on the margin, have no impact on the effective wage and employment levels. In this extreme case, there would be no loss in labor productivity.

researchers have found that minimum wage laws have decreased employment opportunities little. This is because they have had, on balance, little downward effect on the effective wage paid covered workers.

Fourth, the standard view of minimum wages assumes that unemployment arises because the number of workers willing to work expands (that is, workers move up the market supply curve, S_1 in the figures). However, the exact opposite occurs in this new view: the number of workers willing to work falls (that is, workers move down their supply curve). This is because their effective wage falls. It is also because many, but not necessarily all, of the affected workers have better alternatives in other labor markets, one of which is the markets for contraband and other criminal activities.

Minimum wage laws, in short, make many criminal activities relatively profitable by making money wage deals below the mandated minimum wage illegal. Since minimum wages are likely to lead to a marginal increase in the educational and experience requirements of prospective employees, they will tend to encourage differentially the less advantaged workers into criminal activities.

Regardless of its initial adverse impact on employment opportunities of the covered workers, the magnitude of the effect of any real minimum wage should decrease with time. This is because with the passage of time, employers will discover a growing number of ways to circumvent the laws. In addition, competitive pressures will grow, encouraging more and more employers to find ways of cutting their workers' effective wages.

Fifth, conventional analysis reveals that higher minimum wages place many people (especially those who provide a second family income at the minimum wage) in higher marginal tax brackets. However, the higher tax payments only reduce the net benefit received by those who retain their jobs.

The revisions in the analysis presented here suggest that minimum wages not only throw people into higher tax brackets but also increase the money and, hence, taxable income portion of their effective wage rate. This means that the effective marginal tax rate for people covered by the legal minimum is greater than specified in the tax schedules. The after-tax effective income is actually reduced by more than the drop in the effective wage rate; therefore, when the decrease in effective income is recognized, the total marginal tax rate resulting from all explicit and implicit taxes extracted from affected workers can be greater than 100 percent, which hardly seems in accord with the dictates of a progressive tax rate structure.*

The Politics of Minimum Wages

Until the advent of the Reagan presidency, minimum-wage laws have enjoyed broad-based political support. The broad-based political support for minimum wage legislation has been explained with reference to the contrast between, on the one hand, the concentration of the benefits among a relatively small group of affected workers who, in spite of legal minimums, retain their jobs and, on the other hand, the dispersion of the costs among a relatively large group of consumers who are burdened with higher prices for the goods and services they buy.[7] Also, a cost is incurred by some workers who must accept lower wages or unemployment.

The analysis developed here makes the political support for minimum wages somewhat perplexing. This is because it suggests that in the long run all, or practically all, workers in the covered markets are made worse off. Hence, the political support from workers in the targeted markets must stem from the expected short-run benefits of wage minimums. However, the long-run costs incurred by many workers from legal minimum money wage rates that are held permanently above the market-clearing wage will exceed the short-run

---

*Finally, it should be noted that textbooks conventionally demonstrate that in monopsonistic labor markets, a minimum wage that is imposed at any level between the monopsony wage and the wage at the intersection of the marginal cost of and demand for labor curves will result in an expansion of employment. Further, it is argued that for any employment level between the monopsony and competitive employment levels, two minimum wage levels will result in the same level of employment. However, if the monopsonistic employer can adjust the nonmoney wage benefits of employment, then the analysis of monopsony markets needs to be revised in two respects. First, as in the competitive model, the supply of labor will tend to contract by more than the demand curve expands. An increase in the minimum wage will, therefore, result in a reduction in nonmoney wages, a decrease in the effective monopsony wage, and a decrease in the employment level. Second, a higher minimum wage will always provide employers with a greater incentive to make nonmoney wage adjustments and will lead to a greater decrease in demand for labor than will a lower minimum wage. Therefore, two minimum wage levels cannot result in the same employment levels: the higher minimum wage will always cause a greater reduction in employment opportunities than will a lower minimum wage. In summary, the employment effect of minimum wages will tend to be in the same direction in both competitive and monopsonistic labor markets.

gains and will diminish seriously the number of people who support the legislation. Indeed, the analysis developed in this chapter suggests that many of the affected workers who may be fully informed about the consequences of minimum wages are likely to be political opponents of the legislation.

The political support for minimum wage laws must, it would appear, emanate to a large extent from groups other than those in the targeted markets. These beneficiaries may include workers in labor markets that are not covered by the legal minimum and that, as a result of the legal minimums, experience an increase in their employment opportunities. On these grounds, active political support by unions for minimum wage laws can be appreciated. Further, producers of capital equipment who experience an increase in the demand for their products should also be supporters of minimum wage laws.

Still, the extensive support that minimum wage laws enjoy in many countries is difficult to explain, especially when it is recognized that all, or almost all, affected workers may be made worse off as a consequence of the law and that the employed workers must pay unemployment compensation to the affected workers who decided not to work at the prevailing effective wage. Perhaps those persons who are covered by the legislation attribute the increase in their money wage rate to the "humanitarian concerns" of their political leaders and blame decreases in their nonmoney employment benefits on their employers.

Because of the myriad forces operating in the marketplace, affected employees may not be able to make the connection between the increases in their money wage rate and the decreases in their nonmoney employment benefits. Making such a connection may be particularly difficult when nonmoney benefits of employment are on the increase and when rises in the minimum wage only restrict the increase.

Perhaps the most powerful (but theoretically unsettling) explanation for the political acceptance of wage minimums is that people who support them are simply ignorant of their effects. Economists do not seem to have fully understood the market consequences of the laws. In fact, conventional supply and demand analysis of wage minimums may have misled many politicians into believing that such laws are an effective way of helping one segment of their constituency at the expense of another, smaller segment.*

Concluding Comments

The standard analysis of minimum wage legislation was, perhaps, quite applicable to labor markets for menial labor when it was first developed, a time in which the money wage probably represented a substantially larger portion of the effective wage than it now does. And, as noted, the conventional analysis may still be fully applicable to that limited number of jobs for which money wages are the only form of compensation and changes in skill and production demands are impractical. However, times have changed, nonmoney benefits of employment loom much more prominent in workers' compensation than they used to, and theory must accommodate these adjustments in labor compensation.

This is especially true since jobs have become more technical, requiring more on-the-job training. And training can be construed as a fringe benefit of employment. Such a benefit can, because of minimum wage laws, be less available to lower income workers. With the surplus that emerges in response to minimum wage laws, employers can increase the educational and training demands of their employees, requiring workers to secure the necessary education at a higher expense from off-the-job sources. The minimum wage laws effectively bar workers from paying for training through wage reductions. And this is the reason that Professor Richard Epstein (quoted at the head of the chapter) views a minimum wage of zero as much too high. It makes perfectly reasonable employment behavior uneconomical by effectively making it illegal.

The tax code and rising tax rates over time have, no doubt, been a major reason why a growing percentage of workers' compensation has come in nonmoney forms.† The adjustments in the relative share

---

*As an aside, regardless of the reason the government sees fit to control money wages, it is interesting to note that the minimum wage laws may be one of several factors that induced federal and state governments to attempt to control, through regulatory agencies, the health, noise, and safety conditions of work.

†Fringe benefits became a dramatically more important source of worker compensation during World War II when money wages were strictly controlled. Fringe benefits became a device for circumventing the maximum wage controls.

of nonmoney compensation in employment may have lessened the effectiveness of minimum wages as a redistributed policy tool. They have also increased their unfairness, because they deny tax breaks and income to some of the lower-income workers in this economy.

The central lesson of conventional economic analysis of minimum wage rates is that they promote inefficiency—that is, they reduce the nation's income pie subject to distribution among all citizens. The central lesson of this revised view of minimum wage theory is that they promote unfairness; that is, on balance they reduce the portion of the income pie going to lower income workers. Minimum wage laws can be opposed, as they should be opposed, because they have perverse effects.

There is, however, a much broader lesson to be learned from the nation's experience with minimum wage laws: Well-intended controls of prices can have unintended and, ultimately, perverse consequences. This is because under such control arrangements, markets are not controlled very effectively (and cannot be controlled without major problems encountered in centralized control systems[8]) in their entirety. The pressures of competition still escape in some form, often to the detriment of those the controls are intended to help.

This is the reason—simple fairness, not efficiency, to those who are the intended object of market controls—that controls on tenants' rental payments and price controls of most varieties can be opposed. Controls can hurt those they seek to help, a theme that will be raised again in our following discussion of discrimination and comparable worth laws following in chapter 8. These secondary market adjustments can pose serious efficiency-equity obstacles for movements to decontrol regulated markets, a topic that is reserved for chapter 11.

Notes

1. This is a paraphrase of comments made by Richard Epstein, University of Chicago law professor, in a political economy seminar at Washington University in St. Louis (January 23, 1986).
2. Sar A. Levitan and Issac Shapiro, "The Minimum Wage: A Sinking Floor," *New York Times* (January 16, 1986), p. 19.
3. Ibid.
4. For a conventional textbook discussion of the employment and efficiency effects of minimum wage laws, see Armen A. Alchian and William R. Allen, *University Economics* (Belmont, Calif.: Wadsworth Publishing Company, Inc., 1964), pp.

385–388. For a survey of the scholarly literature on the subject, including empirical assessments of theoretical predictions, see Finis Welch, *Minimum Wages: Issues and Evidence* (Washington: American Enterprise Institute, 1978) and Keith B. Leffler, "Minimum Wages, Welfare, and Wealth Transfers," *Journal of Law and Economics* (October 1978), pp. 345–358. Leffler makes the interesting but perverse argument that the poor have a demand for minimum wages because of the positive effect that minimum wages have on welfare benefits.

5. Finis Welch, "The Rising Impact of Minimum Wages," *Regulation* (November/December 1978), pp. 33–34.

6. These predictions have been supported by empirical research. See Wessle, *Economic Inquiry* (to be completed).

7. F. G. Stendle, "The Appeal of Minimum Wage Laws and the Invisible Hand in Government," *Public Choice* (Spring 1973), pp. 133–136; William R. Keech, "More on the Vote Winning and Vote Losing Qualities of Minimum Wage Laws," *Public Choice* (Spring 1977), pp. 133–137.

8. For an elaboration of the problems created by broad-based efforts to centrally control the full breadth of markets, see Richard B. McKenzie, *Competing Visions: The Political Conflict over American Economic Future* (Washington: Cato Institute, 1985), chapter 5.

8
The Discrimination of
Comparable Worth

In a fundamental but limited respect, "fair chances" amount to "equal opportunity." Each person is assured that the claims to economic value assigned to him are determined by elements *within himself* and by chance factors that affect all persons *equally*.
                                                              —James Buchanan[1]

S ocial philosopher and economist Frank Knight once wrote that our ability to earn a living is "based upon a complex mixture of inheritance, luck, and effort, probably in that order of relative importance."[2] Unfortunately, Knight noted, only effort has any ethical validity because the moral merit of what we earn must have at least some remote connection to what we, not circumstances, do.

The luck component of our earning capacity is not only wedded to those ways our incomes are accidentally increased or decreased by more than expected; it is also critically dependent upon where we happened to be born and reared, or, more specifically, under what economic and political system we can try to earn a living. Those of us who happened to be born in the United States have been immensely lucky, for had we been conceived just about anywhere else in the world, our expected incomes unquestionably would have been (on average, at least) much lower than they actually have been and will continue to be.

Our incomes in the United States depend substantially on the market system that was developed long before we appeared. The market system gave rise to the physical and human capital stock on which we draw today, and that gives us and others incentives to produce efficiently and to coordinate our work with many others around the globe. Economists have long stressed that in this market economy we luckily have at our command, our income shares also depend on our marginal contribution to the country's total product, given the system and given the capital stock more or less in place when we arrived on the scene.* The importance of our personal contributions to our welfare relative to the importance of the contribution of the system itself to our welfare can be assessed conceptually by imagining how much we might earn if any one of us were relocated to Tobago or some similarly primitive economy. If we were so transported, most of us would probably live no better than Crusoe did.

Admittedly, when luck is so prominent in determining people's earnings, the distribution of income is hard to justify on fairness grounds. This is especially true for the market system, which prescribes the rules for the process by which incomes are determined. It would appear, therefore, that the fairness of the market system must hinge on the extent to which people consent to the rules of the market process. If they agree to the rules as being fair, then the results should be construed as more or less fair, a concept of fairness that has emerged in earlier chapters. Some may earn more than others (partially because some are luckier than others) as a result of the agreed upon process, but that may have been anticipated and considered acceptable, given the agreed-upon rules. The chance factor that James Buchanan mentions in the quotation at the head of this chapter may be of no particular concern if such a factor could equally affect all within the system (or were not warped to favor some particular people by the rules that are the subject of agreement).

Many political efforts to redistribute the nation's income are founded in part on nothing more noble than private interests, strictly defined, and private greed. Some people simply want more than they have and freely obscure their greedy intentions behind rhetorical veils of moral indignation about the unfairness of the income distribution.

---

*Wages in a competitive labor market tend to equal the marginal contribution (or "marginal revenue product," to use economic jargon) of the last additional worker hired. This is because employers will extend their hiring so long as their workers' marginal contribution to revenues exceeds the wage paid. Since the marginal contribution of workers declines with an increase in their number, there is a point at which the last additional worker hired adds only enough to additional revenues to cover his or her wage. Beyond that point a further expansion of employment is no longer justified, since the wage paid would then exceed the contribution of additional workers to the revenues. For a more detailed discussion of these points and how wages are determined in competitive markets, see Richard B. McKenzie, *Economics* (Boston: Houghton Mifflin Co. 1986), chapter 26.

(People often become distressed at the results of every game even if they considered the rules fair before the play of the game was begun and the results were known.) Still, concern about the fairness of official and unofficial rules of the market process appears to propel many claims of unfairness of the system itself. Some people obviously believe that many rules work, as intended, to the detriment of others and that many participants in the market process do not adhere to the agreed-upon rules.

A case in point are claims of the unfairness of labor market discrimination. For our purposes, labor market discrimination means an employment action based on assessments of the market worth of individuals by reference to characteristics of identified groups into which the individuals may be arbitrarily included. Individual blacks, for example, may be thought to be poorly educated and unproductive not because they individually have exhibited such characteristics, but because blacks as a group are believed, rightly or wrongly, to be less educated or productive than whites or other races. Similarly, individual women may be judged to be uncompetitive or without clearly defined career objectives because women in general are, rightly or wrongly, believed to exhibit such characteristics.

This chapter focuses on how this type of market discrimination may emerge and be tempered by market forces. The central question addressed is not whether discrimination (which we may all agree, for purposes of argument, if nothing else) is unfair in some forms and under some circumstances, but whether the rules of the market process systematically modulate the forces of discrimination sufficiently to avoid recommended governmental means of correcting discrimination.

Of course, to make the examination complete, we must also evaluate the ways governments have sought to correct market discrimination. The world is full of imperfections, so we cannot allow ourselves to evaluate the unfairness of market results devoid of real-world assessments of how government seeks to correct discrimination. The discussion focuses on sexual discrimination, but the principles developed apply generally to other forms of discrimination.

Scarcity and the Necessity of Discrimination

The world is replete with discrimination of all kinds for one simple reason: We as individuals and groups cannot do and have all that we want. Choices are inevitable in a world of scarcity, and those choices are founded on discriminatory preferences and actions. It is an immutable fact of life that we must somehow decide what we do, and we often make picks of products, friends, and jobs based on relatively few discriminatory characteristics: color, size, shape, smell, and softness, for example.

When we walk into a store, we go to certain counters and products because clues tell us how our shopping time will be spent most productively. And in the process, we often totally ignore many counters and products that, if they were considered with care, would, at times, result in superior purchases. We discriminate—rationally and understandably. Most of us would probably agree that it is altogether appropriate for society to adopt an economic system that encourages consumers, investors, workers, and employers to be discriminating.

Most forms of discrimination are generally of little concern because they encourage the wise and efficient management of resources, meaning that, on balance, they do not tend to reduce the welfare of others. Indeed, most forms of discrimination are the product of competitive market forces at the same time that they are a source of competitive market forces.

Competitors who do not get sales because of discriminating buyers are, of course, hurt by the discrimination in those instances. However, most are compensated for their losses in identified settings by the system that allows and encourages discrimination, a point of major concern in chapter 4. Most receive offsetting benefits from the products they buy whose prices are lower and quality higher because of other discriminating consumers and buyers. Labor market discrimination is a different matter, or so many maintain is the case for the sexual and racial discrimination observed in labor markets. There is a sense in antidiscrimination arguments that racial and sexual discrimination is not generally offset by competitive forces elsewhere in the economy.

Without dispute, discrimination exists in labor markets. Some labor market discrimination is patently vicious, based on hatred and ignorance. However, much is not. Some labor-market discrimination is based on simple but sound economic principle that employers and employees pursue their goals in the most cost-effective manner. After all, selecting employees with the right, or at least tolerably suitable, skills is a costly process for most employers. This is because information about employees' skills and their likely contributions to the production process is scarce and difficult to acquire.

Employers may discriminate—choose people based on group characteristics—to reduce their recruitment costs, recognizing that judging individuals by perceived characteristics of their groups will at times lead to mistakes (wrong or unproductive employees) and will also prove over time to be more cost-effective than if the costs of more rigorous recruitment systems were incurred. In the process, however, some individual workers will be discriminated against: They will receive a wage that is not comparable to that of their colleagues who are less productive (or who contribute less to the goals of the business or organization.)

To see this point more clearly, consider figure 8–1, in which the distribution of men and women workers is plotted according to their perceived (hypothetical) productivity along the horizontal axis. The bell-shaped curves indicate that most men and women workers are clustered around a mean productivity level for their gender.

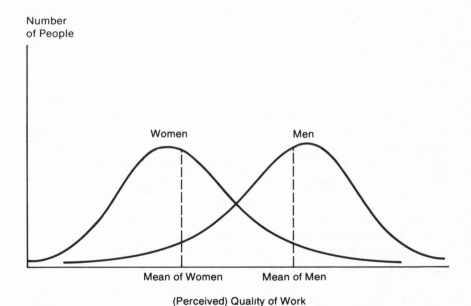

Figure 8–1. *(Perceived) Quality, Distributions of Women and Men*

For purposes of discussion, we assume that the mean productivity level for men is assumed, rightly or wrongly, by all employers to
be higher than the mean productivity level for women. The central
point of the graph, which is that if employers hire their workers more
or less randomly (with little or no information about the workers'
individual skills), the employers will on average obtain a higher average productivity from the men they hire than from the women they
hire.

Under the circumstances described in the figure, we would expect employers to be willing to pay men on average a higher wage
than women (or women a higher wage than men if the relative positions of the men and women distribution were reversed). In the
process, there will be highly productive women in the upper end of
the female distribution who receive a lower wage than their male
counterparts who may be on the lower end of their sex's distribution
(and may actually be below the average productivity for women as a
group).

Let us agree that such a result is unfair, violating the principle
that says that equals should be treated more or less as equals or that
people's pay should generally match their relative worth to their
employers. However, before we jump to the judgment that the
market system in which private-individual judgments prevail should
be subverted by governmental-collective means, there are several
points that must be considered.

First, as noted above, highly detailed information about individual employees' actual position on the productivity spectrum can be
very costly to employers. A system that requires employers to judge
prospective employees exclusively on the basis of their own individual merits will be a system that increases the resources used in
employment and, consequently, reduces the resources available for
expanding the community's total income. Such a requirement may
improve relative positions of employees at the same time that it
undercuts their absolute income standing. It is not at all certain that
such a requirement would result in anything the people involved,
men and women alike, would agree is social betterment.

Second, any social system, such as a market system, must ultimately be judged in terms of how it systematically forestalls or elimi-
nates social evils such as labor-market discrimination compared with

its viable institutional alternatives, for example, comparable pay systems organized by governments, the central concern of following sections of this chapter.

Women's groups hold an understandable disdain for discrimination against their sex, especially when the wage gap seems wide. As acknowledged, labor market discrimination can be caused by suppression and oppression of women and can be a source of depression among women. However, the often quoted statistic that women earn approximately 59 percent of the wages of men is, for two important reasons, a grossly inaccurate measure and a misleading assessment of labor market discrimination and the extent to which free and open competitive markets suppress discrimination.

First, numerous scholarly studies show that the wage rate differential between the sexes can be partially, if not substantially, explained by such factors as differences in age, education, work experience, occupational concentration, career orientation, competitiveness, career interruptions, and cultural backgrounds.[3] These studies do not prove the absence of discrimination; they never could. Nevertheless, the studies strongly suggest that the extent of the labor market discrimination is nowhere near as great as one might suspect by comparing the raw wages earned by men and women.

Second, labor markets as a system must be assessed in part by the extent to which markets eliminate discriminatory tendencies of employers. It is a curious logic that leads many people to believe that "greedy capitalistic employers" would systematically be inclined to forego profitable opportunities in order to hire more expensive men. It would appear that greedy capitalists would be the first to forego their prejudices and hire women who are just as productive as men but who earn a lower wage than men. Such opportunists would be able to outproduce and underprice their prejudiced competitors.

Where significant unwarranted discrimination exists, competitive market forces would lead to an increase in the demand for female workers and to a decrease in the demand for male workers. Relatively speaking, the wages of women would rise and the wages of men would fall. Markets are not perfect, but the fairness case for them is founded partially on the proposition that they do contribute to the elimination of unfairness in pay. Over time, the pay provided to different workers should move toward comparability, as the market participants judge comparability. Again, we should judge the system by how much it accomplishes and how its accomplishments stack up with the fairness of other pay systems.

Yet some pay equity advocates argue that men conspire to suppress the wages of women. If this were flagrantly the case, women in free and open competitive markets could form their own companies and could hire all or mostly women, taking advantage of their special insight about the relative productivity and pay of women and men, and run their male-dominated competitors out of business. The result again should be an increase in the relative wages of women or a decrease in the relative wages of men.

Still, social analysts may fear that women do not have the financial resources to go into business and compete with male-dominated firms. Such a reaction, however, conflicts with the fact that women control more than half of the country's financial assets. Furthermore, it would seem that male and female investors, especially those intent on maximizing their profits, would eagerly invest in companies that demonstrate a profit potential founded on the employment of equally productive women.

The point of this line of argument is not that markets are devoid of prejudice and discrimination. Rather, the point is that free and open labor markets, as social devices for allocating worker time, do not always exacerbate discrimination. Competition in open markets reduces people's tendency to impose their individual preferences on others. To that extent, markets work for the interest of the women's movement. Free and open competitive labor markets may be women's (or any other suppressed groups') greatest social asset in the fight against prejudice and discrimination. We say "may" because we have not yet considered a governmentally backed comparable-pay system. If the system is not sufficiently free and open, then it should be made more free and open.

Is Comparable Worth a Crazy Idea?

While a member of President Ronald Reagan's Council of Economic Advisors, William Niskanen ruffled the feathers of White House chief aides several times for what they considered to be unnecessarily blunt discussions of the Reagan administration's economic policies. In the fall of 1984, he managed to outdo himself by declaring that the concept of comparable worth is a throwback to medieval times and "a truly crazy idea." Media analysts and women's rights advocates, however, suggested that what was crazy was Niskanen: He was crazy to have raised such a sensitive political issue in the midst of the presidential campaign and crazy for not being more sensitive to the concerns of women.

Democratic presidential candidate Walter Mondale used Niskanen's comment as an opportunity to characterize Ronald Reagan and his advisers as virtually "hopeless" when it comes to issues of fairness. After all, comparable worth is the patently simple proposition that people receive equal pay for jobs involving more or less comparable responsibilities.

Nurses, in other words, should be paid comparably to teachers, and secretaries should be paid on par with truck drivers—if those jobs are deemed comparable. Few can disagree with the social objective of comparable worth advocates. Achieving comparable pay for comparable worth is nothing less than noble—given the repeated use of comparable. To do otherwise would seem grossly unfair, since it would suggest that equals are not equals or that we ought to dispense with fairness in discussing wages. It would defy reason to declare that which is comparable to be incomparable.

When any argument is founded on such patently "obvious" conclusions, we must wonder if the reasoning is truly sound and whether it is a sound foundation for building a sense of social fairness. All too frequently obvious conclusions obscure the full complexity of the problem of achieving even a semblence of fairness in a multifaceted society that seeks a host of other conflicting social virtues, not the least of which is a modicum of individual freedom without systematic discrimination.

To begin to understand Niskanen and other opponents of comparable worth, we must first acknowledge that agreement on broad social objectives does not make specific policy proposals sane and workable. General agreement can mask considerable disagreement over what constitutes comparable worth and even comparable pay. This is especially true because the concepts of comparable worth and pay are nowhere near as objective as some might think.

Jobs require collections of skills and attributes, all of which have different values to the same people under different circumstances and to different people under the same circumstances (even if we could agree on what "same" and "different" people and circumstances are). The task of judging comparability in jobs is no less difficult than judging the comparability of different shopping carts filled by different shoppers. The problem of establishing the comparability of jobs, as well as shopping carts, is made even more difficult by the fact that the value of purchases of people's collection of skills, as with shopping carts, depends upon the prices (or wages) that are charged.

The task of establishing comparability among the millions of different jobs in this country is enormous, far more complex than appears to be imagined by comparable worth advocates. The job of a secretary must not only be evaluated relative to the job of a truck driver but also to the jobs of a draftsman and a child care worker. Jobs that are viewed as comparable to a truck driver's job must also be judged in terms of their comparability with secretarial work, if, again, secretarial and truck driving jobs are considered comparable. Of course, there must be some sense of consistency in the relative rankings of all incomparable occupations.

Establishing equal (or comparable) pay is also a deceptively simple problem. As emphasized repeatedly in previous chapters, worker compensation obviously varies not only in terms of salaries, but also in fringe benefits, flexibility of working schedules, difficulty of assignments, risk of accidents and failures, ability to relocate within the same profession, community status and recognition, and a host of other factors that must be subjectively evaluated by people who are actually in the labor market. Even then, we must recognize that our listing of job descriptions masks an immense variety of degrees and variation in what people do for a living and what employers pay to have done.

The conditions of work and pay can, of course, be appraised by people outside the market process, such as by judges, juries, and teams of consultants and labor department experts. But we must wonder if the substitutions of such evaluations are any better, even in terms of fairness, than the evaluations of the people—both employees and employers—actually in the market. They are necessarily subjective in spite of all the facts and figures that may be assembled. Such an evaluation process must rely on fragile and limited democratic and bureaucratic institutions that can be silly as well as slow. In addition, by centralizing and collectivizing decisions, an equal or comparable pay system can impose demands on the intelligence of evaluators that just cannot be done by them in anything approaching a reasonable, nonarbitrary, and consistent manner. We must wonder, in the final analysis, if people can be as smart as a comparable-worth system requires.

Of course, decisions can readily be made to equalize the paychecks of nurses and teachers or secretaries and truck drivers. But such decisions do not mean that total compensation will actually be equalized, for the pay rulings may not adequately account for the nonmoney benefits received by the workers in the different jobs. The resulting total compensation in money and nonmoney forms may be just as unequal after the rulings as before, and may be no more firmly grounded in broadly recognized social ethics or a vision of fairness.

Proponents of comparable pay fail to understand that wages and working conditions established in more or less competitive markets will adjust in response to political efforts to equalize pay. If a pay board determines that secretaries should be paid as much as truck drivers, a market surplus of secretaries can be expected, both because fewer secretaries will be demanded by employers and because more people will be attracted into the secretarial labor market.

Employers, who are willing and able to pay their secretaries less than truck drivers to begin with because of market conditions, can be expected to react to the emerging surplus of secretaries. For example, they may reduce the fringe benefits their secretaries receive or, if they cannot do that, demand that their secretaries have greater skills and work harder and according to more rigid schedules. Secretaries with limited skills will be forced out of the secretarial labor market and into a labor market with less demand. The less preferred group will hardly consider the results fair.

The wage benefits received by some secretaries will be acquired at the expense of other, most likely lower-income, secretaries. The principle is that the very people who are the object of the comparable worth political drives may then be the object of covert discrimination.*

These problems may be partially rectified by government mandated quotas. But then we must wonder how the government can determine what the quotas should be and how it can enforce them without draining resources from other social programs that may also be designed in part to achieve greater social justice. More important, we must worry that quotas cannot be fair for the simple reason that they amount to the type of sex discrimination that is the object of remedy.

Employers will, of course, have to fear continually that their employment and pay decisions on work comparability will be declared illegal and subjected to fines and penalties. This means that they will often be placed in a position of having to second-guess official pay panels that must rule *ex post* on the justice and legality of the established pay structures.

The point of these arguments is not that comparable pay advocates do not have their hearts in the right place. Rather, the point is that laudable policy proposals sometimes have consequences that conflict with their advocates' intentions. Such is the case with comparable pay. Mr. Niskanen could have been more tactful, but not more forthright.

The Incomparability of Comparable Worth Systems

Opponents of market-determined wages often maintain that a comparable pay system organized through government is a "disciplined, objective process for rank-ordering jobs on an agreed compensable

---

*A major point of this discussion is that comparability requirements may actually encourage discrimination in many instances. An official ruling that two jobs are comparable or that given groups of men and women workers are comparable does not eliminate the belief, rightly or wrongly held, that certain categories of people should be paid more than others because of their presumed or measured greater productivity. When asked to choose among prospective employees from the two groups, employers will naturally choose the more productive, thereby increasing the employment opportunities of the more productive and decreasing the employment opportunities of the less productive. For a discussion of the employment effects of equal-pay-for-equal-work laws in supply and demand curve terms, see McKenzie and Tullock, *The New World of Economics*, chapter 16.

value scale."[4] Supposedly, such a process yields accurate and consistent pay rankings—or, at least, more accurate and consistent than the systems they replaced. However, that is a highly dubious conclusion.

In a survey of several comparable pay systems instituted by or proposed to states, Richard Burr found that comparable pay systems are fraught with problems, not the least of which is that comparability does not seem to have any clear meaning to the people who must establish comparability in pay.[5] Burr determined from examining several actual state pay systems that what jobs are deemed comparable or incomparable depend on who does the comparing, how workers describe their jobs, and a host of political considerations that influence what jobs are evaluated and how many points they are assigned. When the evaluation process is undertaken by nine or so representatives of the workforce, it is clearly of some interest exactly who is chosen as representatives, how much time is allowed for the evaluation process, and what types of statistical procedures are deemed appropriate.

Burr uses figure 8-2, which depicts the points three states give to five jobs classifications, to drive home his central point that comparable pay systems lack the accuracy, consistency, and even comparability they supposedly seek. As can be seen in the figure, Vermont's ratings for all job categories, except for librarians, is higher than Iowa's and Minnesota's. Indeed, a social worker is more valuable in Vermont than any of the other sampled jobs in the other two states.

However, a nurse is rated more highly in Iowa than in Minnesota or Vermont, and a librarian is rated more highly in Minnesota than a social worker in Iowa. For that matter, a beautician is rated more highly in Vermont than a social worker is in Iowa or a librarian in Iowa. Confused because of a lack of sense to the ratings across states? If you are, you may understand why Burr concluded, "In short, comparable worth evaluations of jobs are anything else but 'comparable' in practice. The 'worth' ascribed to comparable jobs in the different states are not consistent. As a result, any unbiased party surely must question whether comparable worth truly can deliver on its promises of a scientific, objective determination of a job's worth."[6]

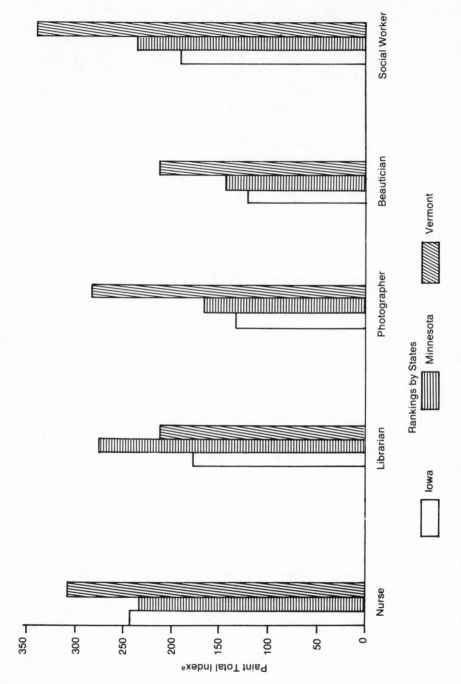

Figure 8–2. *How State Job Evaluations Stack Up against One Another*

Source: Richard E. Burr, *Are Comparable Worth Systems Truly Comparable?* (St. Louis: Center for the Study of American Business, Washington University, 1986).

Concluding Comments

The comparable rights debate is charged with rhetoric of sexism, a veil that tends to confuse opposition to government intervention in labor markets to equalize wages of men and women as support for discrimination. The point of this chapter (or even the rest of the book) is not that markets as they exist today are ideal by any stretch of the imagination. On the contrary, discrimination exists and should be minimized. Nonetheless, to evaluate markets properly we must scrutinize how they will adjust to interventionist measures to ensure they can actually correct the acknowledged problem in ways that are deemed fair. A major function of this chapter has been to explain why not all women support the policy agenda of advocates of comparable worth. Feminist economist Jennifer Roback has concluded that "comparable worth, far from being a help to women, will in fact seriously hinder some of the most important goals that women have established for themselves in the late 20th century."[7]

Clearly, much of the analysis in this chapter is based on competitive models of labor markets that are not fully represented in real world marketplaces. One reason for using such models is prescriptive; that is, if we want discrimination to be minimized, we should consider making labor markets as competitive as possible by eliminating barriers to entry and exit—that is, by ensuring that people have equal access, not equal or comparable pay. This means that government should assume its conventional role of making sure, to the extent feasible, that markets are as open and free as they can be. If people are able to move among jobs reasonably freely, a check will be imposed on people's abilities to judge people arbitrarily and people —employers and employees—can together decide whether their wages are comparable by deciding to stay put, if they are, or move, if they are not.

Notes

1. James M. Buchanan, *Liberty, Market and State: Political Economy in the 1980s* (Washington Square, N.Y.: New York University Press, 1985), p. 140.
2. Frank H. Knight, *The Ethics of Competition* (Chicago: University of Chicago Press, 1935), p. 56.

3. For a quick review of the empirical findings of several of these studies, see Richard B. McKenzie and Gordon Tullock. *The New World of Economics*, 3rd ed. (Homewood, Ill.: Richard D. Irwin, 1981), chapter 16.
4. Alvin Bellak, "Comparable Worth: A Practitioner's View," Hay Management Consultants booklet prepared for the U.S. Commission on Civil Rights (June 6–7, 1984), p. 3.
5. Richard E. Burr, *Are Comparable Worth Systems Truly Comparable?* (St. Louis: Center for the Study of American Business, Washington University, 1986).
6. Ibid., p. 3.
7. Jennifer Roback, "A Skeptical Feminist Looks at Comparable Worth," *Cato Policy Report* (July/August 1986), p. 6.

Part IV
Fairness and
the Welfare State

———

9

The Conservative Case for the Contained Welfare State

The tools of politics . . . [are] to extract resources from the general tax-payer with minimum offense and to distribute the proceeds among innumerable claimants in such a way as to maximize support at the polls. Politics, so far as mobilizing support is concerned, represents the art of calculated cheating—or more precisely how to cheat without *really* getting caught.

—James Schlesinger[1]

The U.S. welfare system has always been the object of heated political conflict. The policy debates have most often been conducted between the political extremes—between the left and right or liberals and conservatives—as if the policy contestants have harbored radically different human values and incompatible social goals for humankind.

The proponents of welfare are frequently characterized as "bleeding hearts," recklessly spending other people's money to satisfy their own heartfelt moral obligations toward others. Welfare opponents, on the other hand, are just as often described as cold-hearted egoists who do not understand the needs of others less fortunate than they and who are too greedy to willingly help others at their own expense.

In short, the welfare debates are all too often conducted as a battle between those who care for others and those who do not. And its political context all too often drives people to adopt the rhetoric, if not the substance, of the political extremes. The opposing political sides in Washington or other seats of government understand that political power ultimately means that some (for example, welfare recipients) will gain at the expense of others (for example, taxpayers) and that the actual policy outcomes (who gains and loses and by how much) will be influenced significantly by whose case is made most dramatic and stark.[2] Casual observers are left to deduce that the schism separating our political leaders and policymakers is broader and deeper than it may really be.

In this chapter the terms of debate are tempered with two primary arguments. First, the welfare state is not only desirable but most likely necessary for the continued collective acceptance of the market system. Welfare, albeit limited in scope and amount, meets goals of efficiency (as economists define efficiency) as well as equity and fairness. Second, the welfare debate typically misses the real issue that forces the debate in the first place because it frequently focuses almost exclusively on the effectiveness of welfare payments and on the motivations of the proponents and opponents. The issue is how does society control the welfare state once all, or virtually all, acknowledge that a welfare state is desirable and necessary?

A central point is that opposition to welfare among many, if not most, conservatives stems not so much from a genuine hostility toward or lack of concern for the poor, but the exact opposite—a genuine fear that the welfare state will be uncontained and that an uncontained welfare state will hurt the poor, the professed central concern of welfare state advocates. From the perspective of many conservatives, the social problem of helping the poor in the long run is one of appropriately regulating government, as opposed to regulation by government.

The Efficiency Case for the Welfare State

Economists have long argued for government-sponsored welfare (meaning poverty relief) on efficiency grounds. Poverty relief is said to correct for a misallocation of resources that will emerge when aid to the poor is the consequence of individual, as opposed to collective, actions. As will be demonstrated, economists' efficiency arguments for welfare ultimately mean the welfare state must be contained or circumscribed by restrictions on how much public aid will be provided. Otherwise, many nonpoor people will be beneficiaries of the aid and many poor people will receive curtailed aid.

Welfare as a Public Good

Welfare has been construed as a classic example of a public good, the benefits of which are externalized to all, or virtually all, within the relevant community.[3] If the poor are provided with aid, then non-poor community residents benefit (or capture external benefits) as well. For example, nonpoor residents' "hearts are warmed" by the aid[4] or by the extent to which the aid leads to less crime and more beautification of impoverished neighborhoods.[5]

Economists conventionally have argued that without governmentally provided welfare, involving forced taxation, many nonpoor community residents who benefit from the welfare system will "free ride" on the generosity of others. This is because the external benefits are received by others regardless of how much they contribute to the aid of the poor. Each potential donor can reason that because of his or her relative unimportance in the context of the entire community, his or her contribution or lack of contribution to aiding the poor will not materially affect the overall level of the poor's well-being and, thereby, his or her own well-being. Because his or her voluntary contribution will most likely be inconsequential, the rational course of action for each individual acting alone is to do nothing or practically nothing.

The potential for widespread free riding convinces many economists to argue that the amount of poverty aid given privately will be suboptimal. Suboptimal aid means, in effect, that less aid will be given than all or virtually all nonpoor people within the community would collectively like to see provided to the poor. Forced welfare contributions can be socially beneficial in the same sense that forced police protection or smallpox vaccination can be. Accordingly, taxpayers do not necessarily see coercion as bad.

Although the public-goods argument for public charity has theoretical merit, it also has serious problems that may make policymakers reluctant to accept it as a basis for welfare.[6] The public-goods argument can also be used to provide state-sponsored aid for many nonpoor, particularly those who do not want to see state involvement in poverty relief. After all, such people suffer external costs by poverty relief that make them feel uneasy. These external costs suffered by the opponents of welfare are no less important, as far as the consistent application of theory is concerned, than the external benefits received by the welfare supporters.

To make the welfare system fully efficient (as economists conceive of efficiency in public policy), the welfare state must necessarily be extended to compensate many nonpoor, those who oppose welfare for the poor or anyone else because of the (psychic or other) costs they incur.* Otherwise, the amount of aid will be superoptimal, or more than that which achieves community consensus.†

While the previous analysis may explain why the contemporary welfare state encompasses welfare benefits that go to people other than those who are truly poor, it also explains the prevailing discontent with the amount of aid actually going to the truly poor. The cost of the welfare system, including the expenditures on the nonpoor, induces or unwittingly permits a reduction in aid available to the truly poor. Because of the aid going to the nonpoor, taxpayers have less income to spend on aid to the truly poor and are induced to spend less on the truly poor to reduce the amount of compensating aid going to the nonpoor. In other words, the conventional economic argument for poverty relief leads to the conclusion that aid going to the poor will be restricted because of a failure to contain the scope of the welfare state to those who, by the standards of misfortune, need the aid.

The Efficiency of Welfare in a Market System

Many proponents and opponents of public charity seem to think welfare remains incompatible with the philosophical dictates of a market system. However, aid to the poor can be fully consistent with the efficiency requirements of the market system.

The market, as a system for allocating resources and goods, is supported by its advocates because it is not only cost effective, but also Pareto efficient. This loosely means that the welfare of all, or virtually all, in the community will in the long run, over a sequence of events and outcomes in an endless variety of markets, be made better off. In its more restrictive sense, Pareto efficiency requires that

---

*In economists' jargon, those who want to see public welfare have positive demands for aiding the poor. Those who dislike welfare have negative demands. Those with positive demands must pay a tax-price, while those with negative demands must receive a payment (a negative tax-price) to make the system efficient. An efficient system is conventionally viewed as one under which the price paid or received by each in the collectivity equals the individual's marginal evaluation. Alternately, the efficient system is one in which the price paid or received is adjusted until all agree on the amount of aid given.

Actually, the amount of aid must be further extended to include aid to those who do not like to see nonpoor opponents of welfare receive payments from the government treasury.

†The real concern is that the collective marginal value of some amount of the poverty relief to all community residents will exceed the social costs of the relief.

the welfare of some be improved without reducing the welfare of others at the same time. The market system is, in other words, a positive-sum game for everyone, or practically everyone.

Pareto efficiency in the adoption of the market system does not require that no one is ever harmed, just that no one is ever harmed on balance over the long run and over the course of a sequence of market events. Clearly, one of the most aggressively touted features of markets is that they promote and accommodate changes; markets are, in other words, dynamic and adaptable.

Because the market system is dynamic and adaptable, it can lead and has led in the long run to an increase in aggregate wealth of nations, a point that has been fully appreciated by economists ranging from Adam Smith to Karl Marx. To that extent, the market system holds out the hope of welfare improvements for everyone.

Just as clearly, at various points in time and in narrowly identified markets, changes in market forces result in a plethora of harms to individual market participants. Some producers are harmed when competitors discover more cost-effective methods of production or develop improved products. Some domestic workers are harmed when foreign firms introduce cheaper products, when robots are developed to take their jobs, and when the dollar appreciates in terms of foreign currencies and increases the competitiveness of foreign producers. Some consumers are harmed when other consumers increase their demands for certain products, diverting resources and raising product prices.

By the standard of Pareto efficiency, many, if not most, individual market changes are hardly Pareto efficient. They help some while hurting others. Opponents of the market system have, of course, effectively focused their criticism on the consequences of individual market changes. They emphasize the distress faced by steelworkers unemployed because of plant closings, by farmers bankrupt by falling crop prices, and by children who are abused by their unemployed parents. In spite of economists' blackboard demonstrations with supply-and-demand curves, individual markets can rarely adjust to changes in market forces and make the adjustments fully efficient, as economists define that term.

The recognition of harms in individual markets is not to say, however, that the system is inefficient. While some producers, workers, and consumers are harmed by competitive changes in their own markets, they are helped by changes in many other markets. They are able to buy more attractive resources, goods, and services at lower prices. A steelworker may be out of work for many weeks because of his plant's closing, but in spite of his suffering during those weeks of unemployment, his lifetime income can be greater than otherwise because of the competitive forces in all other markets that ultimately improve the purchasing power of the unemployed steelworker. The farmer who occasionally has to sell below cost can benefit similarly through the improved purchasing power of his lifetime income, net of all temporary losses.

The case for the market system hinges critically on the contention that for virtually all people the gains received from all market adjustments over the long run will exceed the costs they incur from adverse market changes in their own markets. Most will be like the steelworker and the farmer over the long run when all relevant market changes, not just the adverse market changes, have been considered.

As the length of the relevant time period over which the market system is evaluated is extended further into the future, the net benefits tend to rise because of the potential for growth in the overall economy. People may often lose today because of changes in their own markets, but they also benefit from the enormous capital stock that has been created from the incentives to compete embedded in the market system from previous time periods, a point that was considered in some detail in the discussion of the fairness of economic failure in chapter 4. Similarly, future generations will benefit from current market incentives incorporated into the system to add to the capital stock. The important point is that during any short-time horizon, workers, for example, may lose from job displacement, but they may gain from their higher productivity spurred in part by the growth over time in the capital stock. Economic growth is important to conservatives precisely because it increases the chances that a substantial majority of the population, across generations, will be net gainers from the system.*

---

*A market system understandably may be opposed by a significant percent of the population in any given generation. This is because resources may be diverted from consumption goods, which benefit the current generation, to investment goods, which benefit future generations (to a much greater extent than consumption goods). The market system may, however, be supported by a substantial majority of all generations taken together simply because the future generations that benefit from economic growth encouraged by market incentives represent a large number of voters and an overwhelming percent of all voters over generations.

If left alone, however, the market system over the long run will not in all likelihood be fully Pareto efficient. The sheer number of people, the extraordinary volume of market events covered by the long run, the immense lack of knowledge people have about how market events will unfold through time as others act and react to changing market conditions, and inherent risks and uncertainties involved in private-market plans necessarily imply that not all people will be net gainers from the unfettered operation of the market system.

Over the long run, there will inevitably be net losers. These are people who, because they are in some way incapacitated or are down on their luck, seem be harmed more often than they are helped by market changes. They include people with extraordinarily limited skills who would be better off in, for example, traditional, family and small-group-oriented societies than under market systems, where rewards are tied more directly to productivity, as defined competitively by market participants.

Net losers also include the workers who go from one job to another, repeatedly terminated just as they complete the necessary investment in training and become adjusted to the work demands. Finally, they include all of those people who do everything right in that they attempt to ensure against market losses and develop a portfolio of skills, products, and investments to minimize their losses from market risks, but who fall victim to the dictates of market uncertainties.

Pareto efficiency is a highly demanding criterion for the social acceptance of the market system as a fair system. It requires that everyone or virtually everyone be made better off by the adoption of the market system. This is because Pareto efficiency requires the consent of all, including net losers as well as net gainers. As measured by general agreement, Pareto efficiency demands that fairness prevail.

Theoretically, unanimous consent might be conceived as emanating from a conceptual framework in which everyone agrees to the market system because everyone, not knowing their exact economic status over the long run, expects to be better off from the adoption of the market system than from the status quo or any other viable alternative system. Practically, however, there is no reason to assume that everyone will expect to be better off, if for no other reason than that people vary in their optimism about their long-run status. Furthermore, the prevalence of risks and uncertainties in economic life, founded on the current commitment of resources for future rewards, precludes the attainment of the ideal state in which all are better off by the free flow of market forces. Practically speaking, to ensure the consent of all, including the expected net losers, some welfare or transfer system must be appended to the market system, just to guarantee that all or practically all are, after transfers, net gainers and that all or practically all will accept the market system.

The transfers to the net losers, who might be defined as the truly poor, would be financed through taxation of the gains received by the net gainers. If the market system is truly Pareto efficient, the taxes on the net gainers will be less than their gains from adoption of the market system and the transfers to the net losers will be sufficient to more than cover their net losses. When the market system has a welfare appendix, the system has much to recommend it: The market system is efficient and fair in the sense that no one is made worse off by its adoption.

The Containment of the Welfare State

Making a theoretically sound case for welfare has never been a particularly difficult task for economists, even for devotees of the market system and open opponents of the welfare state. Almost all can agree that welfare has the potential for enhancing economic efficiency. And almost all can imagine individuals who have such limited skills and abilities that they have little or no capacity to compete effectively for either jobs or goods and services in a market system.

Infants and young children unattached to family and friends, the mentally deranged, and the severely physically handicapped are obvious examples of people who do not have a serious chance, much less an equal opportunity, of competing effectively in a market system. These are people who may very well be net losers from the adoption of a market system, who might be under-supported by private charity and who might be obvious beneficiaries of any agreed-on government welfare system.

Still, the welfare system all too often encounters much hostility among market supporters, even among conservatives who may acknowledge the theoretical case for and social desirability of welfare. It may well be that some conservatives oppose welfare from greed and self-interest, as proponents of welfare contend. Others oppose welfare because they fervently believe people have natural rights to their property that cannot be violated under any circumstances. The necessary taxation to finance a welfare system would represent a violation of people's natural rights to their property.

Some conservative opponents harbor a fundamental distrust of democracy, in particular a fear that the majority of people with incomes less than the mean will use their new-found political power to exploit government transfer authority for the benefit of the poor and to the detriment of the rich. Conservative opposition to welfare embraces early eighteenth- and nineteenth-century fear, articulated by Alexis de Tocqueville, of the "tyranny of the majority."[7] As the distinguished English historian Thomas Babington Macaulay has stressed,

> I have long been convinced that institutions purely democratic must, sooner or later, destroy liberty, or civilization, or both . . .
>
> It is quite plain that your government will never be able to restrain a distressed and discontented majority. For with the majority is the government, and has the rich, who are always a minority, absolutely at its mercy. The day will come when in the state of New York a multitude of people, none of whom have had more than half a breakfast, or expect to have more than half a dinner, will choose a legislature. Is it possible to doubt what sort of legislature will be chosen?[8]

A nontrivial number of conservatives oppose welfare, however, because of a genuine concern for the fate of the poor in a world in which government is granted the power of transfer without explicit, nondemocratic constraints on that transfer power. Some conservatives fear an unconstrained welfare state will be exploited by the nonpoor to the detriment of the poor. Granted, the poor and the well off may have one vote per person in their ranks, and there may be more poor voters (with incomes below the mean income level) than wealthy voters (with incomes above the mean). Nonetheless, the well off, by definition, have substantially more economic power than the poor; and economic power can be just as effective, if not more so, than votes in swaying political outcomes. Furthermore, it is important to recognize that the rich tend to vote with greater consistency than the poor, partially offsetting their lack of numbers. As evident in table 9–1, persons eighteen and over in households with less than $12,500 in annual income represented 24 percent of the voting age population but only 36 percent of them voted in 1984.

Table 9–1

Voter Participation by Income Groupings, 1984

Household Annual Income	Percent of Voting Age Population	Percent of Voters in 1984 Election	Percent of Persons Age 18 and Over in Income Group Who Voted, 1984
Less than $12,500	24	16	36
$12,500 to $24,999	27	29	56
$25,000 to $34,999	19	22	62
$35,000 to $49,999	17	19	60
Over $50,000	13	14	58

Source: *New York Times/CBS Poll* published in *New York Times*, November 8, 1984 and Department of Commerce, *Money Income of Households, Families and Persons in the United States: 1983*. Reported in James Gwartney and Richard Stroup, "Equality, the Transfer Society, and the Nature of Redistributive Activity," a paper presented at a conference on "The Political Economy of the Transfer Society" (Policy Sciences Program, Florida State University, March 6–7, 1986).

However, more than 60 percent of the voting-age members of households with more than $25,000 voted in 1984.

Even where the poor may dominate in terms of the number of votes, social analysts have questioned whether political power is not negatively related to the number of potential votes. This is because large groups have a more difficult problem of unifying and cohering to pursue their common interests than small groups. This means that the size of and diversity of interests among the poor may work to their disadvantage in politics.[9]

Researchers have also studied the power of the purse in elections and have concluded what is obvious to even casual political observers. The supply curve of votes is upward sloping with respect to campaign expenditures, and campaign expenditures largely depend upon political contributions from the economically powerful.*

The poor and their political allies have obviously succeeded in establishing an array of government-backed poverty relief programs. Food stamps, Aid to Families with Dependent Children, public education, public housing, free and subsidized school lunches, and Medicaid are several of the more prominent programs focused on the needs of the poor.

---

*Statistical studies show that campaign contributions are likely to be positively related to industry concentration: the more concentrated industries (those more likely to have monopoly power in their markets), the greater the campaign contributions [Russell Pittman, "Market Structure and Campaign Contributions," *Public Choice* (Fall 1977), pp. 31–52; and "Market Structure and Campaign Contributions: Does Contraction Matter?" (Washington: U.S. Department of Justice, September 26, 1985, discussion paper)].

However, the welfare state encompasses much more in the way of transfer benefits. It also includes Social Security; Medicare; rent and interest controls; import restrictions; economic and environmental regulations; direct business grants and subsidized loans; indirect business subsidies through expenditures on streets, bridges, and sewer systems; disguised business subsidies provided in overblown payments for government goods and services; and monopoly privileges.*

Interestingly, the federal government spent in 1983 more than $475 billion on transfer payments. However, only 16.4 percent (or $78 billion) of the total transfers went strictly to poverty (or means-tested) programs, which means that the overwhelming portion of the welfare budget amounted to transfers among the nonpoor. In addition, between 1975 and 1983 the growth in transfers for the nonpoor was greater than the growth in transfers for the poor.[10]

The most challenging question asked by conservative opponents of the welfare state that has been overlooked, sidestepped or ignored by liberal proponents is whether the poor on balance gain from the welfare state when all direct, indirect, and disguised transfer programs are considered.[11] The poor may not pay much in the way of direct income taxes, but they do indirectly pay a significant portion of the costs of the welfare state through the higher consumer prices charged for goods and services they buy because of the sales taxes, business taxes, and personal income taxes imposed on other higher income businesses and people. They also pay through higher prices for goods and services, a part of the transfer costs of import restrictions, economic and environmental regulations, and government-sponsored monopoly power. These implicit welfare taxes imposed through the pricing system, the revenues from which tend to go directly to the nonpoor, tend to be regressive because the poor spend a larger share of their incomes on goods and services.†

---

*Conservatives rightfully insist that poverty programs be cost-effective, meaning, given their budgets, they accomplish as much as possible in relieving the problems of poverty. However, conservatives might reasonably fear that myopic focus of cost-effectiveness studies on the costs and accomplishments of poverty programs may overstate their true social worthiness when *all* costs and benefits are evaluated. Poverty programs might be quite cost-effective, but the establishment of government's transfer authority can result in many programs for the nonpoor, and the costs of the transfer programs for the nonpoor might rightfully be considered costs of the poverty programs that make the cost-benefit ratios of the poverty programs quite perverse.

†If the poor spend 98 percent of their incomes while the rich spend 75 percent of their incomes on goods and services, and if the transfer costs of disguised welfare programs amount to 10 percent of the selling prices of all goods and services, the poor will suffer a tax burden equal to 9.8 percent of their incomes while the rich will endure a tax burden that is a lower percentage of their incomes, 7.5 percent.

Conservatives' concern for the welfare of the poor is particularly applicable to the long run. During the long run, the growth in the nation's capital stock may be seriously eroded by the growing disincentives to invest that may accompany the expansion of the welfare state. And the welfare state may expand because the nonpoor may seek more public aid in the name of the poor. More people may on the margin adjust their behavior to qualify for public assistance.

Welfare programs can be expected to proliferate as more areas of human behavior impose, through the tax system, external costs on the rest of the tax-paying public. Retraining programs can, for example, be justified on the grounds that without them people are unemployed for a longer period of time, and the tax burden on the general public is increased through greater unemployment compensation payments.[12]

Over time, constrained only by the rules of majoritarian democracy, interest groups can be expected to divert more resources to seeking government benefits—that is, exploiting the transfer authority of government powers. As more interest groups use the government transfer authority available to them, the explicit tax rates imposed by the Internal Revenue Service on the incomes of the rich can rise, resulting in reduced incentives to work, save, and invest. The implicit tax rates incorporated into the welfare programs and faced by the poor can also rise as more welfare benefits are provided.*

In addition, the economy may become progressively less competitive and less efficient, dynamic, and adaptable as interest groups from all points on the income distribution take advantage of the government's transfer powers and secure their own monopoly restrictions. The end result can be the development through government of a "public bad": a reduction in the prosperity of all groups through the competitive and destructive use of transfer powers.[13]

Conservatives may understandably oppose the welfare state because the end result assaults their own private interests. They are marginally impoverished by it.

---

*Most welfare benefit programs are devised so benefits are scaled down as the recipients' incomes rise. The reduction in the benefits as a percentage of any given rise in earned income is the implicit tax rate faced by the welfare beneficiaries. If the welfare benefits are raised while the break-even income level is held constant, the implicit tax rate must rise. This is because the benefits must be reduced by greater amounts for given earned income increases to meet the break-even income level. For more on the disincentives of welfare faced by the poor, see Martin Anderson, *Welfare: The Political Economy of Welfare Reform in the United States* (Stanford, Calif.: Hoover Institution Press, 1978).

But, as argued at the start, the rich may also be concerned that the uncontained welfare state will ultimately work to the detriment of the poor and may work against the interests of the poor more so than of any other group. The welfare system may not only be a negative-sum game and Pareto inefficient in the sense that all, or virtually all, are made worse off, but may also be grossly unfair because it achieves, on balance, the exact opposite of its intent: the further impoverishment of some of the poorest people in society. Accordingly, the welfare economy, including the market system and an uncontained welfare state, may be no more fair, and may be more unfair, than the unfettered market system it is designed to supplant.

The problem of the fairness of the welfare state is particularly pressing when welfare policies encourage the very poverty problems they are presumably designed to abate. Much conservative opposition to extensions of the welfare state has been founded on the belief, which has theoretical and empirical foundations, that many welfare programs by indirection have made the poverty problems for some people and groups worse while helping others, a central theme of relatively recent book-length welfare studies by Martin Anderson, Charles Murray, Walter Williams, and Thomas Sowell.[14] At the very least, it can be said that extensions of the welfare state over the past three decades have not been an unmixed blessing for the poor.

For example, as shown in table 9-2, the poverty rate for all Americans was generally on the decline during 1947–1984, whether measured by the official poverty statistics that includes only money income received by the poor or the adjusted poverty rate that accounts for in-kind welfare benefits (housing, medical care, and food) received by the poor. However, the decline in the overall rate was fueled in large measure by a decline in the number of elderly poor. The poverty rate for the nonelderly poor, most notably prime working age adults, began to rise after the late 1960s. This happened in spite of continued increases in per capita real income (also shown in table 9-2) and dramatic growth in welfare benefits.

Clearly, the turnaround in the poverty rate for the working-age poor is the result of many factors, not the least of which is the general rise in the unemployment rate during the 1970s and 1980s. However, one reason that conservatives insist should not be overlooked is the incentive effects of poverty programs to seek, on the marginal, relief instead of work. So much of the disagreement over public welfare is grounded in different assessments of just how strong the

Table 9-2

The Official Poverty Rate and the Poverty Rate Adjusted for In-Kind Benefits for Families by Age of Household Head, 1947–1982

Age of Household Head	1947	1959	1965	1968	1970	1975	1980	1982	1984
Per Capita Real GNP (1972 dollars)	$3263	$4076	$4782	$5271	$5393	$5702	$6480	$6370	$6925
Official Poverty Rate									
Under 25	45.0	26.9	19.4	13.2	15.5	21.0	21.8	26.1	29.4
25–44	27.0	16.5	12.8	9.3	9.5	10.3	11.8	14.2	13.2
45–54	27.0	15.0	9.6	7.0	6.6	6.6	7.6	8.9	8.6
65 and over	57.0	30.0	22.8	17.0	16.5	8.9	9.1	9.3	7.3
All Families	32.0	18.5	13.9	10.0	10.1	9.7	10.3	12.2	11.6
Adjusted Poverty Rate[a]									
Under 25	n.a.	n.a.	19.0	12.3	14.2	18.7	18.8	24.0	26.8
25–44	n.a.	n.a.	12.5	8.6	8.5	8.5	9.5	12.3	11.4
45–54	n.a.	n.a.	9.5	6.7	6.1	5.8	6.2	8.0	7.4
65 and over	n.a.	n.a.	22.4	15.9	14.9	6.0	5.4	5.5	4.3
All Families	n.a.	n.a.	13.7	9.3	9.2	8.1	8.2	10.2	9.8

Source: The 1947 data are from *Economic Report of the President: 1964* (table 7). The other data are from U.S. Department of Commerce: Bureau of the Census, *Estimates of Poverty Including the Value of Noncash Benefits: 1979 to 1982* and *Estimates of Poverty Including the Value of Noncash Benefits: 1984.* Reported in James Gwartney and Richard Stroup, "Equality, the Transfer Society, and the Nature of Redistributive Activity," a paper presented at a conference on "The Political Economy of the Transfer Society" (Policy Sciences Program, Florida State University, March 6–7, 1986).

[a]The poverty rate adjusted for in-kind benefits is based on the recipient value method of valuing in-kind benefits.

disincentives of relief programs are. For example, Lowell Galloway and Richard Veddar have reported startling findings on the effects of federal welfare expenditures on the number of poor. They conclude that by 1984 about one-sixth of the poverty population (or 5.7 million people) were living in poverty "as a result of the generosity of public welfare." In addition, they estimate that a $1 billion increase in welfare spending will increase the poverty population by 250,000. The impact of welfare on the number of poor children is particularly acute, accounting for as many as 20 percent of the children in poverty.*

Concluding Comments

A central message of the previous discussion is that assumed political positions on welfare can be misleading. They may suggest that proponents of welfare, the liberal left, have a monopoly on heartfelt concern for the poor and that opponents of welfare, the conservative right, have little or no concern for the poor.

It is difficult to accept at face value that a significant percentage of conservative opponents of welfare (especially those concerned with economic efficiency) oppose to any meaningful degree welfare for the truly poor, the net losers in society—those who cannot, out of no fault of their own, make a reasonable living in a totally free market economy. As argued, welfare can be efficient, the presumed "Holy Grail" of conservatives. Additionally, there is no reason to believe that liberals have a monopoly on compassion.

Finally, welfare limited to the truly poor would be relatively cheap because the poor now receive less than a third of the transfers

---

*The authors' findings from several studies are summarized in "Paying People to Be Poor" (Dallas: National Center for Policy Analysis, February 1986). Galloway and Veddar adjust for changes in the unemployment rate and income across states. They also point out that seven of the ten states with the highest welfare spending experienced increases in their poverty rates between 1969 and 1979, whereas all of the ten states with the lowest welfare spending had substantial reductions in their poverty rates during the same period.

Although the limitations of data are ever-present, it is also interesting to note that the percent of all poor households that had no working member during the year rose 30.5 percent in 1959 to 44 percent in 1970 and then to 50.6 percent in 1984 (Gwartney and Stroup, "Equality, the Transfer Society, and the Nature of Redistributive Activity," p. 25). Granted, the growth in the number of nonworking poor is an explanation for the growth in the poverty rate as well as a consequence of the growth in the benefits that are intended to benefit the poor. The difficulty of disentangling the interactive effects of the causes of poverty will keep the empirical debate a lively one for some time.

made through the federal treasury.* A social commitment, accompanied by strict controls on the government's transfer authority, to help only the truly poor would probably be accompanied by a massive reduction in taxes along with a reduction in the transfers to the nonpoor that those taxes and additional regulatory authority of governments permit. Growth could be spurred in two ways. First, fewer resources would be wasted in what economists have come to call rent seeking, the search for monopoly profits through government market controls and handouts, and in defending the rents that have already been garnered by interest groups and might be lost with a shift in government policies. Second, marginal tax rates would be lowered, providing greater incentives to work, save, and invest for future returns.

The central problem in getting political conservatives to acknowledge openly the need and social desirability of welfare for the truly poor seems to be one of ensuring that the implied transfer powers for government will be bounded or contained. The containment of the transfer powers can be accomplished through implicitly accepted fiscal norms or explicitly agreed-on constitutional checks on use of government's powers by the nonpoor. The critical need is not to check government per se but to check interest groups who are inevitably driven by the powers of competitive politics to use the government's transfer powers to their own advantage.

In their efforts to enlist the support of conservatives, the admonition to proponents of welfare is simple. It is to rethink the dimensions of the welfare problem, to conceive of welfare as a package of benefits for the truly poor along with a necessary set of accompanying constraints that will check the exploitation of government's welfare powers by the nonpoor. The constraints on the nonpoor are as important in enlisting the cooperation of conservatives and in

---

*In 1982, the federal government spent approximately $125 billion on selected cash and noncash aid categories to the more than 34 million poor people. These aid forms included cash assistance, mainly in the forms of Social Security and Aid to Families with Dependent Children, totaling nearly $26 billion, and noncash benefits, including food, free lunches, public housing, and Medicaid, totaling nearly $99 billion [U.S. Bureau of the Census, *Estimates of Poverty Including the Value of Noncash Benefits: 1983* (Current Population Reports, P-60, No. 145), p. 45]. The federal government's expenditures on human resources for the year totaled $387 billion. However, that expenditure total does not include a variety of other outlays that represent transfers, for example, expenditures on agricultural programs and community and regional development.

alleviating the long-run plight of the poor as is the volume of benefits directed to the poor.

Notes

1. James R. Schlesinger, "Systems Analysis and the Political Process," *Journal of Law and Economics* (October 1968), p. 285.
2. For a discussion of how politics tends to drive people to political extremes and to sharpen the rhetoric of the debate, see Dwight R. Lee, "Malice in Plunderland" (Los Angeles: International Institute for Economic Research, 1984).
3. See Milton Friedman, *Capitalism and Freedom* (Chicago: University of Chicago Press, 1962), chapter 10.
4. Ibid., p. 191.
5. See James M. Buchanan *The Public Finances* (Homewood, Ill.: Richard D. Irwin, Inc., 1970), chapter 9.
6. These flaws are more fully explored in Richard B. McKenzie, "The Construction of the Public Goods Demand Curve and the Theory of Income Redistribution," *Public Choice* (Summer 1981), pp. 337–344.
7. Alexis de Tocqueville, *Democracy in America* (New York: Schocken Books, 1935). For a critical reevaluation of Tocqueville's arguments, see Robert A. Dahl, *A Preface to Economic Democracy* (Los Angeles: University of California, 1985), especially chapters 1 and 2.
8. In a letter dated May 23, 1857 written by Thomas Babington Macaulay to Henry Stephen Randall, author of *Life of Thomas Jefferson*.
9. The seminal works on these topics include Mancur Olson, *The Logic of Collective Action* (Cambridge, Mass.: Harvard University Press, 1967); and George J. Stigler, "A Theory of Economic Regulation," *Bell Journal of Economics and Management* (Spring 1970), pp. 3–21.
10. James Qwartney and Richard Stroup, "Equality, the Transfer Society, and the Nature of Redistributive Activity," a paper presented at a conference on "The Political Economy of the Transfer Society" (Talahassee, Fla.: Policy Science Program, Florida State University, March 6–7, 1986), p. 8.
11. This question has been at the heart of two recent controversial books on poverty, Charles A. Murray, *Losing Ground: American Social Policy, 1950–1980* (New York: Basic Books, Inc., 1984); and Walter E. Williams, *The State against Blacks* (New York: McGraw-Hill, 1982).
12. For an extended discussion of how government welfare programs tend to proliferate because of their effects on federal taxes and expenditures, see Richard B. McKenzie, *Bound to Be Free* (Stanford, Calif.: Hoover Institution Press, 1981) chapter 6.
13. This thesis has been developed and evaluated empirically and historically by Mancur Olson, *The Rise and Decline of Nations: Economic Growth, Stagflation, and Social Rigidities* (New Haven, Conn.: Yale University Press, 1982). See also James M. Buchanan, *The Limits of Liberty* (Chicago: University of Chicago Press, 1975)

for a discussion of the more general and perplexing social dilemma that is at stake in this discussion: How to create a government with real authority for the purpose of accomplishing acknowledged social goals and, at the same time, prevent it from becoming a Leviathan, destructive of its original objectives.

14. Martin Anderson, *Welfare: The Political Economy of Welfare Reform in the United States* (Stanford, Calif.: Hoover Institution Press, 1978); Murray, *Losing Ground; Williams, The State against Blacks;* and Thomas Sowell, *Ethnic America* (New York: Basic Books, Inc., 1981).

10
Eminent Domain: A Useful Tool
for Industrial Reform?

That government can scarcely be deemed to be free, where the rights of property are left solely dependent upon the will of the legislative body, without any restraint. The fundamental maxims of a free government seem to require, that the rights of personal liberty and private property should be sacred.

— Justice Story[1]

No one questions the power of plant closings, especially large ones, to disrupt workers' lives and economically depress whole communities. While there is much agreement in the United States about the adverse social effects of many plant closings, considerable political tension, founded in concern for the fairness as well as efficiency of plant closings, remains over what should be done to remedy the observed problems.

Industrial reformers have traditionally sought to remedy the plant-closing problems, which have tended to be central issues in debates over what should be done about economic dislocation, by following the lead of European governments. They have sought to reduce the number and pace of plant closings by requiring firms to give advance notice of pending plant closings (up to two years), to offer affected workers severance pay (as much as a year's wages), to continue employee health insurance benefits beyond the closing of plants (up to a year), and to provide restitution to the affected communities (up to 25 percent of the firm's previous twelve-month total wage bill).[2] After all, employers have "a responsibility to communicate to employees and the surrounding community on issues relating to the stability of the plant . . . [and] a duty to show cause why they must shut down, move operations, reduce the work force."[3]

So-called plant-closing laws have been introduced in the U.S. Congress just about every two years since 1974,* and more than two dozen state legislatures have, at one time or another over the past decade, considered some form of plant-closing restriction.[4] In 1985, more than forty bills that sought to impose some restriction—prenotification, severance pay, or extended health benefits—on the right of firms to shut down were pending in nineteen state legislatures.[5]

All of these efforts have been directed at mitigating worker hardship and introducing a modicum of fairness into firms' decision-making process. If workers are not given the right to participate in closing decisions, the concern of chapter 5, then firms' decisions should be constrained by government, an outside force that can take account of social values such as justice, equity, and fairness, or so it has been argued.

In recent years, however, proponents of industrial policy have begun to shift the focus of their reform efforts toward the use of states' powers of eminent domain to prevent plants from closing and then relocating. Admittedly, these reform efforts have been primarily directed at keeping professional sports teams from moving their franchises to new, presumably more lucrative, cities. For example, the cities of Oakland, California, and Baltimore, Maryland, threatened to use eminent domain as a means of retaining their professional football teams.† State legislatures in California, Maryland, and New York have considered bills that would clearly legalize municipal seizures of their sports teams under the powers of eminent domain.

Nevertheless, the legal principles and arguments at issue in the cases of relocating sports teams can be easily extended to manufacturing plants or corporate headquarters. Indeed, Montana has considered legislation that would allow plants slated for closing to be

---

*The "National Employment Priorities Act" is the plant-closing bill favored by longtime proponent of closing restrictions, Michigan representative William Ford. In late 1984, Ford planned to reintroduce the plant-closing bill sometime in 1985. See U.S. Congress, House, "National Employment Priorities Act of 1983," H.R. 2847 (ninety-eighth Congress, 1st Session).

†Both the Oakland Raiders and the Baltimore Colts moved. The Raiders moved to Los Angeles, in spite of legal efforts by the National Football League. These legal efforts were not concerned with the issue of eminent domain; rather, they concerned the authority of the NFL to approve or disapprove of team moves. The Colts moved to Indianapolis, Indiana, after packing up and having the moving company pull out in the middle of the night.

condemned and seized under the powers of eminent domain. In 1984, the city fathers of New Bedford, Connecticut, considered using eminent domain to prevent the closing of Morse Tools, a subsidiary of Gulf and Western, which had been up for sale for two years with no buyers in prospect. The issue was settled, prior to the invoking of eminent domain powers, when the employees found a buyer. And the Boston City Council in 1985 studied a proposal from a group of business people to condemn Colonial Provisions, a hot dog plant slated for closing, but turned the issue aside when legal counsel judged the move to be in violation of the Massachusetts constitution.

This chapter evaluates the use of eminent domain as a tool for achieving the industrial policy goals of those concerned with the economic and social consequences of plant closings. Three main questions are addressed:

> First, is there legal precedent in the United States for extending the use of eminent domain to plant closings?

> Second, are conventional arguments for imposing restrictions on plant closings consistent with the dictates of past court rulings?

> Third, is the use of eminent domain as a general policy option in cases of plant closings a wise industrial policy strategy for municipalities in terms of the efficient and fair use of resources?

Two major conclusions emerge from the discussion that follows. Given past extensions of eminent domain powers, especially a 1984 Supreme Court ruling on an extended use of eminent domain in Hawaii, there remains little reason to expect that legislated use of eminent domain powers to prevent plant closings will be struck down on constitutional grounds. However, extending the application of eminent domain powers to plant closures will be counterproductive. That is to say, the condemnation of plants slated for closure will likely exacerbate plant closings and the very social and economic problems confronted by many workers whose plants are closed. When applied as a rule for policy, the extended use of eminent domain powers would not likely be fair policy, especially in the long run.

The Economic Rationale for the
Use of Eminent Domain

In the United States, the power of government to take property is restricted by the eminent domain, or takings, clause of the Fifth Amendment to the Constitution: "private property [shall not] be taken for public use without just compensation." The government's taking powers are, therefore, restricted in two ways. First, the taking must be for some public use. Second, there must be just compensation, as settled in court by a jury trial, if necessary.*

Historically, eminent domain powers have been used for fairly narrowly defined purposes such as the taking of private property to provide public roads and canals, military bases, and national parks. Private railroad systems have, however, been extended at times through the use of eminent domain condemnation proceedings.

Whether such publicly provided goods are sufficiently public to justify the use of the taking powers has been, and continues to be, a highly contentious issue. Proponents contend that the use of eminent domain is often the only way needed property can be obtained by government at reasonable prices. Without eminent domain, highways may follow a highly crooked course. On the other hand, opponents have argued that transportation networks, military bases, and parks could be provided by government through normal market channels, without resorting to condemnation proceedings.

Presumably, there is some price at which most landowners, for example, would sell their holdings to government, regardless of whether the purpose is partially or totally public. If the government cannot buy the property, given its limited budget, then opponents maintain that it must be presumed that the value of the property retained by private owners is greater than its value to government or the polity. Use of eminent domain would be inefficient, resulting in the shift of resources from more highly valued to less highly valued

---

*An eminent domain provision, while circumscribed in these ways, may not necessarily be conceived as a grant of additional power for government. Instead, as Richard Epstein has argued, an eminent domain constitutional provision itself may be viewed as placing "a limitation upon the powers of government that are already in place, including both general powers of taxation and regulation" [Richard A. Epstein, "Taxation, Regulation, and Confiscation," *Osgoode Hall Law Journal*, 20 (September 1982), p. 435.]

uses. Even if the use of eminent domain could be shown to improve economic efficiency, some opponents would object to its employment on grounds of basic rights and fairness in the respect of those rights. For example, libertarian social philosopher Ellen Frankel Paul contends that whether under government police or eminent domain powers,

> The power of eminent domain allowing the state to seize property against the will of its rightful owners, whether accompanied by the payment of compensation or not, is wholly unjustifiable. It is only upon utilitarian or pragmatic grounds and not upon rights system, as defended here, that eminent domain could conceivably be justified. But—and this is important—pragmatic considerations of efficiency and the like cannot touch fundamental rights. That is, the right to property stands on a higher moral ground than consideration of efficiency . . . . How can preventing crooked highways ever rise to such moral significance as to override anyone's fundamental right to property?*

But proponents of eminent domain stress that government needs the power to take private property not only to prevent the extreme preferences of a few to dictate to the many, but also to prevent strategic bargaining by individual property owners whose sole motive is to sell at the maximum gain to themselves.

Consider the highway example already mentioned in more detail. City transportation planners want to run a freeway straight through their city. Their sole purpose may be to minimize construction costs and residents' travel time across the city. However, because of the cost-cutting efforts of the transportation officials, each landowner along the proposed route acquires the status of a monopolist and can

---

*Ellen Frankel Paul, "Taking by Regulation: Resolving the Constitutional Muddle," *Constitutional Economics: Containing the Economic Powers of Government*, edited by Richard B. McKenzie (Lexington, Mass.: Lexington Books, 1984), p. 174. At one time, the Supreme Court appears to have taken views similar to those held by Paul, recognizing that property must be viewed as sacred. See the comments at the head of this chapter made by Justice Story, who also wrote in the same decision that "we know no case in which a legislative act to transfer the property of A to B without his consent, has ever been held a constitutional exercise of legislative power, in any state of the Union. On the contrary, it has been constantly resisted, as inconsistent with just principles, by every judicial tribunal in which it has been attempted to be enforced" [*Wilkinson* v. *Leland* at 657].

hold out. Each landowner can refuse to sell unless the price tendered includes virtually the entire cost savings from the highway project, which means that the sum of the prices asked by all landowners exceeds the total value of the property in public use.

Under a pure market system, the result of strategic bargaining can be that the property is not bought and the road is not constructed (or follows a highly cost-ineffective route), even when all city residents, including the landowners along the most cost-effective route, may prefer that the land be bought and straight road constructed. As the classic free rider would do in the production of any public good, each individual property owner can reason that his or her willingness to bargain strategically on the sale of his property will likely have little effect on whether the road is ever built. This attitude results because a high probability exists that someone else will delay the project by bargaining strategically. Thus, the reasoned position is for each to bargain strategically.*

The Extended Use of Eminent Domain Powers

Regardless of the conceptual arguments for the employment of eminent domain powers, the use of the powers has been considerably extended over recent decades mainly through an expansive interpretation of public use. Since at least 1945, much urban renewal in the United States probably could not have been pursued (except at considerably higher public expenditures) without expanding the meaning of public use to include reductions in crime, city beautification, and economic development. The new definition opened up the ways in which the powers of eminent domain could be used.

In assessing the constitutionality of the District of Columbia Redevelopment Act of 1945, which authorized takings for urban renewal, the U.S. Supreme Court wrote

> We deal, in other words, with what traditionally has been known as the police powers. An attempt to define its reach or trace its limits

---

*Clemson University economist Bruce Yandle argues that the strategic bargaining problem can be overcome by eliminating or undermining the monopoly position of the landowners—that is, by proposing that roads be constructed along several alternative, competing routes. The landowners could then submit bids, both positive and negative prices, at which they would give up their land.

is fruitless, for each case must turn on its own facts. The definition is essentially the product of legislative determinations addressed to the purpose of government, purposes neither abstractly nor historically capable of complete definition. Subject to specific constitutional limitations, when the legislature has spoken, the public interest has been declared in terms well-nigh conclusive. *In such instances the legislature, not the judiciary, is the main guardian of the public needs to be served by social legislation, whether it be Congress legislating concerning the District of Columbia . . . or the States legislating concerning local affairs . . . . This principle admits of no exception merely because the power of eminent domain is involved* [emphasis added].[6]

The Court emphasized the extent to which it intended to leave legislatures alone in defining public use by noting

Once the object is within the authority of Congress, the right to realize the exercise of eminent domain is clear. For the power of eminent domain is merely the means to an end. . . . Once the object is within the authority of Congress, the means by which it will be attained is also for Congress to determine. Here one of the means chosen is the use of private enterprise for redevelopment of the area. Appellants argue that this makes the project one of taking from one businessman for the benefit of another businessman. But the means of executing the project are for Congress and Congress alone to determine, once the public purpose has been established.[7]

Using its powers delegated by the State of Michigan, supported by the above Supreme Court ruling, the City of Detroit in 1981 condemned Poletown, a section of the city with a high concentration of Polish people. The city seized the homes of 1,100 families, tore them down, and sold the land to General Motors at a price far below the cost of the property, all for the declared public purpose of making way for the construction of a new GM Cadillac plant that might eventually provide as many as 6,000 jobs for auto workers in the area.*

---

*See "The Rape of Poletown," *Inquiry* (August 3, 1981), pp. 11–12. Backed with a federal grant, the City of Detroit paid nearly $200 million for the Poletown property but sold the land to GM for approximately $50 million.

Presumably, public use then included creating jobs in the community, as well as the general redevelopment of the community. The question of efficiency arose because the city government thought that the value of the jobs, measured in expected additional city revenues and family incomes as well as in reduced social expenditures on unemployment compensation and welfare benefits, exceeded the value of the property to the owners. The question of fairness arose simply because the land owners said they had a right to their property and that the price paid was not adequate to compensate them for their losses. Many residents had to be forcibly evicted.*

Missouri now has a law, known as Chapter 353, that "allows local government bodies that have approved a developer's plans for a site to pass on to the developer the government's powers to take the properties for just compensation."[8] While the law was supposed to encourage economic development, mainly in blighted areas, the building projects erected under the law, according to an official of an organization in Kansas City, Missouri, "have been less and less speculative and more economically feasible with the provisions of eminent domain and tax abatement in the law; and that what we find now is that almost every development in Kansas City in the last couple of years has taken advantage of 353."[9] Apparently, general economic development is a sufficient public use that private property can be taken, even if redevelopment may have occurred through normal market channels.

The breadth of the current legal meaning of public use in the United States is best exemplified by a 1984 U.S. Supreme Court decision involving the forced sale of Hawaiian land under the authority of the states' taking powers. In 1967, the Hawaiian legislature enacted the Land Reform Act that created "a land condemnation scheme whereby title in real property is taken from lessors and transferred to lessees in order to reduce the concentration of land ownership."[10]

When large Hawaiian landowners were required by the Hawaiian Housing Authority to sell their land to their lessees, the landowners

---

*Proponents of the use of eminent domain in the case of Poletown contend that we cannot conclude necessarily that the use of force in moving people out of Poletown indicates that people were treated unfairly. This is because each person may have been behaving strategically, refusing to move unless a price inflated by the extent of the social savings was paid for the property.

sought legal protection. A U.S. district court held that the purpose of the Land Reform Act came within the bounds of the state's police powers, a position that was reversed by the U.S. Ninth Circuit Court of Appeals. The appeals court ruled that the statute represented a "naked attempt on the part of the State of Hawaii to take private property of A and transfer it to B's private use and benefit."[11] The appeals court held that the taking of the property did not pass the "public use" test. Indeed, the court ruled that the case involved public taking for the private use of the lessees.

In 1984, however, the U.S. Supreme Court in *Hawaiian Housing Authority et al.* v. *Midkiff et al.* reversed the appeals court, determining that the takings clause did not bar any compensated taking "rationally related to a conceivable public purpose." The "conceivable public purpose" in this case was judged to be the destruction of the economic grip that the presumed oligopolistic land market in Hawaii had on lessees, which presumably prevented them from buying the land they farmed for fair market prices.

In 1984, 47 percent of Hawaii's land was in the hands of seventy-two private owners; the federal government owned the vast majority of the remaining land.* The Supreme Court held that the taking under the Land Reform Act was justified because the "legislature concluded that concentrated land ownership was responsible for skewing the State's residential fee simple market, inflating land prices, and injuring the public tranquility and welfare"[12] and because it "presumes that when a sufficiently large number of persons declare that they are willing but unable to buy lots at fair prices the land market is malfunctioning."[13] Besides, the Court notes, the "Hawaii Land Reform Act unambiguously privides that '[t]he use of the power . . . to condemn . . . is for a public use and purpose' "[14] and "[r]egulating oligopoly and the evils associated with it is a classic exercise of a state's police powers."[15]

The court acknowledges that the Land Reform Act may be misguided in the sense that it may not accomplish its professed public purpose. But drawing on an earlier decision, it concluded that "whether *in fact* the provision will accomplish its objectives is not in

---

*The Legislature also found that "18 landholders, with tracts of 21,000 acres or more, owned more than 40% of this land and that, on Oahu, the most urbanized of the islands, 22 land-owners owned 72.5% of the fee simple land [Ibid., at 235]."

question: the [constitutional requirement] is satisfied if . . . the . . . [state] Legislature *rationally could have believed that the [Act] would promote its objective*" [emphasis in the original].[16] The Court then says, in effect, that except under "extremely narrow" circumstances, it will defer to the judgment of legislatures as to what constitutes a public use:

> In short, the Court has made clear that it will not substitute its judgment for a state legislature's judgment as to what constitutes a public use "unless the use be palpably without reasonable foundation."[17]

This is because

> When the legislature's purpose is legitimate and its means are not irrational, our cases make clear that empirical debates over the wisdom of takings—no less than debates over the wisdom of other kinds of socioeconomic legislation—are not to be carried out in the federal courts.[18]

The Case for Plant Closing Controls

Can government's taking powers be applied to plant closures? As far as the precedents reviewed above, the answer would appear to be affirmative, and without much question. A state might quickly declare the saving of jobs and the community's tax base as the necessary "public use and purpose." In addition, the past arguments made for plant-closing restrictions may be redressed for condemnation proceedings, ensuring that the extension of eminent domain powers are not used "palpably without reasonable foundation."

Industrial reformers repeatedly have argued that unemployment, caused most noticeably by plant closings, has resulted in a loss of worker self-esteem and higher than normal rates of child and spouse abuse, suicides, family dissolution, physical and mental illness, and mortality. In addition, plant closings can lead to a disintegration of communities, greater crime, and greater social expenditures to combat all of the greater social problems at the same time that the communities' tax base erodes.[19]

By listing the personal and social problems created by plant closings, especially large ones, industrial reformers in effect are contending that plant closures have external, spillover effects, that, in terms of free market economists' own efficiency-based models of the economy, justify government intervention in plant-closing decisions. Conventionally, plant-closing restrictions have been seen as a means of "internalizing externalities, of making firms compensate workers and communities for the costs they necessarily suffer when their plants close down. The restrictions are presumed to result in fewer and more rational closing decisions and a more efficient allocation of resources.*

The case for doing something about plant closings has been traditionally viewed as virtually analogous to the case for government controls on pollution, for example, effluent standards or taxes on effluents (or the products produced). When firms are able to emit pollutants into the atmosphere at no, or practically no, cost, products will be underpriced; not all costs will be reflected in the market price, and the product will be overconsumed because the total marginal cost to society of producing some of the units will exceed their value to consumers.

When paper plants, for example, do not have to abate the smells from their plants or have to compensate local residents for enduring the smells, paper will be underpriced and, accordingly, overconsumed. Similarly, when those same paper plants do not have to consider the social costs of their plant-closing decisions—the pain endured by families where the primary wage earner is unemployed or the higher taxes imposed on people in the community owing to expanded social expenditures and a lower tax base—plant-closing decisions will also be "too cheap." Too frequently owners, especially far-removed absentee owners, remain unaffected by their own closing decisions. Restrictions on plant closings are not only fair but also efficient, or so the argument goes.

Predicting how courts will react to any category of new law is risky business. However, given the social consequences directly attributable to plant closings, it is hard to see how the Supreme Court would deny states the right to prevent plant closings through the exercise of their taking powers and retain the semblance of consistency with past decisions (although consistence has not always been an abiding virtue in the American legal system).

---

*A more efficient allocation of resources is, to economists, a state in which there are fewer closing decisions for which the private and public costs will exceed all benefits.

Such an extension could, on its face, be construed by the Court as "a comprehensive and rational approach to identifying and correcting market failure,"[20] especially since the effects of such legislation will not likely be of any consequence in the Court's review. There is every reason to believe that Court will reaffirm, as it did in *Hawaii Housing Authority*, that the central question is whether a state legislature rationally could have believed that the use of eminent domain in cases of plant closing would promote its stated public objective. Indeed, it would appear that there are many areas of economic life to which eminent domain could be extended, given that the government that takes the property need not use the property, that the "public use" can be declared with little or no concern that the objective will be disputed by the Supreme Court, and that the means used should not be irrational.

Extending Eminent Domain: Would It Really Be Fair?

The legal rights of states to employ eminent domain in cases of plant closings appears clear and certain in all but the most limited and unusual instances. The remaining interesting economic question is whether states should do it as a general rule. Several reasons, not the least of which is a sense of fairness and justice in industrial reform, can be given for why they should not.

Plants that are closed are generally idled because they are unprofitable or are not expected to remain profitable for long. The lack of profitability at the plant is evident by the lack of a buyer or buyers, including the plant's employees, who are willing to pay the plant's alternative market value and keep it in business. (Presumably, eminent domain would only be exercised when a buyer cannot be found.) Their unwillingness attests to the economic rationality of management's decision to close the plant. But is closure fair?

A common complaint among proponents of plant closing laws is that firms close plants to locate production in more profitable areas of the United States, often the South and Southwest. The presumption is, therefore, that the plant is profitable, meaning viable, which seems to make its closure not only unfair but irrational. However, such a policy position takes a short-run view. It fails to acknowledge that more profitable production locations elsewhere translate into more cost-competitive locations elsewhere, which raises questions about the long-run viability of the plant slated for closing. If the plant is not closed and relocated, then other entrepreneurs will spring up in the more cost-effective location and underprice the firm that refuses (or is unable) to relocate its plant.

If a plant is bought under condemnation proceedings, it would appear that the plant would, on balance, impose net losses on the community, lowering the general welfare of the community. The affected government would have to compensate for the plant's losses through subsidies if it wanted to keep the plant open. If it could be profitably operated without a government subsidy included in the purchase price, then the condemnation proceedings presumably would be unnecessary.

One must question whether it is fair to impose net costs on the rest of the community for net benefits that are received largely by the workers, suppliers, and stockholders, many of whom may not reside in the community where the costs are borne. The rest of the community may work where costs have been kept competitive, in which cases the purchase of the plant slated for closing would amount to a transfer of income and wealth from competitive firms and worker groups (who are made less competitive because of the net tax burden they must share) to the noncompetitive firms and worker groups. Such a transfer scheme may worsen the overall competitiveness of the community simply because of the marginal loss of incentives to remain competitive implied by the transfer programs.

There may be, of course, limited cases in which governments take over plants that were thought to be unprofitable by private buyers but which turn out to be paying propositions. The bailout of the Chrysler Corporation through government guaranteed loans, after all, has, at least to date, allowed Chrysler to earn a profit.* The central virtue of the Chrysler bailout to date has, however, been its exclusiveness. But its exclusiveness makes questions of the fairness of it all the more prominent. Such exclusiveness violates a fundamental

---

*This is not to say the Chrysler bailout has been an unmitigated success. Questions abound over whether Chrysler would have been in much the same economic health if it had officially gone bankrupt and had been reorganized and over whether jobs on balance have been saved. The guaranteed Chrysler loans diverted investment funds from other investment projects and, to that extent, redeployed employment in the economy. See James Hickel, "The Chrysler Bailout Bust," *Backgrounder* (Washington: Heritage Foundation, 1983).

precept of government, which is that government policy should not be used to help identified economic interests but should be directed at following rules for help, regardless of whom it is that is helped. Exclusiveness implies powers of discretion made available for political distribution, and such powers are subject to abuse if not checked.

Setting such concerns aside, other important questions remain. For example, if the same bailout benefits accorded Chrysler were organized into a general policy of industrial reform, should we expect the same favorable results over the course of a number of similar bailouts? This is doubtful. To anticipate that a policy of government bailouts will be profitable requires us to assume that governmental institutions are better equipped than capital markets to judge firm profitability, a dubious presumption, especially when governmental decisions may be biased by the political influence of the workers and others directly involved with the operation of the plant. If people in government were more talented at picking winners (a phrase widely used in the U.S. industrial reform debate), we would expect them to be attracted to private investment markets where they could privatize the benefits.

Therefore, we can only anticipate that while some bailed-out firms would be winners, there would also be losers. It is reasonable to believe that the results of an industrial reform rule, which may bail out firms through eminent domain, would cause losses for the community and increase the tax burden on the remaining economic sectors. In the process, entry of firms that can compete both in capital markets for investment funds and the product markets for the goods and services provided would be discouraged in those communities.

Also, it should be recognized that a normal presumption in discussions of eminent domain is that government "takes" the private property owner by paying something less than the competitive market price for the property. Surely that will not always be the case, especially for large property owners. Conceivably, a small landowner with, for example, one acre of land may not get its full economic value as just compensation. However, the threat of property being taken by government at below-market price should be a risk cost that should work itself into the value of the property, which means that the property owner from whom the property is taken may or may not be the person who is actually "taken." The person from whom the property was purchased may be the one who lost property value by the threat of condemnation.* The large landowner can be in a more fortunate position, since he or she could have this condemnation risk covered through the downward adjustment of the price he or she pays for the various and many pieces of property that he buys.

More important for this chapter, we cannot be sure that the government actually takes the property at a below-market price. We note that the just compensation clause of the Fifth Amendment requires that the lower taking price be the value of the plants or grounds in some other use, if the plant is not kept in production. The price could include the opportunity cost of the plant plus the government's savings on social expenditures (unemployment compensation and welfare benefits, for example). After a series of taking proceedings, we would expect the prices paid to average more than the opportunity costs of the plants themselves. To this extent, the plant owners and their retained employees would be "taking" the taxpayers.

When the costs of saving and protecting the jobs are externalized to the rest of the community, we would anticipate that owners and their employees would, as noted above, tend to be less concerned about protecting their own jobs and companies and would be more inclined than otherwise to allow their costs to become uncompetitive, which would aggravate the problem of the threat of plant closings.† The externalization of such internalities again raises questions of efficiency and fairness.

Granted, just compensation might be less than the opportunity cost of the property for a time. This is apparently what the cities of Oakland and Baltimore had in mind when they threatened to condemn their professional football teams. However, government must be careful not to pay such below-market compensation as a general

*The market value need not always be deflated by the risk that the property will be condemned. Indeed, it may often be inflated by the fact that just compensation is more than its alternative value in private use. Many people seek property that will likely be condemned, say, property along proposed interstate highways, for the conventional purpose of buying low and selling high.

†Indeed, to the extent that government social expenditures rise with plant closings, the bargaining power of companies with their governments would be raised, increasing the tax abatements and public subsidies they can obtain from their governments. Such social expenditures can be expected to inspire "industrial blackmail," involving the threat of closure, for the purpose of obtaining greater benefits from government.

rule. The threat of below-market compensation can work itself into the required rate of return on investment within the governmental jurisdiction, reducing its investment and retarding its residents' job growth in the process. The net result can be, again, that the use of eminent domain is counterproductive and perhaps no more fair than the plant closings.

Concluding Comments

Two points that stand out in this chapter are themes throughout the various social issues considered in this book. First, plant closings often may be unfair, but so can their remedies. Few proponents of plant-closing restrictions appear to have thought through the implications of their recommendations. Plant-closing restrictions that discourage plants from opening (or opening on the scale that they would otherwise) can be just as unfair to the workers who are unable to find a job as plant closings are to the workers who lose their jobs. Since pace of investment would tend to be retarded by the added costs of doing business implied in closing restrictions, we might conclude that such restrictions are on balance unfair, since they would most likely result in a net loss of jobs.

Second, it should be evident from the discussion that policy concerns about plant closings should rise both with the size of plants and with governmental social programs to help distressed workers. Large plant closings can have serious ripple effects throughout governmental jurisdictions. The larger the relative size of the plants, the larger the ripple effects from plant closings and the more sudden and difficult the adjustment process can be. Also, the larger the social programs that are designed to relieve economic and social hardships, the larger the external effects that can be seen as justifying governmental intervention and the more tempting the use of eminent domain powers.

However, eminent domain is a temptation that should be studiously shunned by governments interested in the long-run welfare of their residents on efficiency and fairness grounds. Eminent domain can be a governmental power that is used skillfully by the politically powerful to the detriment of others. To argue that the unfortunate people in our society will benefit from the adoption of such an industrial reform is to assume a result that will very likely have no connection to reality.

Notes

1. *Wilkinson v. Leland*, 2 Pet. 627 (U.S. 1829).
2. The case for plant-closing laws is made effectively and completely in Barry Bluestone and Bennett Harrison, *The Deindustrialization of America: Plant Closings, Community Abandonment, and the Dismantling of Basic Industries* (New York: Basic Books, 1982).
3. From a working draft of "Principles for Responsible Management of Plant Closings and Permanent Layoffs," considered by the U.S. Department of Labor Task Force on Economic Adjustment and Worker Dislocation, Subcommittee on Private Responses, minutes of meeting (April 3, 1986).
4. The past legislative efforts to restrict plant closings have been evaluated extensively in Richard B. McKenzie, ed., *Plant Closings: Public or Private Choices?* (Washington: Cato Institute, 1984); and Richard B. McKenzie, *Fugitive Industry: The Economics and Politics of Deindustrialization* (San Francisco: Pacific Institute for Public Policy Research, 1984).
5. See National Center on Occupational Readjustment, "Summary of Federal and State Bills on Plant Closings" as reported in *DLR* (December 14, 1984), pp. E-1–E-6.
6. *Berman v. Parker*, 348 U.S. 26 (1954), at 32.
7. Ibid., at 33.
8. Wendy Swallow, "Missouri's New Eminent Domain," *Washington Post Weekly* (November 12, 1984), p. 33.
9. Ibid.
10. *Hawaiian Housing Authority v. Midkiff*, 467 U.S. 229 (1984).
11. As quoted in *Hawaiian Housing Authority v. Midkiff*, at 235.
12. Ibid., at 232.
13. Ibid., at 242.
14. Ibid., at 236.
15. Ibid., at 242.
16. Ibid., at 242, as cited from *Western & Southern Life Ins. Co. v. State Bd. of Equalization*, 451 U.S. 648, 671–672 (1981).
17. Ibid., at 241, citing *United States v. Gettysburg Electric R. Co.*, 160 U.S. 668, 680 (1896).
18. Ibid., at 242–243.
19. Task Force on Theology and Economic Justice, "Building Justice in Communities: Doing Theology in the Economic Crisis" (Cleveland: the Ecumenical Great Lakes/Appalachian Project on the Economic Crisis, December 7–9, 1984), pp. 2 and 3.
20. *Hawaii Housing Authority v. Midkiff*, at 242.

11
The Efficiency-Fairness Dilemma
of Deregulation

The deadweight loss caused by government economic policies in the United States reaches an astonishingly large figure. One trillion dollars is a modest estimate of their sum. Current income would be at least 25 percent higher if we had never instituted some of the programs operating in the postwar period.

—Yale Brozen[1]

T he economic case for deregulation of various industries in the United States has been extraordinarily strong, so much so that a liberal Democrat such as Senator Ted Kennedy (D.-Mass.) was a leader in the deregulation movement for such industries as trucking and airlines that gained political momentum in the mid- and late 1970s. Even the bastion of liberalism, the *New York Times*, has at times joined the deregulation forces, including supporters of congressional measures to fully decontrol the natural gas industry:

Speed up decontrol of natural gas prices? Critics call the idea an outrage, a giveaway to producers who are locked into regulated prices and want to rip off consumers. Actually, the decontrol plan now pending in the Senate is not an outrage at all but a brave effort to protect consumers in the economy. What is discouraging in the debate is the simplism of the unions and consumer groups who oppose the measure.[2]

However, elemental but stragetic points of economic and legal analysis can be obscured by the rhetoric of political debate. And the full complexity of policy issues often lies just beneath the surface of public pronouncements of more or less obvious solutions to critical social issues.

Such has certainly been the case in the historic debate over the deregulation of natural gas, trucking, airlines, banking, and energy that occurred in the late 1970s and early 1980s. Political rhetoric probably will shroud any future debate over the deregulation of any other industry such as electric power production, insurance, and agriculture.

Not too many years ago, all the government seemed to be interested in was the regulation of various industries. Now, with much experience in government regulation and with several studies showing that many regulatory efforts of government have not benefited the general public or accomplished the stated objectives, the Nixon, Ford, Carter, and Reagan administrations have made many proposals for deregulation.

This chapter considers the ethical problems the government faces when deregulation of an industry is contemplated. The specific concern here is with the "regulatory trap," which involves questions of fairness as well as efficiency, the government often gets itself into. This means the concern is with the political opposition to deregulation. The chapter focuses on the deregulation of the natural gas industry simply because the deregulation of natural gas was still subject to political dispute in the mid-1980s and remains a reasonably clear example of the regulatory trap of government.* The principles developed in the examination of the decontrol of natural gas apply to a wide range of other products that may be subject to deregulation.

The Economic Case for Deregulation

Economists are quick to support almost any deregulation movement on efficiency grounds as that term is understood in the economic profession. Their argument for deregulation is straightforward: If prices (or services or any other characteristic of products) are allowed to vary freely in response to the forces of supply and demand, scarce commodities like natural gas can be allocated in the least

---

*The *Times* repeated its support of full decontrol of natural gas in another 1986 editorial, "An Everybody-Wins Natural Gas Bill," *New York Times* (April 28, 1986), p. 18.

costly manner to those uses that are most highly valued in a relative sense. Problems of shortages, restricted entry of consumers into the market, and forced production and allocation schemes will be eliminated in deregulated markets.

As Robert Helms, a student of natural-gas regulation, has written: "The main conclusion of the study on regulation of natural gas is that thirteen years of experience with market regulation in the United States provides an example of an unsuccessful attempt to improve social welfare through price controls. Shortages of natural gas are a direct consequence of these price controls. Deregulation of the field market would reduce this country's future energy costs."[3] Heritage Foundation policy analyst Milton Copulus, who concentrates on energy policy issues, estimated in 1983 that continued control of natural gas would cost the U.S. economy an additional $154 billion over the following six years.*

The economic argument of deregulation proponents is decidedly one sided, so much so that the resistance of the political system to the advocated reforms may not be fully understood or appreciated. Some analysts assume that opposition to deregulation of gas stems almost exclusively from natural-gas users who do not wish to see their heating bills raised and from others who mistakenly perceive natural-gas supplies as unresponsive to price changes, in which case deregulation means a movement of (unearned) economic profits from consumers to producers.[4]

The public debate over gas deregulation has failed to grasp important points that reveal the true complexity of deregulation efforts. It has failed to recognize that while gas prices have been regulated, the prices of houses and businesses that have gas connections have not been. Through secondary market adjustments, the perceived benefits of regulation have been reflected into the market values of these freely salable assets. Since these adjustments have occurred,

---

*See Milton R. Copulus, "Natural Gas Deregulation: Giving the Consumer a Choice," *Backgrounder* (Washington: Heritage Foundation, 1983). The partial control system for natural gas employed as a consequence of the Natural Gas Policy Act of 1978 was especially destructive to the economy, since it was founded on different prices for old and new natural gas sources. This pricing system distorted the use of energy resources, caused different users to pay radically different prices for energy, and heaped costs on the consumption of energy of all kinds.

deregulation reduces to a problem of achieving not only efficient results but also fair results (or results that are reasonably consistent with the rules under which market transactions were consummated).*

Although this chapter tries to clarify the conflict between efficiency and fairness in deregulating the natural gas industry, the case of natural gas should be viewed as a convenient means of broaching a much broader objective: How can social reforms be made that are not only efficient but fair? If complete fairness cannot be achieved, how can we make the consequences of change largely fair or sufficiently fair so that efficient changes will be readily accepted and implemented through political process?

These questions force us to consider the merits of alternatives for social change for a sequence of conceived changes across industries and through time. Hence, this chapter is concerned with the presumed need for social change and the problems associated with particular changes; but it is also concerned with the "constitution of social policy change."

In pursuit of these goals, we must be concerned with capitalization which is the process by which anticipated future benefits are captured in the price of an asset that is owned and can be traded. Further, we must explain how and under what circumstances the benefits of regulation can be captured or capitalized in freely traded assets, like houses, that are not subject to control. We can then consider two alternative means of obtaining collective agreement for deregulation: tax-compensation schemes and across-the-board deregulation of a number of industries.†

---

*Gordon Tullock has referred to this problem as the "transitionary gains trap" ["The Transitionary Gains Trap," *Bell Journal of Economics* (Autumn 1975), pp. 671–678]. As the following discussion shows, the problem of capitalized entitlements has also been recognized by Victor Goldberg, who is concerned with the general problem of redistribution as articulated by Tullock and George Stigler. See Victor P. Goldberg, "On Positive Theories of Redistribution," *Journal of Economic Issues* (March 1977), pp. 119–132.

†We assume for purposes of argument that the empirical studies that show inefficiency in many regulated industries are essentially correct. For studies that show the growing recognition of the inefficiencies government regulation has engineered, see Paul W. McAvoy (ed.), *The Crisis of the Regulatory Commissions: Introduction to a Current Issue of Public Policy* (New York: W.W. Norton and Company, Inc., 1970); and Almarin Phillips (ed.), *Promoting Competition in Regulated Markets* (Washington, D.C.: The Brookings Institution, 1975).

The Problem of Capitalized Entitlements

Regulation of natural-gas prices has the commonly acknowledged effects of eventually restricting current supplies of natural gas and increasing the quantity demanded. These effects happen because the price is held below the market-clearing price. However, the effective subsidy per unit of natural gas bought is actually greater than the difference between the market-clearing price and the official control (or ceiling) price. This is because the quantity of natural gas available for sale is reduced by the price control, and that restricted quantity will sell for a price that is higher than the market-clearing price. The effective subsidy granted natural-gas users is, therefore, the difference between the higher price users are willing to pay for the restricted quantity of natural gas and the control price. (These points are clarified with the use of a graph in an appendix at the end of the chapter.)

This subsidy effectively reduces the cost of operating homes and businesses with gas connections. Thus, the market value of gas-supplied homes and businesses increases because the operating costs of natural gas facilities will be relatively lower and the market demand for them will be greater. The critical point is that the benefits of the regulation become capitalized, that is, included in inflated prices for gas-supplied homes and businesses that have gas connections.

However, to be perfectly accurate, it must be added that the distribution of the capitalized benefits of regulation over time depends on two factors: (1) The state of people's expectations through time, which in turn depends on how much people know about the prospects of regulation; and (2) The extent to which the number of natural gas connections can increase with price (technically referred to as "elasticity of supply").* The latter condition means that if the

---

*This latter condition has been considered at length by economists James Buchanan and Nicolaus Tideman, who have evaluated the wealth effects of price controls on gasoline. Their argument can perhaps be more appropriately applied to our discussion of natural gas controls. Buchanan and Tideman have demonstrated that wealth transfers of price controls increase with a decrease in the responsiveness of supply of assets to price. See James M. Buchanan and T. Nicolaus Tideman, "Gasoline Rationing and Market Pricing: Public Choice in Political Economy." *Atlantic Economic Journal* (November 1974), pp. 15–26.

number of gas connections cannot be increased with greater benefits going to those with gas connections associated with suppressed gas prices, then the gas connections (or the homes that have them) will increase in market value.

Although this has not always been the case, the supply of natural gas connections was fixed in many parts of the country for many years. New connections were simply prohibited by government regulators. The prohibition was instituted because the regulated price had been held below the market-clearing price, and the restriction was used as a means of allocating the limited amount of natural gas available. The current supply of natural gas to many areas was restricted by the sheer lack of incentive that firms had to explore for new reserves, and because gas producers, anticipating deregulation, began to withhold a portion of their known reserves from the market and to sell in nonregulated intrastate markets such as Texas. The prohibition on new hookups has been a convenient, politically astute means of disguising the shortage of natural gas at the ceiling price and of attempting to ensure that those homes and businesses with connections will have adequate supplies.

Admittedly, the Federal Power Commission (FPC) was never fully successful in keeping homes and businesses with gas connections adequately supplied. During the unusually cold winters of 1976, 1977, and 1978, there were major interruptions in supplies to gas users, and many businesses and schools had to close for a short time. These shortages were caused by the unexpected severe weather and the long-term growth in demand for gas by those with connections. Regardless of the imperfect results of regulation, the important point for our purposes is that the FPC tried with dedication to eliminate or reduce the revealed shortages among gas users. The result was a fixed supply of gas connections, which provided the basis for more or less full capitalization of benefits of the regulated price in homes and businesses.*

It is important to note here that rights (or entitlements) are fundamentally bundles of expectation about what can be done with "things." These expectations will, however, partially depend upon

---

*The benefits of the regulated prices may have been capitalized prior to the prohibition on new connections. The complete prohibition just made the capitalization process complete.

the information people have concerning the course of future events, including such events as the regulation or deregulation of commodity prices. If regulation has been anticipated, previous owners of gas connections may not receive the capitalized value of regulation at the time of effective regulation.

To the extent that regulation is anticipated, the prices of facilities with gas connections will be bid up prior to effective regulation. It may therefore be said that persons with gas connections at the time of regulation are not necessarily the sole beneficiaries of regulation: they may have already paid out a portion of the benefits to prior owners of the gas connections.

It is useful to note here that in a world of perfect information and fully rational people, there can never be redistribution of wealth due to change in, for example, government policy. The value of change will always be fully and accurately anticipated and capitalized into the value of the entitlements that were the subject of the initial distribution. In a world of perfect ignorance, on the other hand, where in effect no basis exists for evaluating change before the fact, the opposite is true: All changes have redistributional effects; no change can be anticipated and incorporated into the capitalized value of entitlements.

There are two reasons for highlighting the extreme conditions of perfect information and ignorance. First, the wealth effect of change is partially capitalized prior to change and partially captitalized (that portion which is unanticipated) at the time of change. There are, in other words, partial redistributional effects from changes in government policy. This chapter focuses on the wealth effect at times of change to simplify the discussion, but we must recognize that capitalization is not always completed at the time of change.

Second, much regulatory power is intended to help one group at the expense of another because of the dictates of perceived social values or goals. If this kind of regulation is to have the intended redistribution effect, it must be predicated on some user's ignorance or other market imperfections or on the capability of the reform proponents to foster the necessary ignorance, misinformation, or misconception that makes real redistribution possible. Assuming that law is intended to increase the accuracy of expectations, this requirement means that proponents of redistribution must be able to either work outside established laws, whether formal or informal, or create new laws that cannot be fully anticipated from the established procedures (which have the characteristics of law or are themselves laws) for making new law.

Four points, although they are somewhat aside from the main argument, are worth noting to round out the discussion. First, regulation does not necessarily begin at the same time that the regulatory agency is given the power to regulate. In the case of natural gas, the FPC effectively used its newly acquired regulatory powers only after the courts forced it to do so.

Second, shortages do not necessarily emerge immediately after the price is restricted by regulation. When producers are convinced that the price is fixed and there is no reasonable possibility that it will rise in the near or intermediate future, they have less incentive to hold to their known reserves. When no price restriction exists, producers will hold onto a larger portion of their reserves in anticipation of future price rises; they are consequently compensated for the interest foregone on any sales revenue that could have been earned. So we should expect regulated prices to lead at first to greater supplies of a product like natural gas. This producer response will mislead the public about the ultimate consequences of regulation.* The effect of government policy change, that is, regulation, is to increase the level of ignorance.

Third, there is the common (mistaken) presumption in discussions of regulating this or that industry that regulation suppresses the price. Therefore, deregulation will mean a price increase. This conclusion may be true for the meter price of gas; however, it does not follow that the effective price, that is, the meter price plus the price paid in hidden charges, of the product is held down. In the case of the freeze on gasoline prices during the Arab oil boycott during the 1970s, the effective price of gasoline rose, although the pump price

---

*Increased supplies of natural gas at the start of effective regulation will make the shortage worse at some future date. However, one can argue that regulation is, through its effect on the intertemporal flow of gas supplies, a means of redistributing wealth in the form of the natural-gas stock from future generations to present generations. Dwight Lee has developed empirical evidence that shows that effective regulations immediately increase the supplies of the regulated product. Dwight R. Lee, "Price Controls, Binding Constraints, and Intertemporal Economic Decision Making," *Journal of Political Economy*, 86 (April 1978), pp. 293–301.

per gallon was held down. Because people had to waste time in line waiting for their allotted number of gallons, there was a hidden charge on each gallon purchased.

Similarly, the increase in the price of gas-heated and -cooled homes has imposed a hidden addition on the effective price of natural gas. The person who buys a home at a price inflated by the advantage of regulated gas prices realizes the hidden charge in the form of larger mortgage and interest costs on his or her home. The original homeowner, who may not have purchased the home at the inflated price, may not feel the hidden charge, but his or her equity in the home rises nonetheless. By holding onto the home, this homeowner nevertheless forgoes the opportunity to invest his or her greater home equity in interest-bearing assets and, to that extent, suffers an additional cost in terms of foregone interest.

Fourth, it should be noted that the effective price of natural gas, which includes both the meter and hidden charges, will tend to be greater than the market price of natural gas in the long run in the absence of regulation. The long-run supply of natural gas will be greater because producers have the incentive to explore and make available the reserves. The selling price in the absence of regulation will be higher than the regulated meter price; on the other hand, the greater supply will mean that consumers will demand less natural gas. The new meter price of natural gas will be lower than the old effective price.

Seen this way, the attention given to the impact of deregulation on the meter price has caused both opponents and proponents to miss the reason why users oppose deregulation: The effective (as opposed to the meter) price they pay goes down, not up. This is just another way of bringing to light a point to which we can now turn: the capitalization problem associated with regulation and the wealth transfer that will inevitably result from deregulation.

Deregulation and Capitalized Entitlements

On average, Americans move about one every five years. We will assume for purposes of discussions that these moves are evenly distributed among homeowners who have gas connections and those who use other energy sources. In this case, about 20 percent of the homes utilizing natural gas turn over each year. In short, a substantial percentage of natural gas homes and businesses has been sold and resold over the past several years. Many people who now own natural gas homes and businesses did not own them when effective regulation began. These people paid inflated prices for their homes on the assumption that the below-market meter price would continue.

Because of their greater home investment, they have been, perhaps, only marginally better off than they would have been if they had bought, for example, oil-heated homes. Indeed, many who once owned homes with gas connections were no doubt induced to sell their homes in part because they expected they could sell their gas homes at inflated prices, use their greater equity to reduce the mortgage payment of, say, oil-heated homes, and use that differential to pay for higher-priced oil.

Much of the political and ethical opposition to deregulation of natural gas is now apparent.* The problem is that when natural gas prices are deregulated, the meter price will rise. The effective subsidy given gas homes and businesses will evaporate or be substantially reduced, and the demand for natural gas homes will fall, along with their resale values. The effective price of natural gas will also fall. Through these market forces, natural gas companies will receive a wealth transfer from the current owners of homes using natural gas, many of whom bought their homes at prices distorted by past government policies. The wealth increase of gas companies will be reflected in the present value of their higher income stream and in the higher value of gas company stock.

Those who lose wealth because of deregulation will include more than just gas users. An increase in natural gas supplies caused by deregulation and the opening up of the natural gas market to new connections will lead to an increase in the number of gas homes and businesses that can be purchased. The demand for oil- and electric-heated homes and businesses will fall, along with their resale values. These owners will also experience a wealth loss; many of them can be expected to join the forces opposing deregulation.

---

*The lack of interest in deregulation may also emerge from the fact that the deadweight loss from regulation cannot be fully recaptured in deregulation because many resources are wasted in achieving regulation. See Robert E. McCormick, William F. Shughart III, and Robert D. Tollison, "The Disinterest in Deregulation" *American Economic Review* (December 1984), pp. 1075–1XXX.

On the basis of size alone, the group of people who are harmed directly or indirectly from deregulation can formidably oppose the best efforts of the Federal Power Commission and the gas companies that seek deregulation. Furthermore, this group can be expected to oppose deregulation with the moral fervor of anyone who has been harmed, as this group has been, by deliberate government action. Theft may be defined as the act of taking "without right or permission, generally in a surreptitious way" or the act of getting or effecting "secretly or artfully."[5] Deregulation has many of the same characteristics as theft.

If prospects of deregulation were to be fully disclosed, the market would be able to adjust to those prospects and there would not be a wealth transfer problem: there would not be such opposition to deregulation. The prices that people have paid for gas homes and businesses will be reflected only in the present discounted benefits of the period during which regulation was expected to be effective.

As in the case of regulation, the distribution of the wealth loss from deregulation over time depends on expectations and the availability of information on which those expectations are formed. All that is really required for wealth transfers to occur is that the market perceives that deregulation will occur. The prospects of deregulation will cause home buyers and businesses to temper their demands for facilities with gas connections.

Furthermore, gas suppliers, anticipating deregulation, will withhold a portion of their reserves for the purpose of receiving relatively higher profits in the future. These actions will aggravate any existing shortage of fuel and tend to make deregulation all the more certain. Such actions will also make deregulation more palatable to gas users. The gas shortages will decrease the market value of gas homes and businesses and, along with that, the effective price of natural gas.

Many gas users may have already incurred the capital loss by the time the political decision on natural gas is made; others will have bought their homes and businesses in anticipation of deregulation. Still others will have to weigh the benefits of continued regulation against the threat of continual supply interruptions, which may then be seen as a real possibility. After supply interruptions like those which occurred in the winters of the late 1970s, it is understandable why the main opposition to deregulation is likely to come from those who want to reacquire the benefits of regulation. However, it is also understandable why this group wants to couple a revitalized regulatory authority with mandatory allocation schemes that will ensure that the homes and businesses with gas connections will have adequate supplies.

The Efficiency-Fairness Dilemma

Deregulation of the natural gas industry or, for that matter, almost any other industry, poses a real dilemma for government policy makers. On the one hand, continued regulation of natural gas means higher effective prices for gas customers, a continued misallocation of resources, a prohibition against new gas connections, and a continuation of a national income level that is lower that it otherwise would be.

On the other hand, deregulation can mean a capital loss for many gas users. As stressed, many of these owners bought their gas homes and businesses at inflated market values on the presumption, which was deliberately fostered by government policy, that the price of natural gas would be held down below market-clearing levels. Maybe these owners should have known better. Maybe the government should not have misled them into believing that regulation of natural gas is a fixed, long-term policy course. Indeed, if the government were a private company, it seems likely that in the event that it deregulated gas, it could be sued for violating its own laws against misleading advertising. However, in spite of the maybes and ifs, the problem remains a fact of social politics that cannot be ignored by politicians who are concerned with fairness as well as efficiency and who wish to be elected or re-elected.

What can be done to end the dilemma? Unfortunately, economists do not have a store of practical solutions. However, two possible policy courses are discussed here: (1) compensatory payments to those harmed by deregulation, and (2) a broad-based deregulation program that simultaneously will subject several industries to the forces of competitive markets.

Compensatory Payments

The policy remedy most often advocated by economists is tax/compensation arrangements. Clearly, a movement away from a regulated gas industry to a deregulated one will generate benefits that will be reflected in a larger real national income. The problem of deregulation concerns the distributional effects, not the aggregate effects. The government can counter the adverse distributional effects by taxing those who gain from deregulation—for instance, the natural gas producers—and using the revenue collected to compensate the owners of homes and businesses who are harmed.

Those who are taxed, so the argument goes, may not like their greater tax payments; however, they may recognize that deregulation has little chance of passage without higher taxes. So long as the increase in their taxes is less than the higher profits they may make because of deregulation, they gain by agreeing to higher taxes. So long as the affected homeowners and business owners are compensated for their wealth loss, they are at least no worse off from a move to a deregulated gas industry. So long as no one is made worse off but someone is made better off, the tax/compensation scheme can lead to an unequivocal welfare improvement and the shift in policy may be considered fair by all concerned, or so economists have argued.

This solution, however, is not as practical as it first appears. There is the inherent difficulty of determining who is harmed and who is benefited and how much each must be compensated or taxed. The difficulty of determining the distribution will be enormously complicated by the sheer number of people involved, since owners of electric as well as gas homes will suffer a wealth loss from deregulation. Further complicating the distribution is the fact that current owners of natural gas (and electric) homes made their investments under various degrees of uncertainty about whether gas would be deregulated.

In summary, questions that are raised by any tax/compensation proposal are numerous, perhaps too numerous to make tax compensation an even approximately fair or efficient solution. How much do we compensate current homeowners who made their purchases in different locations of the country, under different expectations about government and nongovernment changes in market forces and under different estimations of the probability that gas will be deregulated? How much do we compensate people who, for example, bought their homes in 1968 when continued long-term regulation was a reasonable expectation and sold their homes in 1976 when deregulation was at least contemplated?

Moreover, if the compensation is restricted to those people who bought their homes and businesses at inflated prices after regulation and before deregulation, the homeowners who had their homes when effective regulation began will have an incentive to sell their homes to profit from the announced intentions of government to compensate homeowners for the damages of deregulation.

Similar problems exist in trying to determine the distribution of the tax burden. Do we tax just the gas companies or the stockholders? If we tax the incomes of companies, then problems of fairness are not entirely avoided. Many current stockholders in gas companies bought their shares expecting that gas would soon be deregulated and the prices they paid were inflated for that reason. The incomes of each instance of deregulation can be viewed as efficient but largely unfair; taken collectively, they can be not only efficient but, perhaps, quasi-fair and politically acceptable.*

Across-the-Board Deregulation

If the government does not find the tax/compensation scheme very attractive, it may consider deregulating several industries, including natural gas, at one or at approximately the same time. Economists have identified many industries that benefit from protective regulation; that is, these industries are being protected from competitive forces by government regulators who set monopoly prices, divide the market, and restrict entry into their markets. Trucking, agriculture, electric power, insurance, aviation, banking, and broadcasting are particularly notable markets subject to regulation in the past.

In these markets, the government has been caught in a regulatory trap. If each is deregulated independently of the deregulation of all other protected industries, problems of wealth transfers and of solving the efficiency-fairness dilemma emerge, and formidable political opposition to isolated deregulation efforts can be expected.

---

*There is the additional problem that the compensation may be so generous that the economic returns from regulation are, on balance, increased, which can cause greater efforts by interest groups to have their markets regulated so they are compensated for their future losses when their markets are deregulated. For more on this argument, see Richard B. McKenzie, *Competing Visions: The Political Conflict over America's Economic Future* (Washington, Cato Institute, 1985), chapter 9.

What can be done to make deregulation workable? If all, or even just many regulated industries, including natural gas, are deregulated at approximately the same time, there will be wealth transfers, but some will be offsetting. The losers from the deregulation of natural gas will be compensated in part for their losses in their own markets by gains generated from the deregulation of, say, the trucking and agriculture industries. Similarly, the losers from the deregulation of trucking can be partially compensated for their losses by the deregulation of natural gas, agriculture, and aviation.

In short, such a broad-based deregulation movement should be viewed as a move to reconstitute social and economic policy; it is a proposal to move to a constitutional setting in which the give and take of political bargains can guide social and economic policy across otherwise isolated events. Taken independently, each instance of deregulation can be viewed as efficient but largely unfair; taken collectively, however, they can not only be efficient but, perhaps, reasonably fair, a point that has been at the heart of much that has been written in this volume.

Interestingly, the case for a laissez-faire economy developed by Adam Smith in *The Wealth of Nations* was essentially a constitutional proposal that is strikingly similar to the one made here. It was made at a time similar to ours, the Mercantilist period in which government had extended its regulatory arm into many sectors of the economy. Smith's proposal for laissez-faire can be viewed as an attempt to devise a strategy for social reform that would have political acceptability because of (not in spite of) the breadth of the reform. The breadth of the deregulation movement of the late 1970s and early 1980s may be an important explanation for why the movement was as successful as it was. The very breadth of President Ronald Reagan's free-trade, minimum-government stance may go a long way toward explaining his popularity.

The proposal for across-the-board deregulation is, of course, not without its deficiencies. It will not produce complete fairness; few policies can hope to do so. Many will question whether social welfare after broad-based deregulation is higher or lower than before. There will be people who, on balance, will be caught up in political bargaining. Representatives of various interest groups will attempt to acquire special favors for their consent to deregulation, increasing the cost of developing reform. By the same token, the political bargaining that is likely to emerge makes across-the-board deregulation a plausible proposal.

Explicit vote trading can occur and a package of reforms that would have failed if considered independently may pass. The participants in this reform movement do not have to incur the worry that the political climate will change when isolated reform proposals are considered. Furthermore, the total effects of a broad-based institutional change can then be evaluated, and this would be hard to do if the parts if the total reform movement were taken up at different times.*

Furthermore, if broad-based deregulation is ever completed, it is important that some constitutional restrictions be imposed on the ability of government to reregulate. Otherwise, there will be considerable costs incurred from the deregulation process and even more costs incurred when economic interest groups again seek to use government's unconstrained economic powers to control their markets for the benefits not of the consuming public but of the regulated industry.

Concluding Comments

The capitalization approach to the study of deregulation is instructive mainly because it reveals the true complexity of bringing about reform in government policy. Furthermore, the approach illustrates the distributional effects that policy changes can have and, therefore, forces the reform's proponents and opponents alike to consider the questions of fairness and to devise ways of bringing about change that is fair as well as efficient. It helps explain why getting government out of agriculture is so difficult, when virtually all groups other than agriculture interest groups recognize the enormous waste and inefficiency of agriculture policy.

---

*Still, if politicians meet to devise a broad-based deregulation proposal, we cannot be sure that the participants will agree on a deregulation proposal. As I have argued elsewhere, the participants, although ostensibly interested in deregulation, may agree on more regulation in a constitutional setting. The outcome of such a meeting depends on, among other factors, the makeup of the meeting (i.e., what industries and interest groups are represented) and the pervasiveness of the regulation at the time of the meeting. See Richard B. McKenzie, *A Contractarian Perspective on the Deregulation Movement*, Working Paper Series (Clemson, S.C.: Department of Economics, Clemson University, 1978).

As has been suggested, the analysis we have developed in this chapter is applicable to a wide range of regulated industries that many economists would like to see deregulated, returned to private-market status. These industries include trucking, airlines, agriculture, insurance, banking, and drugs, among others. The benefits of regulation of the trucking industry have, to one extent or another, been capitalized in the value of the trucks and truck terminals that have been erected over the decades. The benefits of government regulation of the agriculture industry have been capitalized in the value of land and equipment farmers have purchased assuming that the regulation (which has come in the form of price-support systems and acreage-allotment programs) will continue into the future. The benefits of regulation of the banking industry have been capitalized in the many branches that banks have constructed to attract deposits. The benefits of regulation in trucking were capitalized in many truck terminals that had been erected to accommodate the regulated route patterns that lost much of their economic value when deregulation occurred.

One overriding conclusion should be drawn from all that has been said: It may be far easier for government to start something, like the regulation of an industry, than to stop it. The government should, therefore, be careful in choosing any course of action to bring about social improvement. It may actually find that it does not really help the intended persons, and it may find termination of the program politically difficult, if not impossible, because of fairness considerations that influence a great many votes.

Notes

1. Yale Brozen, "The Economic Impact of Government Policy," a paper presented at a symposium on Economic Policy in the Market Process: Success or Failure? Slot Zeist, The Netherlands (January 29, 1986), pp. 1–2.
2. *New York Times* (October 27, 1983), p. 26.
3. Robert B. Helms, *Natural Gas Regulation: An Evaluation of FPC Price Controls* (Washington, D.C.: American Enterprise Institute for Public Policy Research, 1974), p. 4.
4. See Copulus, "Natural Gas Deregulation", chapter 5, for an example of the way in which the argument is typically developed.
5. *American Heritage Dictionary of the English Language* (Boston: Houghton Mifflin Company, 1972).

Appendix 11A

Price controls provide homeowners and businesses using natural gas with a subsidy on each unit of gas consumed. This point was stressed in the body of the chapter. As noted, the per-unit subsidy can be approximated by the difference between the regulated price and the price at which the restricted supply would have cleared the market.

These standard conclusions are illustrated in figure 11–1. The supply and demand curves for natural gas in the figure are assumed to take on their normal shapes; that is, the demand curve is downward-sloping and the supply curve is upward-sloping.

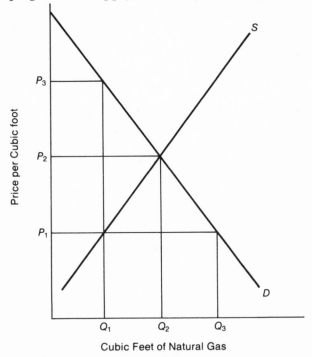

Figure 11–1. A View of the Economics of Natural Gas Regulation

In a completely free, unregulated, competitive market, the price of natural gas will be P_2 and the quantity of gas consumed during each time period will be Q_2. However, if the government believes the free market price is too high or exploits consumers and decides to regulate the price at a lower level of, for example, P_1, a shortage will (eventually) emerge in the market equal to the distance between Q_1 and Q_3. There will not be enough gas to go around. Eventually, the economic effect of natural gas regulation will be that not all potential gas consumers can be served or that there will be times during which homeowners and businesses will not get all the gas they need to heat and cool their homes and work places.

The subsidy to gas users is equal to the difference between the regulated price P_1 and the market clearing price for Q_1 gas, P_3. (As indicated by the demand curve, consumers would be willing to pay as much as P_3 for quantity Q_1.) Recognizing the extent of the subsidy is important because it is this subsidy that feeds into the demand for and prices of houses and businesses with natural gas connections.

Part V
Concluding Comments

12
The Political Economy of Fairness

Economiç man is a clod, heroic man is a fool, but somewhere in between the clod and the fool, human man, if the expression may be pardoned, steers his tottering way.

—Kenneth Boulding[1]

When Judge Richard Posner quipped that terms like fairness and justice have "no content" with respect to so many legal and public policy issues, he was reflecting the general thinking of many of his former academic colleagues in economics.[2] Judge Posner's views are, without question, shared by many other legal scholars and social scientists in the country. As we noted in the first chapter, economists have traditionally focused their scholarly attention on the efficiency, not the fairness and equity, of markets. This was our point of departure for this book. And we really have never escaped from the clutches of efficiency in any of the topics considered. Nevertheless, much has been said of how efficiency and fairness are entangled in the market process.

The Efficiency of Trade, Once Again

Economists' traditional concern with efficiency is understandable. Their primary intellectual turf has largely been trades or exchanges within a given or assumed institutional setting, which could be as large as the whole of society. The assumed social setting specifies the property rights and the rules for trade. Given the setting, trades that are voluntarily undertaken (and affect only the trading parties) may reshuffle property, but they are also efficient because they improve the lot of the traders, by definition, and provide incentive for extended and cost-effective production.

Such exchanges seem hardly objectionable from any perspective, much less from a fairness perspective. In such pristine but narrow settings, fairness and efficiency are virtually indistinguishable and reenforcing. The issues of whether the trading parties should have the right to trade or have the right to the properties that are traded or whether individual trades adversely affect others by price changes or externalities are effectively sidestepped, by assumption.

In addition, conventional economic analysis has been mainly concerned with positive matters; that is, with making correct, empirically verifiable predictions, meaning with what can be expected to happen in given institutional settings, not with normative matters, or with what ought to happen. The issue of fairness of outcomes to the economist/social scientist interested in predictions is no more relevant than the fairness of predicted atmospheric changes is to the meteorologist. The predictions are correct or incorrect and, to that extent, are largely neutral with respect to their fairness. We may quibble over whether economists should devote so much of their professional energies to positive matters to the exclusion of normative concerns; still, we can all agree that much of economists' scientific efforts have been fruitful in informing many public debates. Indeed, even our discussion of the fairness of markets in foregoing chapters has relied extensively on positive methods, which, although incomplete, has been instructive.

The Constitutional Perspective, Once Again

However, the political economist does not have the luxury of assuming exclusively the role of the detached observer/scientist, unconcerned about what people value and want. His natural intellectual turf is that of institutional design, of seeking rules and arrangements for human society that are, at the same time, the means to ends and ends in themselves. As in the cases of policies that are adopted within given rules and arrangements, the discussion of alternative rules and arrangements must be informed by assessments of their likely consequences. Nonetheless, rules and arrangements for human interaction must inevitably be judged normatively, that is, in terms of whether or not they accomplish what they are intended to accomplish; fairness in some form is obviously one such goal for many, if not most, people.

My purpose in this volume has never been to maintain that markets left totally unfettered are, or can be, perfectly fair to all people. In fact, chapter 9 sought to make the point that a welfare state of some size can be intellectually justified on efficiency, as well as on fairness, grounds. There have been, however, three major fairness themes flowing through much of the analysis in this book. First, while markets may be unfair to a degree because someone loses, they can be the product of fair rules and can promote fairness and discourage unfairness by competitively constraining behavior. These points were central to the discussion of, for example, minimum wages in chapter 7. We have, in effect, argued that the fairness of behavior can be evaluated by reflection on the rules for human conduct. The fairness of the rules must fall to the test of agreement.

Second, public policies offered as a solution to unfairness in markets may inadvertently be part of or add to the unfairness problem. This point was especially germane to our discussion of economic democracy in the workplace in chapters 5 and 6 and of regulation and deregulation in the preceding chapter.

Third, the fairness of markets cannot be judged fruitfully from the myopic perspective of individual market events or even individual markets. This is because market changes inevitably produce gainers and losers, and they do that by design. Understandably, the social value of such isolated market changes must be open to questions. And critics of markets are prone to focus on isolated markets and the changes and problems in them.

However, we have sought to emphasize that the fairness of markets is necessarily a problem in system analysis, a matter of summing up the gains and pains, or costs and benefits, that happen to a lot of people across many different markets and across time during which all kinds of things can happen for good and bad to virtually everyone. The acid test for markets, as a system, is how the social ledger tends to balance for people, recognizing that freedom of individual action and initiative and so many consequences of future interaction can only be imagined and never counted very precisely.

Seen from this system perspective, markets appear far more fair than they do in isolation from one another. A stated objective of this book has been to articulate, and even advocate, a shift in intellectual perspective from a policy perspective, in which markets and policies are evaluated in isolation from one another, to a system or constitutional perspective, in which markets are seen as forming an integral part of a social system and policies are not viewed as ad hoc but as consistent with generally applicable principles.

The Politics of Fairness

Admittedly, so much of the public debate over the fairness of markets involves nothing more than disguised expressions of preferences. So many of the people who argue that fairness requires that government provide, for example, a playground are simply stating what they want. The fairness rhetoric may also be nothing more than political puffery or posturing that reflects the advocates' drive to use whatever arguments they can muster to justify and garner support for a transfer of income and wealth from others to themselves. Judge Posner's comment about the vacuous nature of fairness claims was probably intended to apply to such arguments. This is because most fairness claims heard in the political process are, indeed, nothing more than smoke screens for less laudable and even devious private objectives. Accordingly, the textile industry claims that protectionism is only a fair remedy for its employees when the real issue may be corporate profits or survival. The milk lobby claims production restrictions are fair controls, while labor advocates participation rights because, otherwise, workers in the affected markets will be exploited.

The fairness claims that pervade political life are understandable, given political institutions. "Fairness" remains an ambiguous term. And ambiguity is often desirable in politics because passage of many programs requires coalitions of varied interest groups and different people can interpret approvingly the fairness claims to fit their own needs and situations. The banner of fairness promotes the illusion, if not the substance, of political accord.

Political analysis by many taxpaying citizens is necessarily very shallow, extending all too frequently to consideration of only the more obvious policy consequences. This is because voters and their political leaders rarely have the necessary incentive (that is, personal or political reward) to delve very deeply into issues and evaluate the less obvious secondary and adverse market consequences of their policy proposals (such as the ones discussed in chapter 3). Thinking of markets as a system and of policies as matters of generalized principle is no mean intellectual task. The task is especially difficult because the value of principles may only be clearly evident over a long span of time and because finding immediate solutions to observed social ills is politically tempting, if not irresistible, when government is unconstrained in what it can do.

In addition, political combatants are often driven to employ the rhetoric of fairness, even when they know it is inappropriate, because everyone else is using it. Proponents of public policies can rarely be successful by claiming private gains that are generated at public expense when everyone else in the political arena adheres to higher and more lofty standards, at least in rhetorical terms.

The textile industry is no more likely to admit that protectionism reduces the real income of low-income textile consumers than the tobacco industry is likely to admit that medical evidence proves smoking is harmful to health. Both industries know that such admissions will weaken their political support, and the textile industry understands that its political drive for protectionism is a competitive one. After all, most import-competing industries want protection from their foreign competition, and the time of legislators to provide the desired protection is limited. The textile industry knows that it must use the rhetoric of fairness because its political competition in the protectionist struggle will most likely use it.

We can expect that the success some groups have in manipulating government for their own private uses through fairness claims will be followed by other groups using the same fairness rhetoric. In an unconstrained political setting, it should be no surprise that the fairness chorus rises with interest groups competing for the use of governmental powers to redistribute income and wealth.

Fairness, unfortunately, is often touted in political debate as a principle that unifies policies, whereas it may be more accurate to maintain that consistent adherence to principles promotes fairness of conduct. However, when claims of fairness are used excessively in so many contexts to justify government policies that do nothing better than redistribute income and wealth for personal gains, its value can become corrupt and destructive. Politics can make behavior negative-sum by causing back-and-forth movements of income and wealth, with the income and wealth pool being reduced in the process.

Admittedly, this book has had a political, as well as intellectual and professional, purpose. That purpose has been to return to fairness some of the content that Judge Posner, others, and I agree has been lost in the political process. I have, in effect, advocated that fairness should not be sought directly but should emerge as a serendipity, through a process of indirection that seeks, first, governance for free and responsible individuals.

Again, fairness should be construed as adherence to fair rules for the governmental process. These are rules that are not intentionally designed to produce any particular outcome or help any particular person or group and that are generally applicable to all people, regardless of who they are or what their station in life is. The book, in short, has been an appeal to a return of governance by principles that are larger, more fundamental, and more important than the people who govern. In this respect, the book has been in part a call for a return to governance by constraints on the people who govern and, therefore, on the people who would exploit those who govern.

Notes

1. Kenneth E. Boulding, *Economics As a Science* (New York: McGraw-Hill Book Co., 1970), p. 135.
2. As quoted in the *Wall Street Journal* (August 4, 1986), p. 1.

Index

About the Author

Richard B. McKenzie is professor of economics at Clemson University and senior fellow at the Heritage Foundation and Center for the Study of American Business at Washington University in St. Louis. He has written widely on public policy issues. His published works include more than a dozen books and several dozen monographs, pamphlets, and policy papers. His latest books include *Regulating Government: A Preface to Constitutional Economics* (Lexington Books, 1986, with Dwight Lee), *Competing Visions: The Political Conflict over America's Economic Future* (Cato Institute, 1985) and *Fugitive Industry: The Economics and Politics of Deindustrialization* (Pacific Institute, 1984). Professor McKenzie has written for the *New York Times*, the *Wall Street Journal*, the *Washington Post*, and the *Christian Science Monitor*. His textbooks have been published by McGraw-Hill, Houghton Mifflin, and Richard D. Irwin.